WHOSE CRISIS, WHOSE FUTURE?

WHOSE CRISIS, WHOSE FUTURE?

TOWARDS A GREENER, FAIRER, RICHER WORLD

SUSAN GEORGE

polity

First published in French as *Leurs Crises, Nos Solutions* © Editions Albin Michel S.A. – Paris, 2010

This English edition © Polity Press 2010
Reprinted 2010

Polity Press
65 Bridge Street
Cambridge CB2 1UR, UK

Polity Press
350 Main Street
Malden, MA 02148, USA

ISBN-13: 978-0-7456-5137-8
ISBN-13: 978-0-7456-5138-5 (pb)

A catalogue record for this book is available from the British Library.

Typeset in 10.75 on 14 pt Adobe Janson
by Servis Filmsetting Ltd, Stockport, Cheshire
Printed and bound by MPG Books Group, UK

The publisher has used its best endeavours to ensure that the URLs for external websites referred to in this book are correct and active at the time of going to press. However, the publisher has no responsibility for the websites and can make no guarantee that a site will remain live or that the content is or will remain appropriate.

Every effort has been made to trace all copyright holders, but if any have been inadvertently overlooked the publisher will be pleased to include any necessary credits in any subsequent reprint or edition.

For further information on Polity, visit our website: www.politybooks.com

Contents

Aug. 1, 2011 : pp. 1–

INTRODUCTION: CHOOSING FREEDOM

Most people haven't noticed yet but, except for a small minority, we're all in prison. The guards aren't stupid, they let us walk about freely in the sunshine and attend the movies of our choice, but, for many of the most important aspects of our lives, we are not free. *Whose Crisis, Whose Future?* casts a cold eye on the regime of neoliberal globalization under which we live and seeks to explain how we've been incarcerated. Finance governs our economy; finance and the economy together dictate a hugely unequal world; the most basic of all resources – food and water – are disappearing for hundreds of millions and the planet is mostly reduced to the status of an exploited quarry and rubbish tip; for all these reasons, we will continue to fight each other. The last and longest chapter here proposes concrete means and strategies of escape.

I wrote this book because I am angry, perplexed and frightened: angry because so many people are suffering needlessly on account of the economic, social and ecological crisis and because the world's leaders show no signs of bringing about genuine change; perplexed because they don't seem to understand or care much about the public mood, the widespread resentment and the urgency of action; frightened because, if we don't act soon, it may well be too late, particularly where climate change is concerned.

We could enjoy a world that is clean, green and rich, providing a decent and dignified life for everyone on a healthy planet. This is not some far-fetched utopia but a concrete possibility. The world has never been so wealthy, and we have in our hands, right now, all the knowledge, tools and skills we need. The obstacles are not technical, practical or financial but political, intellectual and ideological. The crisis could provide an extraordinary opportunity to build such a world, and the aim of this book is to explain how and why we got into the present mess and how we can get out of it, to the benefit of the planet and of people everywhere.

Although the financial part of the crisis has received the most attention and largely pushed the others off the front pages and the mental landscape, in reality we are in the midst not of a single crisis but of a multifaceted one, which already touches, or will soon touch, nearly every aspect of nearly everyone's life and the destiny of our earthly habitat. Call it a crisis of the system, of civilization, of globalization, of human values, or use some other universal, all-encompassing term; the point is that it has imprisoned us mentally and physically and we must break free.

THE SPHERES

This prison can be looked at in two ways. The first metaphor I find useful is a series of concentric spheres set in a hierarchy of diminishing importance. The outermost and most important one is labelled 'Finance', the next within it 'Economy', then 'Society' and, finally, innermost and least important, the sphere called 'Planet'. That is the order today. For me, the enormous task of people everywhere, an effort never before required in human history, is to reverse the order of these spheres so that it becomes exactly opposite to the existing one. We must look skyward, recall the famous image of the earth seen from space, regain a sense of proportion and set our priorities right.

Our beautiful, finite planet and its biosphere ought to be the outermost sphere because the state of the earth ultimately encompasses and determines the state of all the other spheres within. Next should be human society, which must respect the laws and the limits of the biosphere but should otherwise be free to choose democratically the social organization that best suits the needs of its members. The third sphere, the economy, would figure merely as one aspect of social life, providing for the production and distribution of the concrete means of society's existence; it should be subservient to, and chosen by, society so as to serve its needs. Finally and least important would come the fourth and innermost sphere of finance, only one among many tools at the service of the economy.

Despite incontrovertible proof of impending climate crisis and ecological disaster, mainstream economists and most politicians still don't see things that way – for them, finance and the economy come first. These two outermost spheres together oblige society to submit to their needs and they dictate how society must be organized. In particular, the economic and financial spheres must grow incessantly: their growth is the only measure that counts; their driving mechanism is programmed continually to surpass itself.

Finance and the economy are paramount in the universe of political and mainstream economists. They believe that resource capture, production and consumption have boundless room to expand, and the natural world for them is a mere subsystem, simply the place where we get our raw materials and dump our wastes, including our greenhouse gases. The economists call the systematic destruction of the environment 'externalities' – just unfortunate side effects of economic, revenue-producing activities. In common with many other beliefs of mainstream or neoliberal economics, this view is insane. As the late ecological economist Kenneth Boulding said, 'to believe that one can have infinite growth in a finite system, one must be either a madman or an economist.'

The roots of the crisis that now imprisons us can be traced directly to the way we now order, consciously or unconsciously, the spheres. In the deadly system that has usurped power over human affairs, when finance caves in as it has lately done, it crushes and damages all the others – not just the economy but also society and the biosphere. Over the past three decades, the monetary economy has taken over, neglected the real economy and become virtually separate from it, while the real economy itself increasingly serves the needs of a minority.

Because the economy is unjust and generates vast inequalities, society is necessarily unjust as well. Our beleaguered planet is the object of constant financial, economic and social abuse. We should never forget that, although we can't live without it, it would be much better off without us. This perverse hierarchy and mistaken ordering of the spheres is at the heart of the crisis.

So our daunting goal and the only way to escape the prison is this: we must get from here . . .

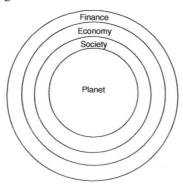

to here:

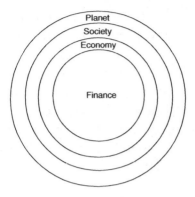

THE WALLS

The spheres are a useful way to think about the present and, I hope, future priorities of our existence, but for the purposes of this book I've chosen the second metaphor that best and most simply describes our plight as prisoners – that is, walls. Every prison has walls that prevent the inmates from escaping, but because the prison I'm describing encloses the whole world, not just the wealthiest countries, parts of its structure may seem less relevant to relatively privileged Western readers, although they are the daily reality for millions. That is why the first wall I will describe is financial and economic – no surprises there. The second is built of longstanding and increasing poverty and inequality in both North and South. The third is shrinking access to vital human necessities, chiefly food and water. These are the subjects of the first three chapters, and you are doubtless expecting that the fourth will be about climate change, destruction of nature and loss of biodiversity.

At first I intended to do what I've done in several previous books and give the environment a separate chapter here as well. Then it dawned on me that 'separate chapters' are part of the problem. The environment and the response to climate change too often figure at best as a subject – or a ministry – apart, at worst as a footnote or an afterthought. Governments still act as if fixing finance were far more important than halting global warming, which they seem to believe can be put off indefinitely, at least until after they've repaired the banks.

So chapter 4 is about conflict. Is it inevitable? And what are the particular features of modern conflicts? I try to suggest solutions to all these problems throughout the book, but chapter 5 is devoted entirely to some quite specific goals. A short conclusion follows.

THE DAVOS CLASS

I think the prison metaphor is a good guide to examining how we might undertake such an enormous task as reversing the spheres because the best way to begin is to ask who now has the keys. Who arms the guards and mans the watch-towers day and night to prevent a breakout? What are the walls made of and who built them? This is where I must introduce the now deeply unfashionable notion of class. In my work I find one of the hardest points to get across to audiences – mine tend to be made up of concerned and decent folk – is that there really are a lot of determined, powerful, well-mannered but truly dangerous people out there; together they have class interests, they profit mightily from the status quo, they know each other, they stick together – and they don't want anything fundamentally changed. But let me make clear I'm not impugning anybody's individual morality – there are surely plenty of kind-hearted bankers, generous traders and socially responsible CEOs. I am simply saying that, *as a class*, they can be counted on to behave in certain ways if only because they serve a single sort of system.

A man of great perspicacity said it far better than I can. In his major work, he wrote: "'All for ourselves and nothing for other people" seems in every age of the world to have been the vile maxim of the masters of mankind.'[1] That was Adam Smith in *The Wealth of Nations*, written in 1776 and universally considered the first comprehensive inquiry into the nature and practice of capitalism. His masterpiece has also been used to justify all manner of mischief and any number of practices Smith would have decried, particularly in his other well-known work, *The Theory of Moral Sentiments*. After announcing the 'vile maxim of the masters of mankind', he goes on to explain how the great proprietors of his day preferred to have a pair of diamond shoe-buckles, or 'something as frivolous and useless', rather than provide the 'maintenance, or what is the same thing, the price of the maintenance of a thousand men for a year'. *Plus ça change . . .*

The masters of mankind are still with us, and for my purposes here I will call them the Davos class because, like the people who meet each January in the Swiss mountain resort, they are nomadic, powerful and interchangeable. Some have economic power and almost always a considerable personal fortune. Others have administrative and political power, mostly exercised on behalf of those with economic power, who reward them in their own way. Contradictions among its members can most certainly exist – the CEO of an industrial company does not always have exactly the same interests as his bankers – but, on the whole, when it comes to societal choices, they will agree.

You can find the Davos class in every country – it is not a conspiracy and its modus operandi can be readily observed and identified. Why bother with conspiracies when the study of power and interests will do the job? The Davos class is always extremely small relative to the society and its members naturally have money – sometimes inherited, sometimes self-made – but more importantly they have their own social institutions – clubs, top schools for their kids,

neighbourhoods, corporate and charity boards, holiday des-
tinations, membership organizations, exclusive fashionable
social events, and so on – all of which help to buttress social
cohesion and collective power. They run our major institutions, including the media, know exactly what they want and
are much more united and better organized than we are. But
this dominant class has weaknesses too; one is that it has an
ideology but virtually no ideas and no imagination.

My argument in this book is that they run the prison we're
in. They still want 'all for themselves and nothing for other
people'. But since Adam Smith's day the 'other people',
through their own struggles, have learned how to read, write
and think critically; they are better informed, they have little
by little captured a measure of power for themselves and
they are thus far more experienced politically than in the
eighteenth century. They must therefore be kept under more
strategic and more intelligent supervision.

The Davos class, despite its members' nice manners and
well-tailored clothes, is predatory. These people cannot
be expected to act logically because they are not thinking
about longer-term interests, usually not even their own, but
about eating, right now. They are also well versed in prison
management and they hire the best-trained and most clever
guards to keep us where we are.

ROUTES OF ESCAPE

As I have already done, I will be continuing to abuse the
much-abused pronoun 'we' because I believe that 'we' – the
decent, honest, 'ordinary' people I meet all the time – have
the numbers (and thus also the votes) on our side. We have
imagination, ideas and rational proposals as well as most of
the skills and the scholarship – meaning we know what needs
to be done and how to do it. We belong to a huge variety

of formal and informal organizations struggling for change in this or that institution, this or that domain. Collectively, we even have money. What we do not have is the unity or the organization of the adversary, and all too often we lack consciousness of our potential power. Leadership is a problem as well. Our political parties are often, as in the United States, financially dependent on the dominant class and either translate the latter's wishes directly into law or, if they are in opposition, go along passively with most of their decisions. And, let's face it, progressives love to bicker and create fratricidal factions so that they become incapable of confronting power other than rhetorically.

To function efficiently, the dominant class requires the state and its machinery, which they shape in so far as they can to meet their own needs. This they did with stunning success from the mid-1970s onwards in order to eliminate any regulations which could hinder the quest to get 'all for themselves'. They wheedled, flattered and pressured and, when that didn't work, paid the politicians to make the necessary arrangements. So that citizens – that is, voters – would go along with their plans, they also spent well over a billion dollars (very little for them) in the United States alone to shape and disseminate their ideology, convincing large majorities that everything they do is benign, that they have our interests at heart and their order is for the best in the best of all possible worlds.

Although hardly Marxists, they followed the Italian Marxist thinker Antonio Gramsci, who formulated the concept of cultural hegemony. I devoted a book to explaining how in the United States the dominant class used media, management, marketing and money to manufacture and spread the new common sense, aiming at the topmost institutions where ideas are forged and then trickle down to the rest of society.[2] President Obama is certainly a welcome replacement for

George W. Bush, but I think it would be mistaken to assume that he can – or even that he wants to – erase at a stroke thirty years of neoliberal transformation. In 2008 he also received over $4 million in campaign contributions from the upper echelon employees of the now bailed-out banks.

PRISON PRINCIPLES AND PRACTICE

Davos Man (including, of course, Davos Woman) has specific characteristics in each country but is now also an international species, and his ideas, such as they are, are pretty much the same everywhere. Because he necessarily follows capitalist rules, he maintains the economy in a chronic state of overproduction and does not need most of the world's workforce. Democracy gets in his way, and if dragging us all back into the miseries of the nineteenth century is what it takes, and if he is free to do so, that is what he will do. If he destroys society and the earth in the process, that's tough. Better luck next time, perhaps on some other planet; he won't be around as an individual. Take Adam Smith's word for it if you don't want to take mine: this class really does seek 'all for itself and nothing for other people'.

Like the ideological shift and the ascent of Davos Man, the present stage of global capitalism dates approximately from the early to mid-1970s and is generally called 'neoliberalism'; it is based on freedom for financial innovation, no matter where it may lead, and on privatization, deregulation, unlimited growth, the free, supposedly self-regulating market and free trade. It gave birth to the casino economy, which has failed and is thoroughly discredited, at least in the public mind.

Most people ask for no further proof; they can see that the system works neither for them, nor for their families and friends, nor for their country. Many also recognize that it's bad for the immense majority of the earth's people and for the earth itself. The ideological and political scaffolding holding it up has collapsed, along with the financial structure, smashing millions of lives, forcing the global establishment to adopt unprecedented remedies at enormous cost to citizens, with no guarantees that their hastily contrived schemes will suffice.

It's time to update Lenin's 'The capitalists will sell us the rope with which we will hang them.' Today it's worse than that – the capitalists now sell each other the rope with which to hang themselves and drag the rest of us down with them. That's how they provoked the present catastrophe – selling each other ropes, which they called by fancy names and acronyms, but which turned out to be dangerously risky financial products. Governments rushed in to save them from an ignominious end before they could expire.

Never fear, however: they may have botched their first suicide attempt but they will give it another go. Already, not much more than a year after Black September 2008, the bankers are inventing hitherto unheard-of financial products and peddling them worldwide. The most macabre I have read about is based on their purchase of the life insurance policies, at a substantial discount, of old and seriously ill people, which they package as they did subprime mortgages and sell as financial products.[3] Their remuneration and bonuses have once more become obscene. Their system is designed to surpass itself continually: to go further, faster, higher, richer, until it crashes. As it will crash again.

At the G-20 meeting in April 2009, political leaders pretentiously claimed to have invented a new world order. It was nothing of the kind but rather a grab-bag of stopgap measures designed to keep the old world order ticking over a bit longer, using institutions such as the International Monetary Fund (IMF) – which helped to create the crisis to begin with – to which they handed over hundreds of billions. I am prepared to bet whatever you like that their solutions won't work, not even on their own terms. In September 2009, they gave a repeat performance.

This leadership has also made its priorities crystal clear. They have now legitimized themselves as the world's government, leaving out 172 countries that don't count. When people marched in London and other cities before the April 2009 G-20 meeting to proclaim 'We won't pay for your crisis' and 'Put people and the planet first', they responded 'Oh yes you will' and 'No way'.

Such governments and their communicators are experts in packaging, concerned with making the status quo look brand new. Since they normally govern on behalf of the Davos class they take the line of least resistance, and so far this has always meant enlisting the rest of us to pay and shut up. Refusal to obey should be our first line of defence. Nothing will change fundamentally without popular action because nothing ever does.

WHAT NOT TO EXPECT FROM THIS BOOK

Here a few things I won't attempt in the 'solutions' chapter. As soon as one even mentions the word, calls for revolution resound. The revolutionary myth is tenacious, but, for me to believe in it, I would first need to know the name of the tsar we are supposed to overthrow this time and the address of the Winter Palace where he and his close advisors can be found and strung up from the nearest lamp post. All I know is that the palace isn't on Wall Street or in the City of London, which, thanks to government bailouts, are still open for business despite their own fecklessness, recklessness and stupidity.

As for 'an end to capitalism', accompanied or not by revolution, I am sympathetic but again would be more at ease if I knew what was meant. To be honest, I can't see a big bang, a once-for-all end to our present economic system, but rather an ongoing process of transformation fuelled by constant public pressure – local, national and, when possible, international – that forces governments to rein in the private sector, particularly the financial conglomerates, and put people and the planet ahead of accumulation and profit in a far more cooperative social context. In any event, the present crisis and the virtual collapse of the financial edifice has not yet been enough to provoke this fabled end.

I don't believe that violence can provide a lasting solution or advance human emancipation, but I do fear it could overtake us unless we can quickly reduce the glaring injustices of the present. I quote some surveys in these pages, but you don't need to consult opinion polls to feel the public mood growing uglier. One's thoughts are drawn irresistibly to the 1930s and the rise of fascism and dictatorships in the wake of an earlier financial crisis. It's tempting for people who are hurting to blame scapegoats such as immigrants, rather than the real culprits, who are too far away to provide easy targets. Some people also fear 'eco-fascism' arising to impose drastic measures as the unmistakeable effects of global warming take hold.

I won't be recommending that one 'abolish the market' either. Markets play a useful role, and archaeological evidence shows they have existed for millennia, for as long as people have been able to travel and exchange. From at least 2500 BC on the Indian–Middle Eastern–Egyptian trade routes, merchants were used to dealing simultaneously with at least ten systems of weights, measures and currencies to exchange valuable commodities such as tin, copper, silver, gold and lapis lazuli and verify that they were not being cheated.[4]

A capitalist economy implies the existence of the market, but the opposite is not true – it all depends on what kind of market you mean. The neoliberal dream of the 'self-regulating market' has finally been revealed as a nightmare and a mythical beast – one hopes, but doubts, that the present crisis has finally put it down. The debate should not centre on saying yes or no to the market but rather on which goods ought to be bought and sold with prices fixed according to supply and demand and which ones should be treated as public or common goods and services, the latter priced according to their social usefulness.

 This means that the role of the individual state remains crucial for the simple reason that we have no democracy to speak of above the state level. For Adam Smith, it was an unspoken truism that the reach of the capitalist marketplace and the reach of the state were identical, but today this is far from the case. For example, Europeans have virtually no control over the decisions of the European Union, which seems bent on destroying as many public services as possible and rejecting democracy at every turn. Nowhere do citizens exert any influence at all over the global architecture of institutions such as the World Bank, the IMF, the World Trade Organization and their acolytes.

My own list of public or common goods would start with a new kind which would not have appeared a decade ago: a climate fit for human beings. Our climate is now a common good because everyone's well-being depends on it. This does not prevent attempts to make it a profitable, marketable commodity via pollution permits and offsets. This is the wrong approach if only because the market presupposes the continued existence of the commodity marketed, in this case CO_2 emissions, which are exactly what we ought to get rid of. We talk all the time about saving 'the planet', but in fact we are talking about saving ourselves. The planet will continue to turn on its axis and orbit the sun – it just may do so without us. If we had a wider range of tolerance for heat and cold,

droughts and floods, we might be OK. But we don't – nor
do most of the species we depend on. Those that will survive
the longest are those with the widest ranges, and they are
nobody's first choice for companionship – flies, mosquitoes,
cockroaches, pigeons, crows, nettles . . .

The next, more conventional roster of public goods would
try to repair the damage of decades of privatization, and
would include not only obvious choices such as health, education and water but also energy, a good part of scientific
research and pharmaceuticals, plus financial credit and the
banking system. To avoid misunderstandings, please note
that 'common' and 'public' do not necessarily mean 'free',
although they should mean that in some areas, for example
education. Nor do they mean 'organized by central planners
and managed by bureaucrats'. Many different organizational
models are possible: decentralization is an obvious choice in
many cases – for example water – and could be used in many
others. Popular participation in the management of many of
them would be not only welcome but indispensable.

The jailbreak in practical terms will require that people
of good will come together, form alliances nationally and
internationally, and use the financial crisis in order to solve
the others. Don't listen to anyone who claims that 'we can't
afford it'. Despite the crisis and the bailouts, the world is still
awash in money. It was only a matter of days before hundreds
of billions were discovered in bottom drawers or buried in
back gardens and used to save the banks. By the year 2010
probably (estimates vary rather wildly) some $14,000 billion
– $14,000,000,000,000 – had magically materialized to prop
up the financial institutions.* This inconceivably huge sum

---

* Estimates begin at about $5 trillion. The most reliable seems to me that
of two researchers at the Bank of England (Piergiorgio Alessandri and
Andrew G. Haldane, *Banking on the State*, Bank of England, November
2009), a report previously presented at a colloquium of the Federal Reserve

is mostly borrowed from the future. It will be paid back by today's citizens and their children and grandchildren – paid back in taxes, of course, but also in unemployment, in services forfeited and doubtless through other hardships we have not yet even begun to imagine.

Amounts a hundredth or a thousandth as large have been perennially unavailable for health, education, job creation, environmental protection and various other worthy endeavours. There are ways to stop that from happening again and places where money is to be found. Citizens, however, must demand a lot more than simple regulation around the edges of the financial system if they hope to limit the dictatorship of the economy. The G-20 is not the body that will impose any of the necessary decisions.

Finally, let me confess freely that there are a great many things I don't know. I don't know if 'we' can vanquish the solidly established Davos predator class and put a more equitable and democratic social order in its place. I don't know if it's possible to alter the present *rapport de forces* and cause the pendulum to swing back towards a fairer, more stable, greener and more habitable world. I am betting that we can – otherwise there is nothing left to do except to imitate those who lived in the time of plague, who feasted, drank and caroused in the public squares while awaiting the Grim Reaper. I think we have better uses for our time than gluttony and drunken revelry – and, even if we fail, at least we have a chance to fail honourably.

Here's another admission: I don't know the ultimate, desirable state of society and I'm wary of those who think they do. In fact, I don't believe there *is* an 'ultimate' state, which would also be static, a dead-end, either unbearably

Bank of Chicago in September 2009. The $14 trillion is their figure for all currencies taken together, worldwide.

boring or simply unbearable. All the twentieth-century 'isms' knew exactly what society should be like and forced everyone to agree; if they didn't, they were sent to re-education camps or liquidated. Thank you, but I can do without the end of history.

Just as I believe that biodiversity is the source of nature's vitality and our guarantee of survival, so I defend social diversity. Different futures will and should be determined by different histories, cultures, geographical constraints and degrees of struggle. We can show solidarity for the struggles of others; we cannot replace them or dictate their outcomes. I believe that human emancipation will be a never ending effort – to secure it where it is missing; to protect it where it is under threat; to perfect it where it is, or seems, most secure.

The more often people anywhere win, the easier it becomes for people everywhere to win as well. However, the common element of these different histories, cultures and capacities to alter their present circumstances must be democracy. Democracy is both the goal and the means one must employ to attain it. We must face the fact that it is often messy and takes a long time. Some people will always try to abuse it, but every other path has invariably led to unspeakable horrors. In this case, ends not only justify means; they are the same. To refuse democratic means is to refuse democratic and diverse outcomes.

A final qualification: although like everybody else I've used and will continue to use the word, I don't really believe we are living through a 'crisis'. 'Crisis' has a long history of elastic meanings: my Oxford Dictionary gives its derivation as the Greek for 'decision' but also stresses the crucial moment or turning point, particularly in an illness, whose resolution will be either recovery or death. In the theatre, it's the moment when the Gordian knot, the dilemma, is sliced through.

According to the noted French sinologist François Jullien,

the oft-quoted assertion that the Chinese ideogram for 'crisis' combines the notions of 'danger' and 'opportunity' is actually a Western construct. The Chinese character is more like the trigger of the crossbow, a release mechanism.[5] Thus in Greek, in Chinese and as far as I know in other languages, the word conveys a sense of before and after, a build-up of tension and a short, sharp passage between possible paths, the crucial crossroads moment that determines the future.

Can it be such a short and decisive moment in our own time for a jailbreak? Perhaps from the viewpoint of the 500-year history of capitalism, the acutely dangerous time we are presently experiencing can be considered 'brief'. I still fear that the 'crisis' which built up over decades, began to unfold in 2007, and was still lumbering along towards the end of 2009 will go on for a while longer. Crises are coming closer together than ever before. Tension will surely build, but there may be no sudden release of the trigger that launches the bolt from the crossbow. The search for a different future is likely to be a long endeavour.

The governing elites will not seize the moment of decision but try to patch up and reinstate a failed system in the face of popular protest; their system will fail again. Perhaps to maintain it they will be obliged to use ever harsher methods to ensure that the prisoners are kept frightened, quiet and cowed. One word more accurate than 'crisis' might be 'depression', as in the 1930s, but in the psychological sense as well as the economic one, this time experienced both by individuals and by entire societies. But another, better word is 'opening' – allowing us a glimpse, despite today's wreckage and the blighted landscape in which it lies, of the clean, green, rich world beyond.

The crash was as inevitable as it was predictable, though few foresaw it. Those who did believe they now know what must be done. Through no special merit of my own, I was part of the social movement that foresaw the crisis, so now, as far as I can tell, my job is to explain its causes and its remedies as clearly as I can – to put my words on the right side of the scales and thus to place whatever influence I can command in the balance. The breakout itself is up to each of us – and to us all.

A NOTE ABOUT NUMBERS

The financial crisis has placed enormous, virtually incomprehensible numbers on the front pages, and one needs some sort of alternative scale to gain a rough idea of what they represent. If you think in terms of the number of seconds your watch ticks, and if each second represents 1 dollar (euro, pound, etc.), the relationship is the following:

a day = $86,400;
a year = $31,536,000; 10 years = $315,536,000; 100 years = $3,153,600,000.

Or, put the other way around:

a billion (or 1000 million in some languages; that is, 1 followed by 9 zeros) is a little less than 32 years;
a hundred billion is nearly 3,200 years;
a trillion (one thousand billion; 1 followed by 12 zeros) is nearly 32,000 years.

The lowest estimates of total financial rescues are around $5 trillion (160,000 years); the one I find most reliable – that of Alessandri and Haldane at the Bank of England (see footnote pp. 15–16) – is $14 trillion (448,000 years).

1

THE WALL OF FINANCE

We had to struggle with the old enemies of peace: business and financial monopoly, speculation, reckless banking, class antagonism . . . they had begun to consider the government of the United States as a mere appendage to their own affairs. We know now that government by organized money is just as dangerous as government by organized mob.

Franklin Delano Roosevelt, final speech at Madison Square Garden in the presidential campaign, announcing the Second New Deal, 31 October 1936

Despite appearances, the financial saga that led to the mega-meta-crisis the world still endures is not particularly difficult to understand. A specialized vocabulary and the array of confusing acronyms such as SIVs, CDOs and CDSs give the issue an aura of complexity, but in reality the unfolding of the drama is underpinned in quite a banal way by base instincts like greed and the everyday actions of intelligent people 'just doing their jobs', as well as wilful negligence on the part of governments imbued with the ideology of the self-regulating market. Animal spirits, as the great British economist John Maynard Keynes called them, or hormones such as testosterone, as chemistry would now interpret them, also played a part. So did the will to power. The banks lobbied and manoeuvred until they became literally 'too big to fail', as the standard phrase now has it, which unfortunately did not mean 'too big to bail'. Private financial power completely overtook public capacity to regulate or even to understand what was happening.

'To bail out' means three things in non-financial English: to use a receptacle to empty water out of a boat so that it doesn't sink; to parachute out of a distressed aircraft; and to pay a large cash deposit in order to release an accused person from jail while awaiting trial. Figuratively it can mean to help someone out of a bad predicament.

The huge bank bailouts across the world fit all these definitions. Governments have emptied the banks' boats of a lot of their stupid loans and toxic assets; they have helped the bankers strap on their golden parachutes and float gently down to solid ground with large sums of money in their jumpsuits; they have kept the bankers out of jail (Bernard Madoff doesn't count, he was the sacrificial wolf); and they have coughed up astronomical sums to extract the banks from a nasty predicament of their own making.

The risky loans and fancy financial products that precipitated the crisis were intellectually justified at the time by a pious belief in market self-regulation, the patent fiction that all participants were perfectly rational, possessed of equal knowledge, and that markets could not lie. Whatever people were willing to pay for was valuable. The financial products sold rested on impenetrable mathematical formulae whose inventors were too smart for their own good and that of their banks. Apparently only ten or twelve people inside a given

bank even pretended fully to understand the complex products they were flogging all over the world.

The banks wanted the government out of their affairs;
they lobbied and manoeuvred until they got their wish for
near total deregulation; disaster followed – at least for some.
The bankers responsible have rarely suffered because governments have intervened just when it mattered, although tens of
thousands of lower-level employees have lost their jobs. That
is the whole point of being 'too big to fail'. And when you
know that is what you are, you have an incentive to take huge
risks, since someone else can be counted on to clean up after
you. Such risks are risky not for those who take them, but for
society collectively. Heads I win, tails you lose.

We will make no attempt to cover all the details,[1] but we
will meet some of the main actors, examine their behaviour
and contemplate with suitable knowledge the devastation they
have wrought. I believe that the remedies prescribed so far
will not and cannot work, if by 'working' one means devising
a financial system that serves the needs of the real economy
and of society and avoids irremediable damage to innocent
bystanders. We need different strategies if something other
than a swift return to business as usual – and renewed crisis
– is the goal. The obvious solution, in my opinion, would
start by getting our system under control, treating finance
and credit as common or public goods operating under well-
understood, democratically established rules and serving the
needs of individuals, families and businesses and considered
as services, not profit-making activities in themselves. The
crisis could have been – could still be – used to achieve such
an outcome, but governments are taking an opposite path.
At the very least, and in the hope that it may not be too late,
concerned people can help to promote genuine democratic
solutions better than those on offer today. I shall elaborate on
these points in the final chapter.

HOW WE GOT HERE FROM THERE

Although events accelerated especially after 2001, the financial meltdown was a long time building up, and understanding it requires a bit of background. It's important to examine first the ideology of neoliberal globalization, then some recent history.

Recall what Adam Smith said about the Davos class: "'All for ourselves and nothing for other people" seems in every age of the world to have been the vile maxim of the masters of mankind.' If you don't tell people who wrote it, they generally attribute it to Marx, Hobbes or Machiavelli. Smith is usually referred to as 'an economist' but considered himself a 'moral philosopher'. We shall try to show how his vile maxim applies to the twenty-first-century masters of mankind, the golden boys, traders, investment bankers and assorted financial hucksters in New York, London and other major centres, and how the world of finance and the real economy followed them like lemmings over the cliff.

Another sharp-witted commentator who regularly deals with the same subject as Adam Smith and reveals the nature of this class is the artist William Hamilton in the *New Yorker*, the sophisticated US weekly which has been publishing his cartoons for decades. Hamilton casts a cold but amused eye on the doings of New York's upper echelons and captures their essence.[2] Unsurprisingly, a lot of his drawings are of wealthy people talking about money – who has it, who hasn't, how much, how they got it, how they go after more, what they do with it. I provide here a few random samples of his observations.

Two 1980s college students walking in the woods; young woman replies to young man, 'That is incredible. Do you know that I, too, want as much as I can get as fast as I can get it?'

Two executive types drinking in a crowded upscale bar: 'The point is to get so much money that money's not the point anymore.'

Woman explains to man at black-tie party, 'Of course they're clever. They have to be clever. They haven't got any money.'

One businessman to another as they gaze out the window of a private jet: 'How little we really own, Tom, when you think of all there is to own.'

In the world Hamilton knows inside out, money invariably figures in the language of seduction, courtship, friendship, marriage, party-going, child-rearing, shopping, divorce and, of course, the everyday business of business. If you want to understand from an insider the present masters of mankind, the mentality, mores and manners of the exotic tribe of New York bankers, top corporate executives, their wives and even their children,* Hamilton is your man – a better guide than any anthropologist.

To get 'All for themselves', this class had to accomplish several tasks, and let me make clear once more that I am not talking about conspiracies. Dark and secret plots are unnecessary when the common interests of the rich and powerful are at stake. Their first order of business was to change the redistributive model of the welfare state that developed in both Europe and the United States after the Second World War and made societies much less unequal than they had previously been. In those days, governments knew they had been

---

* The offspring of the rich learn fast:

Recess at an exclusive private school, small girl to her friend at the approach of another classmate: 'Be careful what you say. She's never been to Europe.'

Two sleek teenage girls riding on a bridle path together: 'Daddy just got sick of money for money's sake, so here we are in Washington.'

elected with a mandate to tax the better off so as to spread at least part of the wealth and to give the 'other people' some financial security, education, health care, pensions and decent public services. Let us recall that, in the era of Republican President Eisenhower in the 1950s, the topmost income bracket was taxed at 90 per cent. In 2009, the top tax rate which applies to income above $372,950 is 35 per cent. The member states of the European Union are already engaged in a kind of race to the bottom where taxes are concerned, both for individuals and businesses, and the treaties make harmonization virtually impossible. Such steep declines represent one of many neoliberal victories.*

In the USA in particular, the wealthy always saw themselves as the victims of the welfare model and complained bitterly that it 'confiscated' their advantages. They wanted this model abolished, but were no longer totally in command. Right-wing intellectuals serving the interests of these elites helped them to understand that the only way to bring about lasting change in favour of those at the top and return them to the position they had – in their view, rightfully – occupied in the earlier twentieth century, before the Depression and the Second World War, was to transform the redistributive culture of the welfare state. These intellectuals found a willing audience and financial support among business leaders, private family foundations and other right-wingers who were also offended by the growing power of the anti-Vietnam War, civil rights, feminist and gay liberation movements that then dominated popular culture, especially among the young.

The right undertook the transformation of society in a systematic way, targeting the centres of production and

---

* At such levels, the taxpayers usually have smart accountants and lawyers who can avoid for their clients taxation at 35 per cent – or indeed any percentage at all.

dissemination of ideas, the manufacture of persuasive images and the creation of popular myths. Purchasing top, politically reliable talent and skilled communicators, conservative foundations based on large industrial fortunes financed the ideological crusade; they showered generous rewards on these professional idea-mongers and patiently built their institutional infrastructure and ideological superstructure. They nurtured think tanks, such as the Heritage Foundation and the American Enterprise Institute, or smaller, more specialized organizations to campaign for conservative causes. They created publications of their own, financed everything from scholarly quarterlies to campus news-sheets, inundated the media, and manipulated the public using management and marketing skills to spread the message.

While the right was busy changing the whole atmosphere, indeed the character, of the United States by funding the development and spread of ideas, the few left-of-centre foundations and philanthropists were funding projects to improve some aspect of disadvantaged people's lives. In the context of an increasingly unfavourable ideological and political climate, most of these projects eventually failed.[3]

THE DOCTRINE

George Soros is credited with inventing the phrase 'market fundamentalism', which tells us in capsule form that the doctrine spread by these intellectual mercenaries is akin to a religious one. Perhaps neoliberal holy writ was easy to sell because it was so simple, ideological, and had little to do with genuine knowledge or sound economics. In any case it sold. Part of the doctrine came from the émigré Austrian economist turned social philosopher Friedrich von Hayek, who trained generations of ultra-conservative monetarist economists such as Milton Friedman at the University of

Chicago. Hayek taught his 'Chicago Boys' that government intervention in individual or social life would put nations on 'The Road to Serfdom', the title of his most famous book. Economic freedom, meaning the right to gain and to dispose of one's wealth without outside interference, was placed on the same pedestal as hard-won political, religious or personal freedoms enshrined in the Constitution and the Bill of Rights.

In Hayek's view, the law should be limited to forbidding certain actions. It should not be used for positive prescriptive purposes such as mandating programmes for poor people or even obliging rich people, through their taxes, to pay for common goods such as public schools and hospitals. Thus, in Hayekian language, the sentence 'I can eat, you can eat' means simply that we are free to do so because no law forbids it, but tells us nothing about the presence or absence of food on a family's table. His basic principle is that people exercising their individual choices will make far better collective decisions than any government, because no centralized bureaucracy can ever be in possession of enough information to know what people really want and need. Hayek's doctrine was an updated and harsher version of Adam Smith's famous 'invisible hand'.

The ideology purveyors concentrated on spreading such beliefs as these:

- The private sector always outperforms the public sector in terms of costs, efficiency, quality and price to the consumer.
- The government (sometimes disparagingly referred to as 'the nanny state') should not interfere in people's lives by enmeshing them in bureaucracies, particularly bureaucracies intended to 'help' them.
- The individual should be self-reliant and free to make his or her own choices and thereby to succeed or fail.

- The market, bringing together all these individual decisions, will be omniscient and thus make wise judgements, draw correct conclusions, value goods and services fairly, and ensure that the public gets exactly what it wants.
- In order to attain optimum equilibrium and thus to reach optimum decisions, markets should be self-regulated, not regulated by any external body.
- The rich are rich because they are smarter, harder working, more daring and more entrepreneurial than you and me; they are creators of wealth and providers of employment, so they and their businesses should be minimally taxed, if at all. The same goes for shareholders, and the aim of every business is to create 'shareholder value' (essentially higher dividends and market prices for the company's shares).
- Philosophically, the individual is sovereign, owes nothing to others, and is looked upon primarily as a consumer rather than as a citizen. Margaret Thatcher pithily expressed the neoliberal bottom line when in 1987 she told *Woman's Own* magazine that we were living in a period when 'too many children and people have been given to understand "I have a problem, it is the government's job to cope with it!" . . . "I am homeless, the government must house me!", and so they are casting their problems on society – and who is society? There is no such thing! There are individual men and women . . .'

In *Hijacking America*, I described the quite awesome material means, machinery, methods and messianic zeal of the ideological workforce that succeeded in making such notions commonplace and generally accepted. Following Antonio Gramsci, and taking seriously his concept of cultural hegemony as the key to domination, the culture warriors understood that real political power was best kept invisible.

It cannot be durably acquired through violence and coercion; rather, you must undertake what Gramsci called the 'long march through the institutions' in order to make your own ideas the 'common sense' of your time. Get into people's heads – their hearts, hands and votes will follow.

The election of Barack Obama gave millions of us, whether Americans or not, a thrilling and euphoric moment of hope after the violent, intensely neoliberal years of George Bush. We can also admit – at least I can – that we tended to project all our long-held, frustrated dreams and fantasies onto this charismatic man, who, despite rumours, does not walk on water or cure lepers with his touch. I fear that, despite such inspiring events as his election, neoliberal ideology is far from dead and can even be found stalking the White House corridors that lead to the Oval Office.

How else can one explain the renascent power and great rivers of money unfailingly flowing towards the very people and institutions that got us into the present mess by devout adherence to neoliberal principles and the interests of the rich? But here I am getting ahead of the story. The 'All for ourselves' crowd and their hired help concentrated on embedding their doctrine in the schools and universities, the press, radio and television, the law schools and the courts, even the churches and family institutions. They often succeeded in convincing people to vote massively against their own economic interests.[4]

THE TRIUMPH OF CAPITAL

Neoliberal doctrine, coupled with accelerating globalization and a simple desire for maximum profits, also favoured foreign investment wherever salaries were low in relation to workers' productivity. Capital naturally preferred jurisdictions where governments did not badger business with unwelcome rules concerning labour, taxes or the environment. Once the Cold War ended and the Berlin Wall came down, investors were increasingly free to go where they liked and do as they pleased. This trend was reinforced when ten, then twelve, new Eastern European countries joined the EU. The new freedoms for capital included the right to speculate against weak currencies and to withdraw one's money instantly and without notice. Many countries learned this to their cost when foreign investors got cold feet and fled, often disinvesting millions overnight. The result of this new capital mobility was one of the greatest hold-ups ever perpetrated.

First, it caused innumerable crises, especially in the poorer countries of the global South and in Eastern Europe. The International Labour Organization calculated that, between 1990 and 2002, over ninety countries experienced serious financial turmoil, defined as a drop in the value of their currency by at least 35 per cent over a two-month period.[5] Whereas our crisis in the West really takes hold in 2007–8, the Asians, Latin Americans and others got theirs a decade earlier – and are now suffering once more from ours. At the end of the 1990s, formerly high-growth emerging countries such as Thailand or Korea suddenly came to a standstill. Their banks were in trouble and businesses could not get credit. Ships refused to deliver cargo without cash payment on the spot. In Indonesia, over 30,000 bank employees were sacked in a single week; throughout Asia, hundreds of unemployed workers no longer able to feed their families committed suicide.

This wave of crisis spread and plunged countries as different as Turkey, Russia and Argentina into prolonged slumps, compounded by the harsh adjustment policies of the International Monetary Fund and the World Bank. In Argentina, once the IMF's star pupil, half the population woke up one morning to discover they were now classed as poor because they had lost their bank accounts, pensions and savings. The IMF and the bank, faithful to the doctrine despite its brutal impact, continued to privatize massively while slashing any remaining safety nets that might help the poor to survive. In Russia, life-expectancy rates plummeted as poverty and alcoholism escalated and social services were gutted.

Such disasters seemed confined to the poorer or emerging countries, and for a while the better-off ones of the OECD escaped harm: in these comparatively wealthy countries the changes were more gradual and the social cushions against the blows were thicker. However, over three decades, Europe and the United States saw major industries shut down and move offshore to poorer, less regulated places, causing massive job losses. The de-industrialization was visible; anyone could see a closed factory and read the unemployment statistics. Not many noticed, however, that over several decades Europe was transferring at least ten points of Gross Domestic Product (GDP), the total national wealth, from labour to the owners of capital.

Economists measure what they call the 'value added' annually in the course of economic activity: in the early to mid-1970s, by far the largest share of this value in Europe went to salaries and wages. Working people captured between two-thirds and three-quarters of the wealth created; the rest went to investors as rents, dividends and interest.

Most shareholders of most enterprises quoted on the world's stock markets are not small investors like the proverbial Chicago dentist or her counterpart in Paris, Singapore or Leeds. They are, rather, extremely large investment banks, hedge funds or pension funds, known collectively as institutional investors. In France some like to call them 'zinzins' because of the sibilant 's's' in 'les investisseurs institutionnels'.

Many top investors are not national institutions (and would probably not practise economic patriotism if they were): for example, more than 40 per cent of the investments in the 'CAC 40' companies quoted on the French stock exchange are made by foreigners. The incessant demands of the zinzins for greater 'shareholder value' have become greedier with each passing year. They cheerfully endorse mass sacking of workers and encourage tax avoidance as beneficial cost-cutting, profit-enhancing measures.

In the United States, the rich also went about system-atically divesting the poor, although the mechanism was simpler and more brutal. They simply kept wages stagnant for decades. Workers were not allowed to share in their own productivity gains, which went instead to shareholders and executives. This is the main reason that people borrowed so heavily, using the value of their houses as collateral – to keep on consuming. Contrary to received opinion, US citizens were not on a buying binge to acquire 'stuff': two-thirds of their increased spending went to higher bills for health care and energy.

From 2001 to 2007, the flow of money borrowed from mortgages was over three times as great as growth in wage and salary income. With the sharp drop in the housing market, people can no longer borrow, and one need look no further for an explanation of the sharpest drop in US con-sumer spending in sixty years.

These are some of the reasons that, at the dawn of the Reagan–Thatcher years, the shares of 'value added' began gradually to shift. Three decades later, European labour's share had dropped by ten points and capital owners had pocketed the corresponding windfall. In many of the twelve new EU member states, the shares are now down, or up, to 50–50, and even in a mature capitalist economy such as France labour's share now stands at only about 58 per cent.* This is not exactly small change: it represents 10 per cent of the wealth in the EU, which in 2008 amounted to €11,245 trillion ($15,293 trillion). Such transfers from jobholders to stock- and bondholders have continued for decades. Nor is this just an ongoing get-rich-quick scheme favouring investors; it also means there is that much less cash in the pockets of working people whose wages fuel the motors of consumption.

Seventy per cent of economic turnover in the United States depends on the consumption of the mass of US citizens. The small minority of wealthy people among them already have most of the things they need, so they put a high proportion of their abundant spare cash into more investments, not goods and services. Working people usually consume most or all of their salaries, particularly where wages are stagnant, as they have been in the USA for decades.

With wages stuck fast and people borrowing in order to continue consuming at the same level, the economic boom kept on going longer than it could otherwise have done: it was running on credit. Savings in the United States fell to zero, then became negative. Meanwhile, capital, especially corporate capital, and the richest citizens were taxed less and less: the middle class and consumers were supplying most of the government's revenues through income and sales taxes.

Less money in all those pockets means fewer purchases,

* A cautionary remark: one can get different results for calculations of value-added shares depending on how they are measured and which years one starts and ends with – I found one credible estimate of a 14-point drop in labour's share over a thirty-year period. Some biased sources manipulate the dates to extremes, trying to pretend that nothing of the kind has happened. Economists enjoy a good academic skirmish over such issues, but what is not in dispute among reputable authorities is the transfer itself. Except for the ideologically oriented calculations that choose the poorest years in postwar Europe as a starting point, I know of no estimate of the transfer that is less than 9 points, or 9 per cent of European GDP, although 10 is more common.

which in turn mean less economic activity, which results in overproduction compared to the solvent demand. Recall the immortal words of Henry Ford: 'I pay my workers so they can buy my cars.' In the globalized world, we pay Chinese or Vietnamese workers who can't buy our cars – or even, on the whole, the mobile phones they produce. The result is a glut of unsold goods and too much unused factory capacity, especially when the economic balloon starts to deflate.

'FINANCIALIZATION' AND LEVERAGE

Transfers of wealth from bottom to top, greatly reduced taxes for the rich and overproduction helped to provoke the current crisis, but by themselves were not enough. For that, two other huge changes were needed. One was what some call the 'financialization' of the economy. To avoid such a barbaric term, let's just say that you could make a lot more money and much higher profits in the financial sector than by producing actual *things* or providing standard services, which, as we have just seen, were beginning to suffer anyway from oversupply, lack of demand and the huge influx of foreign-produced goods at bargain prices.

During the first decade of the twenty-first century, the profits of the financial industry in the USA routinely outstripped profits in manufacturing by multiples of two or three; in Britain, the financial sector's annual profits hit an unprecedented 20 per cent. All the smartest young men and women seemed to be joining investment banks and hedge funds instead of becoming doctors, lawyers, engineers, professors or business executives. Collective year-end bonuses on Wall Street and in the City of London were measured in billions; major institutional shareholders held most of the cards and could dictate their demands to industrial companies. In a word, you could have a lot more power and excitement

making money from money without ever having to go
through the boring process of actual production and sales.
The 'real economy' was just *so* last decade, so passé. Although
it is logically and structurally impossible to detach finance
permanently from the real economy, this was a truth no one
wanted to hear and a lesson yet to be learned.

The second huge factor in the crisis build-up was 'leverage'
– meaning easy access to credit, often at stratospheric levels.
Everybody was madly borrowing – not only consumers but
also, indeed especially, the largest investment houses. The
banks were creating money out of the air and helping to blow
up bubble after bubble. To explain leverage here, we will
keep the numbers manageable by economizing on zeros, but
in the financial casino the big players were routinely gambling huge multiples of the modest amounts in the following
example.

Here's how it worked. Let's say you have a thousand dollars, euros or pounds to spare. Bernie Madoff or one of his
clones tells you he has a terrific investment that will bring
you 10 per cent a year. Your first thought is 'Great. In a year,
I can have 1,100 instead of 1,000.' But then you think, 'How
stupid. Why should I be satisfied with a lousy extra hundred
and a miserable 10 per cent when I could borrow and get
many times that?' So you visit your friendly banker and ask
for a loan of 9,000 so as to bet 10,000 altogether. The banker
says OK, announces that she will charge you 5 per cent interest per annum, gives you the 9,000 in cash, and you hand over
the 10,000 to Bernie.

A year goes by and Bernie comes through: you liquidate
the investment and he gives you back your original 10,000
plus the 1,000 it has earned. You now have 11,000. You pay
back the bank the 9,000 you borrowed plus the 5 per cent
interest charge of 450, and, instead of a profit of only 100 on
the money that actually belonged to you to begin with, you

have made a profit of 550. Instead of receiving 100, or 10 per cent, on your initial 1,000, you have raked in 550, or 55 per cent on your investment *because you borrowed*.

That's if all goes well. If all does not go well, you could break even, or perhaps make a small profit if Bernie's sure-fire investment earns only 5, rather than 10 per cent. In that case, you would get 50, whether you originally bet 1,000 or 10,000. But what if Bernie absconds to the Bahamas, or loses the money altogether? What if some really bad news hits the financial markets? What if your house, which you used as collateral for the loan, starts dropping in value? You knew you were taking a risk, because any investment is a bet on the future, and Bernie never promised he would give you back your capital or the interest under any and all circumstances – the entire transaction was based on your trust in Bernie and in the market itself. In that case, as a borrower you are in a deep hole. If you borrowed 9,000 at 5 per cent, you still owe the bank a total of 9,450, but now you have lost everything – including your own initial 1,000.

In this example, we chose a modest 10 to 1 ratio of bor-rowed money to the initial cash of 1,000 that was really yours. But try working out the same calculation for greater multiples: if at 10 to 1 you can make 55 per cent on your initial investment; at 20 to 1 (when you borrow 19,000 on the strength of your own 1,000) you can more than double your initial money for a return of 105 per cent; at 30 to 1, you will receive at the end of the year 3,000 in interest, pay back the loan of 29,000 plus 1,450 in interest to the bank, and pocket 1,550, a return of 155 per cent. Magic.

The big players in the Wall Street or City gambling dens knew no fear and had no scruples about leveraging. Why should they? They were 'too big to fail'. Some of them, for example Bear Stearns, the earliest of the Wall Street giants to bite the dust, leveraged their bets at up to 33 or more.

Great heaps of money could be made so long as the Bernies, the Citigroups and the Lehman Brothers kept their word, their investments remained productive and they could keep on selling – so long as the markets in houses and all kinds of securities were going up.

But when a bubble begins to seep air and can be seen to shrivel, all bets are off. If you are leveraged at, say, 30 to 1 and the investment turns bad, you owe the bank the 29,000 you borrowed on the strength of your 1,000, plus 1,450 in interest, or 30,450. Investment houses and banks very often owe money to each other – the interbank market is indeed the bedrock of the banking industry. It is therefore a disaster for everyone when one or several banks suddenly discover they can't repay their loans. They then try to sell off other assets to raise the cash they owe their creditors, but, since so many others are trying to do the same thing at the same time, the markets for all kinds of assets are also in free fall. This is why Bear Stearns had to be saved from falling into the abyss. The Federal Reserve stepped in and handed another financial giant, JPMorgan Chase, $30 billion worth of credit so that it could buy Bear Stearns at a tiny price compared with what the BS stock had been worth just a week before, and probably less than the market price of its midtown Manhattan office building. JPMorgan Chase got a very good deal.

The phenomenon feeds on itself: the more cash investors try to raise to repay their loans by selling off their assets, the more the prices of those assets drop. When it gets bad enough, it's known as deflation. The process can easily lead to generalized ruin; prestigious houses such as Lehman Brothers can quickly go from riches to rags. One bankruptcy can engender another in a deadly domino effect. Consumers stop consuming, investors stop investing and bankers stop lending to businesses and to each other.

Despite the obvious risks of a crash, high-leverage bor-rowing was not generally monitored or regulated by anyone. There were supposed to be some rules, those of the so-called Basel agreement (Basel I, because Basel II after several years has still not been universally adopted, although some banks followed it). This agreement dates from 1988 and was drawn up by the Basel Committee on Banking Supervision, which is itself attached to the Bank for International Settlements (BIS), often called the central bank of central banks, located in Basel, Switzerland. It stipulated that banks should hold 'enough capital to equal at least 8 percent of risk-weighted assets'.

As soon as a rule, any rule, is proclaimed, financial wiz-ards immediately seek a way to get around it. The simplest way to get around this very general, not very demanding rule was either to undervalue drastically the risk they really had on their books, or – and this was the new and seemingly brilliant way – persuade someone else to take on the risk for them. Welcome to the casino – but of a particularly perverse kind, because here at the Fabulous Universal Casino the high rollers mostly emerge richer and happier. The ones who lose their shirts are the workers inside dealing cards or serving drinks; it's ordinary passers-by in the street just heading to their offices or shops; it's the bus drivers, factory workers, shoe salesmen, clerks, butchers and bakers who bet little or nothing and are massively losing their jobs as more and more enterprises collapse for lack of credit or shrinking sales. They are doubly robbed because they are also going to be paying for years in order to wipe up the mess the hugely leveraged losers created. The government soon learns that, although they were too big to fail, they are not too big to bail, and steps in rather than risk total economic meltdown.

WHEN A BANK IS NOT A BANK

In the long-dead past, banking was a matter of making loans and keeping them on your own books, meaning that you as a banker were responsible for taking the risk. It's like the post-war Jimmy Stewart–Frank Capra movie *It's a Wonderful Life*, where the banker knows his depositors and his borrowers. When it's your own money you could lose it concentrates the mind, and as a prudent banker you tend not to make overly risky loans, but you support local businesses and homeowners as best you can. For this time-tested banking practice, the Casino Kids substituted the 'originate and distribute' model, meaning that they invented financial products based on mixtures of loans and then, rather than keeping the loans on their own books, 'distributed' them, or sold them on, to someone else, neatly spreading the risk and avoiding the Basel rule.

Those who had plenty of spare cash, often in the form of a fat balance-of-payments surplus – the Chinese, the Japanese or the Koreans – bought this paper; banks themselves in a great many countries bought lots of each other's risks. We'll see in a moment how they packaged debt, got it approved by the specialized ratings agencies and then conned any number of institutions worldwide into buying it. Their CDOs, or 'collateralized debt obligations', were all the rage, and, if they seemed too good to be true, it's because they were.

But first it's important to explain the politics of becoming too big to fail. The story goes back to the days of the New Deal and the Great Depression. One of the first laws Congress passed after President Franklin Delano Roosevelt assumed office in 1933 was called the Glass–Steagall Act, after its principal sponsors in the Senate and the House. Roosevelt made a priority of this perfectly sensible law which specified that commercial banks and investment banks must be kept separate – a sound idea, because institutions performing both functions had seriously hurt investors and contributed to the crash of 1929.

A commercial bank is the retail bank where you deposit your salary and write cheques or use a debit card against your account, where you ask for a loan to buy a car or a home. The traditional Jimmy Stewart–Frank Capra commercial banker made loans using his own or his shareholders' capital plus a fraction of the deposits of his commercial customers. He could not draw on these deposits in excess of a certain percentage and had to make sure the loans were backed, usually with 10 per cent of tangible, in-the-vault capital (Basel made the ratio of 8 per cent official). He made loans only to those individuals and companies he judged offered an acceptable risk and charged them interest for the privilege of using the bank's money. The loans stayed on the banker's books and, because they were made on the basis of rational criteria, nearly all of them were paid back. The bank's income and profits came from interest and service charges, so if the banker made too many risky loans he did not remain a banker for long.

The investment bank makes deals, large deals, like raising money for corporations and governments through issuing and selling securities in capital markets. It handles important matters of corporate finance such as public offerings of shares; it floats corporate bonds but also the treasury bonds of sovereign governments on the appropriate markets; it underwrites mergers and acquisitions. The investment bank makes money through fees and commissions and, increasingly, from its own trading. That was banking theory and practice for generations, but the go-go neoliberal years changed them completely.

BUYING THE GOVERNMENT

Although the two kinds of banks performed different functions, many banks and investment houses had long chafed at the restrictions keeping them separate. Little by little, under political pressure, the Federal Reserve relaxed the provisions of the Glass–Steagall Act to the point that Citicorp (banking) and the Travelers Group (insurance and securities) in 1998 made the biggest, most costly corporate merger in history. Their action was completely illegal at the time, but they got a waiver from the Fed by promising that within two years they would comply with certain provisions of the Glass–Steagall Act that they had just blithely ignored. Citicorp and Travelers were in fact betting they could get rid of this onerous law in time to ride roughshod over the last few restrictions the Fed had imposed, and in this they were encouraged by the attitude of Federal Reserve chair, Alan Greenspan, Treasury secretary, Robert Rubin (former co-chair of the investment house Goldman Sachs), who had followed Bill Clinton to Washington, and President Clinton himself, all of whom approved the manoeuvre and the merger.

With Rubin already on board at the Treasury, the financial industry then spent an additional $300 million on lobbying and handed out more than $150 million in political campaign contributions to strategically placed members of Congress, particularly those on the House and Senate banking committees. At last, after twelve failed attempts over twenty-five years to repeal Glass–Steagall, Congress finally said OK and threw it out.[6] The banks were jubilant. Citicorp and Travelers, newly baptized Citigroup, were home free; they had prised open the door, and now the huge mergers game began in earnest, creating monster institutions that observers instantly labelled 'too big to fail'. These new giants concentrated commercial banking, investment, securities and insurance under a single roof and under the same management; they no longer called themselves 'banks' – how dull! – but 'financial services corporations'.

Immediately after Glass–Steagall was tossed into the dustbin of history, Treasury Secretary Rubin did not even allow the passage of a decent interval but accepted immediately the offer of a top job at Citicorp and headed back to New York. Wall Street lore says that, at one point during the Glass–Steagall saga, the then secretary had received a phone call from the then president of Citicorp, who announced that he had important news. 'You're buying the government?', quipped Rubin in response.*

This turned out not to be a joke. They really could buy the government now. Not only did Wall Street manage to change the law, but, since the financial services industry could henceforward be all things to all people, the top talent, knowing its employers had become too big to fail, began to invent more and more exotic products. The bankers gave these products various imaginative names, for instance 'structured investment vehicles' (SIVs), 'collateralized debt obligations' (CDOs), 'credit default swaps' (CDSs) and others.

The common denominator of these financial instruments is that they were all 'derivatives', because their value was derived from the value of the underlying assets on which they were based. These underlying assets were usually some kind of debt, very often mortgage debt. The process of anchoring the new products to underlying assets – whatever they were – was called 'securitization', because they got attached to something that seemed – at least to financial types

---

* Famous for his personal fortune and financial success, Rubin is also known for nurturing and forming close relationships with promising younger men, such as Larry Summers and Tim Geithner, who by 2009 had become President Obama's closest economic adviser and Treasury secretary, respectively.

– somewhat more tangible, like a stock, a bond or a mortgage. The new generic name for these derivatives was 'vehicles', as in structured investment vehicles or SIVs, possibly because they really did act like moving vans – transporting money, underlying assets and new products from one place to another. The bankers saw them as embodying many cardinal virtues because the vehicles could move financial products off the banks' books and shift the risk to someone else. Recall that the Basel rule stipulated that banks should hold 'enough capital to equal at least 8 percent of risk-weighted assets'. In practical terms this meant that banks had to limit their risk, something they were loath to do because it also limited their profits. SIVs overcame this limitation handily; they were risk dispersers and diffusers. That was the 'distribute' part of the 'originate and distribute' model: the originator shifted the risk from his own balance sheet to someone else's because that someone else bought the repackaged assets along with the risk they represented.

But the buyer also wanted to thwart the Basel rule. No problem: the other miraculous property of SIVs was their near total opacity. They fed what became known as the 'shadow banking system', a vast storeroom of totally unregulated packages of debt-based assets, notably mortgage debts. Sometimes the banks created and managed the new funds themselves, in-house but 'off balance sheet' – that is, not on their books. Sometimes they hired outside fund managers to do it for them. By mid-2007, well over $1,200 billion of these products were hidden in various dark corners, ready to implode. Regulators, had they worried about this at all or tried to do anything about it, would have looked like the Keystone Cops in a Model T Ford chasing a very smart gang in a 220 hp BMW. These investments were touted to perform at such amazing levels that supposedly sober bankers were frantic to borrow great multiples of the money they actually had on hand in order to cash in on the bonanza. That was the main reason they became so highly leveraged.

From the mid-1990s, and especially after the merger mania that the demise of Glass–Steagall stimulated, the most important banks and bankers increasingly abandoned their traditional profession and hired either wizard mathematicians or glorified salespeople to sell their SIVs and CDOs to other financial institutions all over the world. These products were bets that it was possible to make money indefinitely from different kinds of debt, that the value of underlying values of things like houses would continue to inflate much faster than the growth rate in the real economy. But the most essential function performed by CDOs was to make someone else shoulder the risk of as yet unpaid debt on which these assets were based. One player cited in a revealing article in the *Financial Times* about the shadow banking system gave the example of $10 million of real cash in a hedge fund that supported an $850 million mortgage-backed deal: 85 to 1 – now *that's* leverage. Where, then, did the initial $10 million in real money come from? Perhaps from you. Pension funds, universities, hospital endowments, even charities put billions into these products in the belief that they were every bit as safe as bank deposits.[7]

Another innovation was the credit default swap. The basic rule of banking used to be that the banker assumed the risk of defaults on all loans made. The new breed of bankers, however, found a way to package default risk so that it, too, could be traded. If they no longer had to assume that risk, they could make more loans yet not take on the losses if those loans defaulted. They shifted, or 'swapped', their risk to an insurer. As with an ordinary insurance policy, they paid the insurer a premium to assume that risk for them. Ordinary insurance companies have to follow rules limiting how much insurance they can sell, but there were, and are, no regulations applying to these financial products and therefore no limits on how many CDSs a financial institution can issue. This is how the banks collectively became the biggest casino in history. CDSs became so popular that the 'notional' amount outstanding was nearly $60,000 billion, which is more than the GDP of the entire world.

A word of caution: when I think I understand a subject thoroughly, I feel I can write about it; when I don't, I tell the reader. I don't fully understand these things, so please let me first quote part of the explanation of the UN Conference on Trade and Development, UNCTAD. One can say for sure that the CDS craze contributed mightily to the general collapse, because any model that enshrines risks that one need never assume oneself is a disastrous model for a financial system.

In order to buy a CDS on a given security, investors do not need to hold the security. Most CDSs were bought by people who were betting on the fortune of a given security and not by investors who needed to hedge a certain exposure to risk. In fact, there seemed to be betting over betting, with gross exposure of a CDS being about ten times its net exposure. As a result, nobody knew who was insured against or exposed to any type of risk.[8]

Imagine that you could take out an insurance policy on your neighbour's house, torch the house and collect the insurance. This is what you can do against government bonds using CDSs you don't own. As *Financial Times* columnist Wolfgang Münchau puts it, 'A naked CDS purchase . . . [i.e. one which is not backed by a bond you own] is a purely speculative gamble. There is not one social or economic benefit . . . the case for banning them is about as strong as that for banning bank robberies.'[9]

PRIMES, SUBPRIMES, CRIMES AND SUBCRIMES

To concoct their CDOs, the bankers' innovative idea was to throw various debt ingredients into a great financial cauldron, stir well, pour out the mixture, roll it into a sausage shape, slice the sausage, then sell the slices as profitable new financial products. These debt ingredients could be of any nature. They were at first high-end ('prime') mortgages, but later also student loans, credit card debt, loans for big-ticket consumer goods such as automobiles, and so on. The sausage slices were rated 'senior' or even 'super-senior' (meaning you're going to get paid unless there's a communist takeover of Wall Street), and on down the scale; the more certain repayment appeared to be, the more expensive the product.

The raw material of outstanding loans – that is, trillions of dollars in debt – was never in short supply. In the United States, it is virtually impossible to attend university without going deeply into debt and paying back for years after graduation. As for credit card debt, many people hold numerous cards that all charge outrageous high interest rates but allow you to keep on borrowing and rolling over your debt month after month. Mortgages, however, made up by far the greatest proportion of the debt that could be turned into sausage and sold on by the slice. The American Dream, as in many other countries, is to own your own house, especially if its value is going up steadily and you can borrow on that value, no matter how much you still owe the bank. So long as your 'equity', or capital – the amount for which you could sell the house at the current market price – is higher than your remaining debt on it, you're OK.

Watching house prices shoot up, others felt they would be stupid not to borrow themselves. Even if they already owned their own house, they might buy another for rental purposes or simply speculate that they could sell a while later at what they assumed would be a nice profit. That is why mortgages in the United States were a huge industry in themselves. At the time of the ultimate crash, the total US housing bubble of mortgage debt, which had begun in earnest in 2001, reached a staggering $8,000 billion, or $8 trillion. In seconds ticked by your watch, that would come to 248,000 years.

How did this bubble first start to inflate? In 2000 and 2001, the USA experienced the 'dot.com' stock market meltdown, in which dozens of start-up computer and related high-tech firms used up all their capital and went bust. The stock markets were plunging, and the Fed chairman, Alan Greenspan, fearing a severe recession, cut interest rates to a laughable 1 per cent. There they remained until 2004 and even after that only went up at a snail's pace.

This was an open invitation to exchange one bubble for another – dot.com stocks for housing. Americans wanted in on the bonanza, and between 1997 and 2005, according to *The Economist*'s house price index, the value of their houses increased by 73 per cent. The phenomenon became international: increases in US housing values were matched or surpassed in Belgium, the Netherlands and Sweden but were as nothing compared with those in France (+87 per cent) Australia (+114), Spain (+145) and league champions Britain (+154) and phenomenal Ireland (+192).

Banks were generally happy to accept the now more valuable house as collateral for new debt. The housing market had been going up for so long that virtually everyone assumed it could only continue in the same direction. There was no lack of outstanding credit for the bankers to grind up and mix into different sorts of sausage in line with various arcane mathematical formulae according to the debt content and the seniority of the slice. Back in the old Glass–Steagall days, when the commercial banker staked his own business on 'performing' loans, most outstanding mortgages were completely safe because bankers wouldn't lend to borrowers they knew to be, or feared could become, insolvent. In the brave new financial world of the twenty-first century, however, if the loans failed to perform it was no longer your problem, because you had shifted the risk to someone else.

These debt-based financial products were in such great demand that, for people 'originating and distributing', it was a quasi-divine moment, and the more debt outstanding the better. To provide more and more underlying debt for the CDOs, legitimate banks, but also upstart specialized mortgage companies, began descending lower and lower down the social ladder of borrowers. Instead of making only low-risk 'prime' loans to solvent people, they ventured into the 'subprime' territory of the poor and vulnerable, anxious to become American dreamers themselves. George Bush encouraged people to buy into the dream, and creditors knew that, if these people defaulted, they could always foreclose on, or repossess, the mortgaged house, throw the occupants out and resell the property. That was the theory.

The practice was something else. The loans to poor, often minority borrowers were fundamentally dishonest because the people who signed on for them often did not understand the legalese in the fine print, nor had they probably ever heard the Latin phrase *caveat emptor*, or even its translation, 'let the buyer beware'. Aggressive salespeople attracted the unwary with 'teaser rates' – very low interest rates and small monthly payments to begin with, which then quickly doubled or tripled. Formally known as ARMs, or adjustable rate mortgages, they became weapons of mass destruction as the rates escalated.

Banks and mortgage shops stopped bothering with background checks on these new customers. In the space in the contract that said 'Annual Income', you could write $300,000 if you wanted to, even though you were earning ten times less. Why should the lenders worry? Among themselves, they jokingly referred to their NINJA loans, because they had been granted to people with No Income, No Job or Assets. Sometimes, just as cynically, they called them neutron loans: like the neutron bomb, they killed people but left buildings intact. Since these loans were all made during the same go-go years (starting in a big way in about 2003), the higher payments all kicked in at about the same time, and thus the defaults inexorably spread.

Under the terms of the Home Mortgage Disclosure Act, data was collected showing that, between 2005 and 2007, the subprime mortgage purveyors classed as 'high-interest lenders' made nearly 7.2 million subprime loans for a total of $1,380 billion – nearly 1.4 trillion dollars' worth. The top twenty-five lenders alone were responsible for nearly a trillion of that amount. They included specialized divisions of major blue-chip banks such as Citigroup, JPMorgan Chase or Crédit Suisse First Boston, high-flying investment houses such as Lehman Brothers, Goldman Sachs or Merrill-Lynch, and newly minted companies such as Countrywide Financial and Ameriquest. These last two were the biggest lenders of all, explicitly set up to exploit the subprime market.[10]

These financial raptors specialized in preying on the poor, often blacks and Latinos. Desperate families who thought they were on their way to the security of owning their home, and believed that its value could only go up, suddenly saw their monthly payments soar way beyond their means. They couldn't possibly reimburse what the contract said they owed; hundreds of thousands fell behind on their payments.

Meanwhile, the number of student-loan and automobile-loan defaults also rose sharply. By then the savings rate in the United States had dropped below zero and people had nothing left to fall back on. The first warning signs that something was decidedly rotten in the mortgage markets came in 2006.

In early 2007, the bank HSBC took a multi-million dollar loss because in 2002 it had purchased a big US subprime lender called Household International. Then came Bear Stearns. Two of BS's hedge funds were based on huge exposure to the US housing market, and it blew up in March 2008.

Dean Baker, a very smart economist who is co-director of the Center for Economic and Policy Research in Washington, is extremely clear on what the housing bubble actually was.

> This bubble was driving the economy ever since the recession in 2001. [It] led to an enormous boom in construction, as builders made huge profits selling new homes at bubble-inflated prices. It also led to a huge surge in consumption as homeowners spent a large portion of their bubble-generated housing equity . . . When this bubble burst, it was inevitable that housing construction would collapse and consumption would plummet, throwing the economy into a steep recession.[11]

The crisis was predictable because house prices were going up much, much faster than the overall rate of inflation. The law of supply and demand was also at work: the supply of houses on the market was abundant but demand was no greater than previously. Subprime mortgages kept the boom going a while longer, but nothing can sustain a bubble forever.

The financial industry, however, was in denial – or simply didn't care. Despite abundant forewarnings, everyone was having too good a time to put down the champagne bottle and stare reality in the face. Readers of the non-specialized press first began to hear about subprime problems during the spring and summer of 2007, but anyone whose job it was to pay attention to default rates and other economic indicators had all the information they needed at least a year earlier.

In mid-2006, prices for new homes had dropped by nearly

10 per cent; this ought normally to have been a warning sign of oversupply. Already some of the upstart subprime specialist lenders were going bankrupt or sacking hundreds, even thousands of employees. In 2006, foreclosures hit 1.2 million American families; this figure shot up to 2.2 million in 2007. Maybe this was 'nothing' compared with the 3.2 million houses repossessed by the creditors in 2008, but it still represented a huge number of people forcibly awakened from the American Dream.*

WHAT DO YOU MEAN, 'NOBODY SAW THIS COMING'?

I get very tired of hearing or reading claims that 'Nobody saw this coming'. Sorry: lots of people saw it coming, including people in the United States such as Dean Baker, quoted above, Nouriel Roubini, who was labelled 'Dr Doom' for his pains, and the French economists speaking at every Attac summer university since at least 2004.

In the United States, Consumer Affairs, the Comptroller of the Currency and the National Bureau of Economic Research kept tabs on the number of loans of all types in default. The NBER even reported in 2007 that over *half* of subprime automobile loans were in default, the great majority within the first year of repayment. In other words, anyone who wanted to read the bad omens could read them, and any competent economist should have done so. But bubbles are such lovely iridescent things; they also ensure salaries and bonuses as inflated as the bubbles themselves to those who are continually blowing them up.

---

* These frightening numbers continued to mount: foreclosure filings for the month of April 2009, at 342,000, were a third above the filings for the same month the previous year.

You are probably wondering why anyone would want to buy CDOs based entirely on different kinds of debt – those slices of sausage cooked up in the great financial kitchen. The reasons are several. First, they promised huge returns, and that is always tantalizing to an investor. Second, they were put on the market mostly by top banks with solid reputations. But, most important, they were highly rated – one could say countersigned and vouched for –by the ratings agencies, particularly the offerings the bankers called 'senior tranches', or best-quality slices of the sausage.*

The function of the ratings agencies, of which the top three are Standard & Poor's, Moody's Investors Service and Fitch, is to tell investors how safe or risky a given investment is. The highest rating is AAA, then AA+, AA, AA– and so on down the line, through subtle gradations of pluses and minuses into the Bs and finally to junk bond status, meaning super-high risk. Triple A is supposed to be solid gold, and it was systematically stamped on most of the CDOs on offer, meaning you could buy them blindfolded and sleep soundly.

How, then, could so many of them turn toxic and become securities so insecure that even today no one knows what they are worth, if anything? Before the crisis really took hold, I was asked to participate in a debate on France 24, the French answer to CNN, which also broadcasts in English, and was paired with the chief economist of one of the ratings agencies speaking from New York. Pointing out that the agencies

---

* At an OECD forum at which I was invited to speak, I met the governor of the Central Bank of the Czech Republic and asked him if the banks in his country had succumbed to the lure of CDOs. He told me that they had indeed been approached and had asked the Central Bank for guidance. The latter asked them a simple question: 'Do you understand these products?' When the Czech banks replied that actually, no, they didn't, the Central Bank advised them not to touch the CDOs with a bargepole.

were paid by the very companies issuing the securities they
were called upon to rate, I asked him if he didn't feel this
could create a perverse incentive to give high ratings. Wasn't
it impossible under such circumstances to be impartial?
'Yes', he admitted, 'they pay us, but they don't pay us very
much.' Somehow I found this response unconvincing, and I
expect the viewers did too. We turned out to be right. Since
the ratings agencies are private, profit-oriented companies
competing with each other for business, which agency do
you think would receive the most calls for its services? The
one that says (a) 'Your paper is a piece of junk'; (b) 'We can't
even understand what's in this black box'; (c) 'This is a triple
A investment we can heartily recommend.' You get only one
guess.

In October 2008, with the crisis in full spate, a former
managing director at Moody's testified before the US House
Committee on Oversight and Government Reform that
the bankers who originated the CDOs 'typically chose the
agency with the lowest standards, engendering a race to the
bottom in terms of rating quality'. The agency economist
who informed me via France 24 that 'They don't pay us very
much' was also a shade disingenuous: in fact they were paid
far more to rate complex mortgage-based securities than to
assess more traditional kinds of debt.

Congressman Henry Waxman, chair of a House committee investigation, said 'the credit ratings agencies occupy a
special place in our financial markets [and they] broke this
bond of trust'. He also cited internal rating agency documents
obtained by his committee showing they were 'clearly aware
of the problem of conflict of interest'. One such document,
dating from October 2007, baldly stated that 'unchecked
competition . . . can place the entire financial system at risk',
which is precisely what it did. Now the agencies have downgraded thousands of debt issues – they refuse to say how many

– which were originally worth, if that's the word, hundreds of billions of dollars.

Europe has now approved rules which will oblige ratings agencies that want to do business in the EU to register and be supervised by public bodies of the relevant national securities regulators. But in the United States, despite the public outcry and the congressional hearings, little has changed. An apparently technical piece in the *Financial Times* in late July 2009 is enough to give the shivers to anyone informed about the ratings agencies, which now includes you, dear reader. Using exactly the same business model as before, the agencies are raking in money to the point that financial advisers are encouraging clients to buy their stock.

Why? Because these agencies, which are private companies, are now rating great stacks of new debt, partly issued by banks but also by the US government in the form of bonds and government-backed funding programmes. Maybe we can look forward in a couple of years to a nice fat bubble of Treasury debt and a subsequent crash in US government paper and then the dollar.* This scarcely bears contemplating, but who is to say it's not a possibility? It is already happening in Europe.

Most of the 'originate and distribute' products were invented in the USA and Britain, but others wanted in on

---

* Many newspapers published information on these congressional hearings on 23 October 2008. The mid-2009 financial comeback of the agencies is in Aline van Duyn and Joanna Chung, 'Ratings agency model left largely intact', *Financial Times*, 23 July 2009. The agencies can make record profits despite the fact that they are being sued by dozens of investors, such as the California Public Employees Retirement pension fund (CALPERS), which claims it lost more than a billion dollars as a result of 'wildly inaccurate' ratings. It seems bizarre, but the US legal system treats corporations as 'persons', which gives them the same freedoms granted to individuals by the First Amendment, including freedom of speech. So far, the agencies have won all the law suits against them because their ratings are classed as 'opinions' and are therefore constitutionally protected as 'speech'.

the bonanza. Recall that the sausage slices in a given CDO were also rated as 'senior' or even 'super-senior', implying that the owner would always be paid back first even if owners lower down in the pecking order were not paid at all. The combination of a triple A rating and a super-senior label lulled other bankers into abandoning prudence. Why should they bother to verify? As one of them from Union Bank of Switzerland (UBS) told the *Financial Times* journalist Gillian Tett, 'Frankly, most of us had not even heard the word 'super-senior' until the summer of 2007. We were just told by our risk people that these instruments are triple A, like Treasury bonds. People did not ask too many questions.'[12]

REGULATION, SHMEGULATION

As we know, the ratings agencies were passing out triple As like bonbons at Christmas time. But what were the regulators up to, especially in the places these things were invented? Weren't they supposed to be disinterested watchdogs, looking out for the general good and quick to act at any sign of impending crisis? And what about the grandest regulator of them all, the one who became chair of the Federal Reserve in 1987 and remained there for nineteen years? Was not Alan Greenspan at least partly responsible for the debacle? Yes, absolutely. Despite his near-godlike reputation and financial rock-star status, Greenspan has a lot to answer for.

Greenspan had once been a director at JPMorgan, and from the moment he arrived at the Fed he encouraged a series of bubbles, fuelled by the magical mystery money which he also helped to create through ultra-low interest rates. He thought leverage was a great idea, and during his entire Fed career gave the bankers exactly what they wanted while benignly blessing every defeat of government regulation. His severely rationed testimony before Congress and occasional

Delphic utterances at the highest-level revels of the capitalist elites increased his aura and his mystique. He got away with murder. Today, he accepts that there might have been a flaw in his reasoning. This old JPMorgan hand also claimed to experience 'shocked disbelief' as the crisis unfolded. It was inconceivable, wasn't it, that bankers could allow greed and recklessness to overcome their rational selves?

But what really rankles is the way Greenspan laid the blame for the crisis on – you'll never guess – China! Trying to escape responsibility for the disaster, he published a piece in the *Wall Street Journal* where he argued that Chinese growth led to an 'excess' of savings, and this is what kept global interest rates low, which is why the housing bubble inflated. Let us all smack our foreheads in unison. Of course! Why didn't we see it? Greenspan himself had no power at all: he couldn't set interest rates; he was but a tempest-tossed victim on an ocean of overwhelming global forces. This is nonsense, and a former colleague of Greenspan's at the Fed, now a professor at Stanford, tears his arguments to shreds in a manner too technical to reproduce here. The bottom line is that Greenspan's cheap and easy credit policy blew the bubble up to monstrous size, period.[13]

One factor does in some measure exonerate the regulators: they no longer had enough rules to work with. The $150 million contributed to the campaigns of key congressmen and women in order to get rid of Glass–Steagall turned out to be an insignificant fraction of the total funds Wall Street spent between 1998 and 2008 to buy the laws it wanted. These outlays prove once more that Robert Rubin wasn't joking about buying the government. A report entitled *Sold Out: How Wall Street and Washington Betrayed America* describes in detail twelve major deregulation measures that financial industry lobbyists were able to push through Congress with the enthusiastic cooperation of the legislators. It's hard to decide whether their achievement should be called 'deregulation' or 'reregulation' in favour of the financial services corporations. Over the decade 1998–2008, this industry, including banking, securities, insurance and accounting firms, spent $5,000 million – yes, 5 billion – on politicians and lobbyists, not an unduly large amount of money from their point of view. By 2007 the financial industry employed almost 3,000 lobbyists – 2,996 to be precise. Shooting down Glass–Steagall was just their opening salvo.[14]

What else did the financial services wrecking crew get in exchange for their $5,000,000,000 in lobbying and political contributions? Plenty. They were allowed, incredibly, to remove any money-losing assets from their balance sheets, so as to hide them from investors. They were allowed to create and trade financial derivative products, subject to no regulation whatever. Trillions of dollars were subsequently bet on these exotic products. As we will see in the chapter on the food crisis, the commodities markets were also stripped of regulation through the Commodities Markets Modernization Act, allowing uncontrolled speculation and contributing heavily to food riots in more than thirty countries and the hunger of additional millions. Whenever the lobbyists or legislators set out to eliminate a useful law, they call it 'modernization' or 'reform'.

THE WORLD'S GREATEST SALVAGE OPERATION

All this debt-encouraging, transparency-discouraging, risk-promoting deregulation led to the crashes that at first seemed to be isolated events but soon became systemic. Let us sum up the situation, relying here on the ever clear-sighted Paul Krugman.[15] First, the housing bubble bursts, bringing with it a surge of defaults on mortgages and foreclosures on homes.

This leads to a plunge in prices of mortgage-backed securities, whose value ultimately depends on the mortgage payments of millions of home-buyers. These losses leave many financial institutions with too little capital and too much debt, especially because they were so highly leveraged and took on far too much debt during the bubble years. Lacking capital, they are unable or unwilling to provide credit to the economy. They try to pay down their debts by selling assets, including their mortgage-backed securities, but, since everyone else is trying to do the same thing at the same time, prices fall and, in a vicious circle, everyone's financial position becomes worse.

But, at the beginning of 2008, few were prepared to recognize how dire the situation had already become. Those who knew didn't talk for fear of provoking panic. Bear Stearns had to be saved in March 2008 because it held at least $46 billion in mortgage-related securities that were imploding. If it tried to raise money by dumping them all on the market, there could be a chain reaction. So, as we noted earlier, the Fed gave a big credit line ($30 billion) to JPMorgan Chase to buy Bear on the cheap – and at the same time sent a loud signal that no large investment bank with a lot of toxic mortgage securities on its books would be allowed to go under. Or so it seemed.

After Bear, some sizeable hedge funds collapsed, including one belonging to the Carlyle Group, whose capital came in part from wealthy Bush I administration officials and cronies.* More cracks appeared; most dangerous was the shaky condition of the two mortgage financing giants known as

---

* One of the many things I have not attempted in this book is to keep up with hedge funds. If you want to do so, you should read the *Financial Times* Weekly Review of the Fund Management Industry, which appears as a supplement every Monday. But, I warn you, at last count there were 33,543 of these things, although the total numbers were said to have stopped growing (numbers from the Weekly Review for 24 August 2009).

Fannie Mae and Freddie Mac. These two corporations are government sponsored but owned by private shareholders. Their stock prices were steadily falling because investors were afraid they might not withstand losses on the monstrous $5,300 billion worth of mortgages in their portfolios: they absolutely had to be shored up for both financial and political reasons.*

Every weekend there seemed to be another round-the-clock meeting where Treasury, the Fed and elite Wall Street bankers huddled, lived on pizza and saved some institution or other before the markets opened on Monday morning and went berserk. Once the downfalls began, their rhythm accelerated. Fannie and Freddie were snatched from the jaws of certain death on 7 September and nationalized, although the government called it a 'conservatorship'.

The shock that finally snapped everyone out of denial mode and brought home the gravity of the moment was the mid-September 2008 collapse of the venerable house of Lehman Brothers, which held as much as $600 billion worth of bad debt. Throughout the world, all those 'rational investors' whose existence the economists love to postulate ran headlong in herd formation for the emergency exits. Next day, the *International Herald Tribune* featured four front-page photos of traders, captioned 'Nervous in New York, Frantic in Frankfort, Distressed in Dubai, Tense in Tokyo'. Investors

* East Asian and Gulf country governments with large supplies of surplus dollars held nearly a trillion dollars' worth of Fannie and Freddie shares, which they had purchased because the shares paid higher interest rates than Treasury bonds but were supposed to be just as safe. The US government could not allow a Fannie/Freddie share debacle, much less a default, which would have caused a massive sell-off and collapse of the dollar – not to mention an international political crisis. The full truth about the Fannie/Freddie rescue has not come out, but it was clear that these corporations had to be saved at all costs. See Martin Mayer, 'Mortgaged to the world', *International Herald Tribune*, 30 July 2008.

had decided it was better to sell first and ask questions later. Markets were in freefall; bank stocks were dropping to the ground like autumn leaves.

The pizza deliveries stopped. The Fed couldn't pull off a deal. No other bank would buy Lehman even if they could borrow all they needed to buy it, and its death warrant was signed. Lehman Brothers, founded in 1850, declared bankruptcy on 15 September, and the provision of credit throughout the United States and the world came to a screeching halt. Granted, this was a very important bank – but how could the fall of one house, however great and venerable, stop the whole financial system in its tracks? It happened because short-term loans from one bank to another, often as short as overnight, keep the credit system oiled and functioning; but they froze on 15 September because nobody knew what anybody else's balance sheet was really worth. No one was going to lend to a bank that had a string of toxic sausages in its vaults or wrapped around its neck, and if a prestigious bank such as Lehman could disintegrate, who knew what other institutions might perish tomorrow, leaving their creditors holding the bag.

When banks refuse to lend to one another, they also refuse to lend to you and me. Contrary to the freewheeling days of the subprimes, banks came to resemble perfectly the old joke about being institutions that will lend only to people who don't need the money (and, in this case, sometimes not even to them). For the most part, we still have no idea what the toxic sausage CDO slices are really worth, or even which ones are worthless, because there is no market to speak of in these products that would allow the forces of supply and demand to set a price. This is one reason I believe that, despite government intervention and purchases of the toxic assets, we are in for a much longer downturn than many will admit.

Since I am not looking for a libel suit, I shall simply point out in passing that Henry Paulson was the Bush administration's Treasury secretary at the time that this failure, unlike earlier and later ones, was allowed to occur. Paulson, whose personal fortune is estimated at some $700 million, was the former chairman of Goldman Sachs. Like Goldman, Lehman Brothers was one of a handful of the most prominent US investment banks that habitually issued and marketed United States Treasury bonds.

Now that the field of competitors has been narrowed, Goldman is able to charge the US government higher fees to market its paper. These earnings allowed it to declare in June 2009 that it would pay the highest bonuses in its entire history. This windfall should continue for some time as the United States government is obliged to sell *a lot* of Treasury bills – that is, borrow from investors to cover the huge cost of bailing out the banks, including Goldman Sachs. Someone, somewhere, seems to have made some very smart moves.

One might also want to ask the Treasury and the Fed why, just two days after Lehman succumbed, the government consented to a bailout far more massive than even Lehman would have needed and gave the ailing financial insurance giant AIG (American International Group) a whopping $85 billion, which it quickly ran through. It later came back three times for more – a total of $185 billion. AIG insured lots of banks against defaults on the securities they held, promising, like any other insurance company, to pay up if others defaulted. It turned out that it had made such promises to the tune of $560 billion – and all the contracts that sum represented were in worse and worse shape as that week progressed.

Treasury Secretary Paulson could delay no longer – he had to rush in with a defence that had a chance of stopping the avalanche. This was the TARP, the Troubled Assets Relief Program, a trifling matter of $700 billion of taxpayers' money to hand over to the banks. The TARP could easily be seen as the Davos class solution: privatize profit but socialize loss by dumping your problems on ordinary citizens. The lobbies of the usual suspects pushed this solution as the best way to get rotten securities removed from their balance sheets by the government; Paulson was happy to oblige.

Normally, if you hand over a lot of money to someone, you own something in exchange, even if it's something intangible such as corporate shares. None of that for Paulson: initially all the funds were to go to the people who made the mess, with no strings of any kind attached. That was so outrageous it had to be changed, so that the US Treasury, in exchange for hundreds of billions of dollars, now owns shares of preferred stock in a number of banks. In other respects, the Obama administration has continued Bush practices, and recipients of TARP money are still not obliged to report on how they spend it. At first, Paulson also demanded immunity from review 'by any court of law or any administrative agency', but this smacked too much of tyranny even for a Congress that had believed Paulson every time he had said during the past two years that the crisis was 'contained'.

The TARP began immediately handing out staggering amounts of taxpayers' cash to the banks, but also to insurer AIG and to General Motors. Within a few months it had propped up more than 500 banks. The Center for Responsive Politics, a non-partisan think tank in Washington, has published a long and astonishing list correlating the amounts that twenty-six corporations spent on campaign contributions ($37 million) and lobbying ($77 million) and which subsequently received huge amounts in bailout funds from the TARP. These were beyond any doubt the smartest investments these companies ever made: they yielded a return of 258,449 per cent and close to $300 billion. The representatives and senators who received the most in contributions happen to chair congressional committees that deal with financial regulation, but this is probably fortuitous.[16]

Given Paulson's no-strings approach, it was predictable that the TARP would be rife with mismanagement and provide a lot of incentives for fraud, but you will be pleasantly surprised to learn that there is now a Zorro, a noble avenger, at the Treasury, whose name is Neil Barofsky, the special inspector general of the TARP, or SIGTARP. This is the man who should get a bonus, but he seems bent simply on serving the public, and, as if that were not unusual enough, he produces scathing, sometimes scary reports and has successfully stood up to Treasury Secretary Tim Geithner, who is not happy to have a watchdog on the premises. Geithner tried and failed to curb Barofsky's independence, and one understands why the secretary would breathe easier without him. Barofsky has made clear, for example, that the Treasury so far hasn't even tried to value the corporate shares it has received in exchange for the hundreds of billions it has handed over to banks – shares which, in the final analysis, belong to American taxpayers. Barofsky is only thirty-eight years old, spares no one's feelings and, as a federal prosecutor, spent years chasing white-collar criminals. He now has the legal power to do the same on behalf of the Treasury.

The SIGTARP quarterly report published in April 2009 revealed that Barofsky's office had already initiated twenty criminal investigations and six audits to determine whether tax dollars were being stolen or wasted.[17] It also explained how, within a short six months, the TARP had morphed from a payout fund to banks of 'only' $700 billion into a huge, unwieldy conglomerate of twelve different funds amounting to nearly $3 trillion – about the equivalent of the entire Federal budget in 2008. In other words, the TARP has evolved into a program of unprecedented scope, scale and complexity. Before the American people and their representatives in Congress can meaningfully evaluate the effectiveness of this historic program, that scope and scale must be placed into proper context, and the complexity must be made understandable.'

Making things understandable and reporting on it is Barofsky's mission, and he and his team are doing so every quarter. In July 2009 they had some more stunning news about 'scope, scale and complexity'. By then, the SIGTARP was adding up the figures of not twelve but *fifty* separate government programmes to fix the economy. These involved commitments of $23.7 trillion – $23,700,000,000,000 – a mere thirty-four times the size of the TARP. That is the value of *potential* government guarantees and commitments, and no one expects every single risk to go bad at the same time or ever oblige the government to make good on all its guarantees and pay up. It is still a frightening number, and Geithner's spokesperson heaped criticism on the SIGTARP report, calling it, among other things, 'inflated'. Barofsky shot back that, 'if these numbers are inflated, it's because they inflated them when they put them out in public, not because of us.' All his team had done was to 'gather the 50 programs, put them in one place and [tell] the American people what the government has said about the maximum of each of these programs. Perhaps their criticism is that we dare to do math.'[18]

Some of these fifty programmes have either since been cancelled or never got under way, and for the 23 trillion figure to come true every bank in the United States would have to fail. The point of the report was to shine a light on a very murky area of government policy. There is still a great deal of danger lurking out there despite progress, since the post-Lehman salvaging operation. Fannie and Freddie cannot stand on their own feet and Obama's economic stimulus package ('The Recovery Act', also known as 'Son of TARP') has added another whopping $787 billion to the total spending commitments, much of which will be disbursed in 2010. Several commentators, including Paul Krugman and the *Financial Times* journalist Martin Wolf, already doubt that Obama's programmes can work.

British and continental European rescues have been far more modest in scope, and the eurozone is hampered, paralysed even, by the incredibly static policy and behaviour of the European Central Bank and its president, Jean-Claude Trichet, so obsessed with inflation that he actually *raised* interest rates in July 2008 instead of lowering them as one tool that could stimulate the economy.

One understands that the ECB is in Frankfurt in the shadow of the Bundesbank and must be particularly sensitive to the requirements of Germany, the largest and richest of the EU members. One further understands that Germans remain traumatized by the runaway inflation of the 1930s that directly facilitated the rise of Hitler. But there are limits! Unfortunately, the only statutory instruction given the ECB, which is completely independent politically, is its duty to watch over 'price stability'. It has no mandate at all to promote employment or even to help boost European exports. This being the case, the value of the euro against the dollar was punishingly strong for long periods, although it has subsided markedly in the wake of the public debt crises of Southern Europe.

So there was no hope for a coordinated European response: Nicolas Sarkozy declared a €26 billion stimulus package of which the Germans disapproved. Trichet himself fights every step of the way against stimulus packages*. His other obsession besides inflation is staying within the 3 per cent permitted deficit level and making cuts in social spending

---

* In May 2010, Trichet was forced to bend the rules by buying the sovereign debt of weak eurozone countries such as Greece and Portugal.

to keep within that boundary – fortunately a lot of governments are now ignoring him. At the end of February 2009, however, when all the indicators showed Europe slipping deeper into recession and unemployment rising faster than previously foreseen, Trichet announced with a straight face and, I presume, a scowl that governments should 'pursue courageous policies of spending restraint especially in the case of public wages'. This comforted the Irish government trying to impose pay cuts on public employees. I'm not an economist, but I thought that if wages and government spending are lowered it encourages deflation, the last thing I would have thought one wanted in the midst of an economic crisis.

Trichet is fighting back, and the European Union, which shares his goals, intends to have a uniform system of tighter regulation. The model will be that proposed in the Larosière Group's report delivered at the end of 2008 and approved by the European Council (heads of state and government) as its framework in June of 2009. Four members of the eight-member group had close ties to major banks – BNP Paribas, Goldman Sachs, Lehman and Citigroup; there are no real surprises in its recommendations, but it is doubtless better to have more regulation rather than less. The European Council also supplied an exceptionally disappointing decision on funding for climate change, reiterating that 'the private sector will be the main source of financing for mitigation' and that there should be a 'broad and liquid carbon market'.

In the final chapter I will return to what Europe could and should be doing, particularly in the light of the sovereign debt crisis of eurozone countries.

BONUS HORMONES = HORMONE BONUSES

I promised at the beginning to tell you something else about our friends the traders, and here it is, straight from the *New*

Scientist: 'Winning traders are running on a testosterone high.' Policy-makers and economic theorists of the 'self-regulating-market-fully-informed-rational-investor' school ought to keep up with developments in biology – they would learn that we're not just up against untrustworthy mathematics but also battling swarming hormones. Briefly stated, we have left our economic affairs in the hands of people about as dependable as impulsive teenagers. They run on testosterone, linked to aggressive behaviour, and on cortisol, the 'stress hormone'. These are what make them good at their jobs.

Two researchers at Cambridge, one of them a former trader himself, monitored hormonal changes in the saliva of seventeen City traders, then compared the levels with the amounts the trader made or lost as well as with market variations. The eight-day experiment showed that testosterone levels were higher when the traders made more money, while cortisol levels were higher when markets were more volatile. Traders who started their days with extra testosterone made more money than the others; one 'saw his testosterone levels soar by 74 per cent during a six-day winning streak'. Too much testosterone can lead to aggression and reckless decisions, while high levels of cortisol over the longer term can 'lead to shrinkage in brain regions associated with decision making'.

A few months later, the same scientists discovered that high-frequency or 'flash' traders, who buy and sell over ultra-short periods of minutes or seconds, had probably experienced greater exposure to testosterone while in their mothers' wombs. The investigators used a marker previously identified by many researchers as a sign of prenatal testosterone exposure: the ratio of index to ring finger. It turned out that, in their sample of forty-nine high-frequency traders, those with longer ring fingers (denoting higher prenatal exposure) made on average six times the profits of traders with shorter ring fingers.[19] Doesn't that make you feel better about their bonuses?

2

THE WALL OF POVERTY AND INEQUALITY

The price which society pays for the law of competition
. . . is also great; but the advantages of this law are greater
still, for it is to this law that we owe our wonderful material development . . . But, whether the law be benign or
not, we must say of it . . .: It is here; we cannot evade it; no
substitutes for it have been found; and while the law may
be sometimes hard for the individual, it is best for the race,
because it insures the survival of the fittest in every department. We accept and welcome, therefore, as conditions to
which we must accommodate ourselves, great inequality
of environment, the concentration of business, industrial
and commercial, in the hands of a few, and the law of competition between these, as being not only beneficial, but
essential for the future progress of the race.

Andrew Carnegie, 'Wealth', *North American Review*,
June 1889

In his time, Andrew Carnegie was the richest man in America, possibly in the world, and a great admirer, even an apostle, of Herbert Spencer, the English philosopher who invented social Darwinism. Darwin himself never used the phrase 'survival of the fittest', an expression which betrays a fundamental misinterpretation of his work and of natural selection – but that is another story.*

Ever since Spencer and Carnegie, this misinterpretation has been a godsend for the rich, a justification of innumerable collective or individual cruelties and regressive government policies. We hear echoes of Carnegie in Margaret Thatcher's 'There is no alternative' – the law of competition is 'here, we cannot evade it, no substitutes for it have been found', and it will enrich the hard-working rich even though it may seem unduly 'hard for the individual'.

This approach also illustrates perfectly my argument in the introduction: we are presently governed by 'concentric spheres' set in precisely the opposite sequence from the one that would be healthiest for human beings and the planet. As I tried to show in the previous chapter, the sphere of finance governs that of the economy. In this chapter, we will see how the economy, in our case the one that results from the preferences of those who are richest and most powerful, decides how society will function. These choices have built the prison wall of poverty and inequality.

---

* Living creatures must adapt as best they can to the environment in which they find themselves, whether favourable to them or not: a recent case in point is the species of white moth adapting in a few generations to a dirty environment by becoming through natural selection grey and sooty looking, so as to escape predators. Humans are supposed to be able to shape their own environments – that's what social choices and politics are about – and Carnegie's and Spencer's arguments are specious: 'You must adapt to the environment we have imposed upon you because it is the one most favourable to our interests and we have the power to impose it. If you accept it, it proves we are right. If you don't, it proves you are stupid, lazy and dysfunctional.' As usual in human affairs, it's not a question of science but of the *rapport de forces*.

Carnegie is not quite the monster he may seem: at least he argued that wealth should be given away in one's own lifetime after having provided modestly for wives and daughters (but precious little for sons), and he proceeded to cover the United States with public libraries. A library was not, perhaps, the first desire society's worst-off members might have expressed had they been asked, but Carnegie never considered seeking their views. He knew best, and he had firm views about squandering money on the undeserving poor who would surely spend it on unworthy pursuits. Libraries, on the other hand, would give them a chance to improve themselves.

A hundred and twenty years later, Bill Gates is probably the most Carnegian specimen in our contemporary culture, having chosen to give away billions in his own lifetime. However, as a perfect exemplar of the era of globalization, the United States is only one of Gates's philanthropic territories: many of those billions are earmarked to promote a Green Revolution in Africa, the poorest continent with the poorest farmers in the world, at least this side of Haiti. Who will benefit from this largesse?

Gates compares plants to software, and his foundation's programme, called AGRA, or Alliance for a Green Revolution for Africa, is a classic technological fix. Undertaken in cooperation with the Rockefeller Foundation, which was the initiator of the Asian and Mexican green revolutions in the 1960s and 1970s, AGRA is programmed to develop agricultural technology, engage in biotechnology research, increase use of chemical fertilizers, promote access to seeds and other inputs through commercial distribution networks, and create a 'policy environment favourable to market-driven, export-oriented agriculture'.[1]

To understand what this is likely to mean for poor Africans, but also for rich corporations, it is useful briefly to revisit the first Green Revolution. There is no doubt that it increased production – at least for a while. It also evicted innumerable small farmers who could not afford the high-tech inputs – in that earlier case, hybrid seeds selected to produce short-stem plants that could bear more grain without toppling over. These crops were dependent on fertilizers, pesticides and irrigation to bring out the full potential of the new HYVs, or high-yielding varieties. The farmers who couldn't afford to keep up disappeared into urban slums, and the landless labourers were replaced by machinery as holdings grew larger and more concentrated.

Thanks to persistent researchers, it has since come to light that what was touted as the 'Asian miracle' was also the agribusiness bonanza. In those days, Asia and Latin America were receiving massive Northern aid, which helped to build roads, fund agricultural subsidies and price supports, provide cheap credit and organize R&D systems to spread HYVs. These investments were not in vain: 'The germplasm collected from peasants by Green Revolution scientists contributed $10.2 billion a year to US corn and soya production in the 1970s–1980s.'[2] The USA then dumped its own surpluses of cheap grain on Southern countries, ruining small farmers and helping 'major corporations – Cargill and Archer Daniels Midland – capture three-quarters of the world grain trade'. The supposedly high-minded Green Revolution research system for improved cereals also indirectly fed the ambitions and the lined the pockets of private seed corporations.

At the time, the voices of those who opposed the Green Revolution on social, humanitarian and ecological grounds were drowned out by the chorus of the high-productivity, high-yield lobby; top HYV seed scientist Norman Borlaug even won the Nobel Peace Prize (Peace, not Biology) in 1970. From the 1990s, however, loss of productivity and Green Revolution-induced environmental degradation had become all too visible, and the vaunted research institutes were losing both their scientific status and their donors.

Even in its heyday, however, there was one big hole in the coverage of the Green Revolution: it never took hold in Africa. Perhaps the export agriculture imposed throughout the continent by the IMF and the World Bank as part of structural adjustment crowded out any attention to food crops; perhaps the agribusiness corporations – and the funders – simply did not believe that the game was worth the candle.

Decades later, enter the Gates Foundation. AGRA is going to be the Green Revolution in spades, and now that so many former state and public functions, including research, have been privatized in Africa, the market and the private sector will do the whole job. Will AGRA avoid or repeat the social and ecological mistakes of the first revolutions? It is by far the Gates Foundation's most ambitious project, with multiple components. It has a lot of fervent supporters, official or not, inside and outside Africa. Its many detractors, however, fear the worst because AGRA will rely exclusively on technological and market solutions. This is the mix Bill Gates calls 'creative capitalism'.

AGRA hopes to release 1,000 conventionally bred or genetically modified new crop varieties over the next ten years; thanks to the programme, hundreds of African scientists are already being trained to develop new high-yielding plants. Research is especially advanced for transgenic bananas, tomatoes, potatoes and rice, plus GM corn and cotton already planted. It will also build a network of 'agro-input dealers' to deliver seeds, fertilizer (supplied by Yara, a Norwegian company) and other inputs. To fill any gaps, industry presence will include Monsanto, Syngenta and Dupont.

Most of the new varieties will rely on hybrid or GM seeds, whose common characteristic is their non-reproducibility. A Ugandan farmer explains the peasants' dilemma:

> Hybrid cabbage takes only three months and then you can
> harvest it. Our traditional variety takes six months. . . .With
> the hybrid cabbage we can have more harvests. But the seed
> can only be used once . . . we could use our traditional seeds
> over and over again. [If] we have to buy new seeds, those of
> us who are poor and can't go to the market then cannot eat
> . . . the hybrid seeds are high-yielding but we cannot afford
> to buy the technology and maintain it.[3]

To avoid such problems, the foundation also plans a system
of credit guarantees that should encourage local banks to lend
to farmers. Some of these technical, educational and financial
services may be free initially, but it is hard to see how that can
remain the case indefinitely.

There are other problems as well. Monsanto's GM seeds
have a chequered history, including some spectacular failures in Africa. In Uganda, a GM sweet potato supposed to
be virus-resistant proved no more resistant than traditional
varieties and also gave smaller yields. In South Africa, where
three varieties of GM corn were planted on thousands of hectares, the plants looked lush but the corncobs bore little or no
grain.[4]

The Director of AGRA claims he 'wants to learn from
everyone', but a visiting journalist from the *New York Times*
reported that the director of the seeds programme 'seemed
contemptuous of the Foundation's critics'.[5] Some of the
former indeed pull no punches. Vandana Shiva, the well-
known Indian scientist and campaigner for peasant farmers'
agriculture and the conservation of biodiversity, calls the
foundation nothing less than the 'greatest threat to farmers in
the developing world'.[6]

Initially AGRA will target 4 million farmers, but this is
just a tiny fraction of the '150 million smallholder households
in sub-Saharan Africa', most of them headed by women, the

Gates Foundation intends to reach. It makes no secret of its intention to concentrate on 'market-oriented farmers operating profitable farms ... [and] over time this will require some degree of land mobility and a lower percentage of total employment'. The meaning of 'land mobility' everywhere else the revolution has penetrated has been land concentration and eviction of the poor and weak.

Once more, voices with any other suggestions have been outshouted. Despite the existence of a thriving agro-ecology movement, present throughout Africa and using low-cost local solutions for local problems, AGRA is ignoring it. The fact remains that 'A survey of 45 sustainable agriculture projects in 17 African countries covering some 730,000 households, revealed that agro-ecological approaches substantially improved food production and household food security. In 95 percent of these projects, cereal yields improved by 50 to 100 percent.'[7]

Here are a few more instances of successful agro-ecological change:

- Soil and water conservation in the driest parts of Sahelian countries Burkina Faso and Niger has helped the average family shift from a cereal deficit for over six months of the year to an annual surplus of 153 kilos.
- Between 2003 and 2006, grain yields of the Tigray region of Ethiopia nearly doubled because more and more farmers are making and using compost.
- Projects in Senegal using composting, green manures, water harvesting, rock phosphates and other components have increased harvests of several crops by 75 to 195 per cent.[8]

One could add to such a list, but the point is that AGRA did not try to learn from existing successful alternatives or to

consult African farmers' organizations, despite the presence
of such organizations in all the countries where the project
will operate. Not only does it leave out the representative
organizations of the supposed beneficiaries, the farmers
themselves, but there seem to be no plans for safeguarding
biodiversity and local seed varieties, which could be replaced
by hybrid or GM seeds and lost over vast swathes of the continent within a single generation.

GM foods may or may not be bad for one's health – I
don't know, and the case against them on these grounds has
not been proven to my satisfaction. But I oppose them on
environmental grounds, and here the science supporting my
position is extremely solid. Above all, it is economically foolhardy to allow a few giant corporations to exercise oligopoly
control over any resource as important as seeds. But, in the
case of Africa, one need not even invoke such arguments. It
is enough to know that GM seeds can't be saved and must be
purchased for each planting, often from a single, monopoly
supplier. Why else would Monsanto try to give away seeds in
Africa and elsewhere, as it has already done?* Worse, these
varieties grow properly only under certain well-defined conditions – for instance, the proposed 'drought-resistant corn'
will work if there actually is a drought, but not if the rainfall
is normal. Pests, unlike most GM scientists, understand
Darwin, and they adapt in a few generations to their new
plant hosts, so that the pests end up much more resistant and
the GM crops end up being no higher yielding than others –
sometimes less.

---

* When I had the good fortune to attend the World Social Forum in
Bamako, Mali, in January 2006, I asked some members of African farmers'
organizations present about this practice. They were well aware of it, and
their members refuse the seeds, but it is quite possible that farmers who
don't belong to the associations are uninformed and can be tempted by
what appears to be a gift.

The earlier Green Revolution has in many places proved to be an environmental disaster: no safeguards against a similar fate for this one seem to be in place. Once the GM genie is out of the bottle, no one can put him back in – pollens will spread, plants will have lasting effects on bio-systems, from soil bacteria to earthworms to butterflies, and the local environment will be contaminated over far greater distances than scientists initially thought possible. Yet the AGRA programme is, according to the Gates Foundation, 'the African face and voice for our work'. That face, so far, is not an attractive one.*

I am hardly alone in criticizing the AGRA approach, and the programme has begun to pay attention to its PR problem by organizing public 'consultations' with African NGOs and farm leaders. Here is what one of them says: 'You come. You buy the land. You make a plan. You build a house. Now you ask me what colour do I want to paint the kitchen? This is not participation.'[9]

There is a further issue – the increasing privatization of development aid. Gates has the money – far more than the great majority of the official donors of overseas development aid, the countries that belong to the OECD. So, as one Canadian NGO observes, 'Where Bill Gates goes, so go governments. Every head of every aid agency in the OECD wants a photo-op announcing a joint venture with the megabillionaire.'[10]

Why have I put this story in the 'poverty and inequality' chapter and not in the 'food' section of the following 'most basic resources' chapter? Although it is sadly true that the AGRA programme will probably in the mid- to longer term

---

* The Gates Foundation is also financing research and therapeutic measures for several diseases prevalent in Africa, including malaria and HIV/AIDS. I have not examined such programmes, which for all I know may be perfectly well conceived and executed.

aggravate rather than reduce hunger in Africa, I put the case here because, although some African farmers will surely prosper, at least initially, the new Green Revolution 'software' is programmed to widen even further the gap between rich and poor, between winners and losers, just as it did in Asia, Mexico and elsewhere. Interactions between billionaires and poor people along Carnegie–Gates lines have been a rare phenomenon in American or world history, but when they occur they have a common characteristic: the billionaires necessarily know best. And, because they are surrounded by yes men and women, they need never re-examine their assumptions and prejudices. Others may suffer from their Good Works, but they can move on with a clear conscience and hubris intact. In the final analysis, one should perhaps be thankful that philanthropic billionaires are so thin on the ground.

LET THEM EAT RESEARCH

Usually the inhabitants of the highest financial echelons have no thoughts at all about the less fortunate. In the Gilded Age, Carnegie's contemporaries, known as robber barons, pursued their conspicuous consumption and made sure their children inherited the money. Today, the bankers–traders–casino–Davos crowd is not noted for its compassion for the downtrodden, but, contrary to the Gilded Age, its deficiencies in this respect are balanced by the constant concern of a large international bureaucracy. If research, publications, conferences and exhortations are any measure, the world has grown extremely rich in knowledge of, and scholarly attention to, the poor.

Indeed, no subject has been so central to the work of the vast aid and development system as the poor – it knows their numbers, their location, the number of pennies they have to spend per day, how they live and mostly die, how educated and healthy they are (not very), their access to wells, pumps, sinks and toilets, their intake of basic cereals – the list is long. Every year since the United Nations was founded inequality has increased, and every year the pile of studies has grown higher. These are not without value – if only because no respectable journalist or thinking citizen can say 'I didn't realize it was that bad'.

Since 1990, the UN Development Programme (UNDP) has published its *Human Development Report* in which the components of poverty are measured, analysed and weighted and every member country given a ranking. The reports also feature a particular theme, for example climate change in the 2007–8 report, showing how that variable figures in the poverty–inequality equation. The International Labour Organization has rated countries according to the degree of economic security they can provide for their citizens. The UN University branch in Helsinki (UNU-WIDER, or World Institute for Development Economic Research) in 2007 published the definitive study on 'the global distribution of household wealth' to great academic fanfare. There is now even an International Poverty Centre in Brasilia, a project of the UN and the Brazilian government.

The UN's Millennium Development Goals, known to those in the business simply as 'the MDGs', were set after a long process that included a major effort by the rich-country Organization for Economic Cooperation and Development (OECD) and subsequently involved innumerable conferences and the usual fervent promises that poverty and inequality would be attacked forthwith. In 2000, the MDG conferees thought they were being realistic by not shooting for the moon: their stated objective was not to eliminate poverty altogether but to cut it in half by 2015. The various subgoals concerning health, maternal and child health, education, hunger, and so on were also carefully calibrated, and governments everywhere signed up to them. These too have provoked innumerable follow-up conferences inside and outside the UN system. None of the MDGs now looks like being met.

The subjects of poverty and inequality are also standard fare for the World Bank, but if you're after accurate information you would do well to steer clear of it. A review of its research by a team of outstanding development economists was exceptionally hard on this institution, even though the Bank possesses the largest development research capacity in the world and is undoubtedly the most frequently cited authority on such matters. The reviewing panel of academic luminaries declared that:

> much of [the Bank's research on globalization, aid and poverty] appears to have such deep flaws that, at present, the results cannot be regarded as remotely reliable, much as one might want to believe the results. . . . The problem is that in major Bank policy speeches and publications, it proselytized the new work without appropriate caveats on its reliability. Unfortunately, as one reads the research more carefully, and as new results come in, it is becoming clear that the Bank seriously over-reached in prematurely putting its globalization, aid and poverty publications on a pedestal. Nor has it corrected itself to this day.[11]

A university that allowed its PR and communications department to fix the results researchers are expected to highlight would soon be discredited and laughed off the street, but the Bank just rolls merrily along, using when necessary its standard excuse: 'That was then; this is now; we have changed'. For as long as I have known it, it has always been the Bank that is changing.

I'm undoubtedly missing a lot of other poverty/inequality studies, particularly the work of the specialized agencies whose output I haven't necessarily trawled. UNICEF's brief is child poverty and welfare; the World Health Organization works on water/sanitation inequalities and the 'global burden of disease', which is far heavier for the poor; UNESCO deals with unequal access to education. Nearly everyone now has a finger on the pulse of female poverty and gender inequality, a fashionable topic in the UN, in official national development aid agencies and in a great many NGOs, all of which shower attention and funds on anyone proposing to study or do something about the status of poor (rural, urban, hungry, pregnant, working, unemployed . . .) women. Today, the simple expedient of attaching the phrase 'and women' to any conceivable topic will almost always buy a winning ticket. Anyone who worked in the development field two or three decades ago and returned to the scene after a long absence would be amazed.

So we know about poverty and inequality, or if we don't we have no excuse. NGOs have duly spread the word, as have authors like myself. If the brain power expended, statistics compiled, forests of paper and vats of ink used in printing the news about these permanent and worsening features of the global landscape could by themselves solve the problem, everyone on earth would have enough, and no one would have vastly more than the people on the other side of town or of the earth.

The outcome of these decades of thorough examinations, consciousness-raising, hand-wringing and admonishment is clear: it has been the polar opposite of the outcome called for by the UN. Particularly if China and India are excluded (gains against poverty have indeed been made by both), poverty is in many places worse than it was forty years ago, but inequality has unequivocally increased everywhere except for the occasional and truly exceptional country such as Denmark.* Poverty has also become a genuine scourge in some supposedly rich countries, affecting up to 20 per cent of their populations.

If I sound a shade impatient, it's because I'm fed up. The research institutes, especially the rich ones in rich countries, ought to be studying the rich. It's because we don't study the rich and know what they're up to that virtually the whole academic establishment fell off its collective chair in surprise when the crisis struck. I haven't changed my mind since I published my first book in 1976. In the chapter called 'What Can I Do?' I wrote, '*Study the rich and powerful, not the poor and powerless.*' I still find the paragraph important enough to reproduce here almost in its entirety:

> *Study the rich and powerful, not the poor and powerless.* Any good work done on peasants' organisations, small farmer resistance to oppression or workers in agribusiness can invariably be used against them. One of France's best anthropologists found his work on Indochina being avidly read by the Green Berets . . . Meanwhile, not nearly enough work is being done on those who hold the power and pull the strings. As their tactics become more subtle and their public pronouncements more guarded, the need for better spade-work becomes crucial . . . Let the poor study themselves. They already know what is wrong with their lives and if you truly want to help them, the best you can do is to give them a clearer idea of how their oppressors are working now and can be expected to work in the future.[12]

---

* Some argue, although many disagree, that 'the rising tide lifts all boats', the poverty floor has thus been raised, and therefore greater inequality doesn't matter because the status even of the worst off has improved. I would counter that the rising tide can swamp or sink a lot of old, leaky, fragile boats.

We still lack sufficient knowledge of those who make the decisions that affect countless lives and are in a position to manipulate the rules to suit themselves – that is, transnational corporations and banks, international financial institutions, global and regional trade bodies, right-wing think tanks and cultural institutions, major state bureaucracies, the media, and so on.

But, as part of the price of this book, you've paid for a chapter on poverty and inequality and, because they do represent a genuine crisis no one wants to see prolonged, I feel bound to give you the standard contrasts. They are intended to deliver the usual shocks, probably for the nth time. Here we go. The richest 10 per cent of adults worldwide own 85 per cent of global household wealth, with the richest 2 per cent among them capturing more than half that wealth. The poorest half of the world population owns barely 1 per cent. The average person in the top 10 per cent owns nearly 3,000 times the wealth of the average person in the bottom 10 per cent.

That's from the scholars at WIDER mentioned above, part of the UN University. They define 'wealth' as everything you have – the clothes on your back or in your closet, your refrigerator, your radio, your books, and so on – so I'm reasonably sure you are in that top 10 per cent with 3,000 times the wealth of the person at the bottom – I know I am. The good news is that, to belong to the category of the 'top half' of the human race, you needed only a modest $2,200 worth of such tangible assets. The bad news is that most people would still feel exceedingly poor at that level, even in terms of purchasing power parity (PPP), the measure now used in most official comparisons, because similar things don't cost the same in different countries. Within this definition, top 10 per cent membership meant owning $61,000 worth of stuff while the top 1 per cent required $500,000 plus: 37 million people around the world are in this top 1 per cent, according to WIDER. I would have thought the number was far more than that, considering the value of houses, but I'm just giving the figures they provide.

The higher and lower you go in the hierarchy, the greater the contrasts. The first 5 per cent of the world population gets over a third of the income (income, not wealth) and the last 5 per cent gets only 0.2 per cent – in other words, the top slice makes 165 times as much as the bottom one, or earns as much in forty-eight hours as the lowest do in a year. Your status in your own society is more important than where you live. A third of all Brazilians are richer than the bottom 5 per cent of Germans; so, more surprisingly, are 200 million Chinese. Probably the most famous image of these inequalities appeared in an early UNDP *Human Development Report* and came to be known as the 'champagne glass graph' that divided the world into slices of 20 per cent: nearly all the champagne was in the wide bulge at the top representing the first 20 per cent of the world, with the stem narrowing to imperceptibility for the bottom-most people. It used to be that 84 per cent of the wealth went to the top 20 per cent of the world's people. Now wealth is even more skewed: the top 10, not 20, per cent get 85 per cent of the wealth. When no firewalls are erected to prevent it, money, like champagne bubbles and CO_2, heads for the stratosphere.

Gaps between countries in terms of gross domestic product (GDP) per capita have also been published for many years, so that it is easy to measure the wealth differences between the average citizen of Switzerland and Swaziland or of Luxembourg and Lesotho.[13] I am able to inform you on good authority, for example, that the difference between the United States and Malawi in terms of purchasing power per average person is 72 to 1. North–South, rich–poor country contrasts have long been, and remain, horrendous.

More revealing, however, are inequalities of income and wealth within individual countries. They measure differences between social strata and show that a Davos class now exists nearly everywhere. In other words, averages tell us very little: there are a few rich people in Malawi and a lot of very poor ones in the United States. No country is without its more or less affluent elite, but the most rapid and startling changes have probably taken place in the United States, where the richest citizens, thanks to neoliberal 'reforms', have managed to claw back the position they held just before the Crash of 1929.* When Ronald Reagan was elected president in 1980, the top 1 per cent of Americans got 9 per cent of the income. Three decades later they were getting 23 per cent.

None of this should come as a surprise, because this kind of outcome is what neoliberal policies are *for*. Now it may use less blatant language than Herbert Spencer did with the 'survival of the fittest'; in our own day pious pronouncements of concern are expected, but that is a cultural, not a fundamental, change. The same policies are intended to produce the same results, and they do so regularly: the rich get richer unless serious legal obstacles are placed in their way. Erecting those obstacles is doubly difficult now because, to work in a globalized world, they must be transnational.†

---

* Huge differences in wealth exist in China as well, but it's difficult to find reliable information on class divides.
† If you are interested in comparing inequalities in different countries, the standard measure is called the 'Gini coefficient', a number between 0 and 1. Zero is when each person in the society has the same amount, 1 is when one person has everything; so, the lower the figure, the more equal the society. Averages are between 0.3 and 0.5. This will tell you nothing about how much wealth exists in the country, only how whatever wealth there is gets distributed. The most unequal country in the world today is unguessable: Namibia.

STUDYING THE RICH, NOT THE POOR

This is why I'm a fan of Merrill Lynch – yes, the famous financial services corporation recently purchased by Bank of America when it was nearly comatose and ready to expire. Merrill Lynch is upfront about its interest in the rich – and why not? It wants to manage their money and therefore needs to know who and where they are. For thirteen years now, ML, in partnership with Cap Gemini, has published the *World Wealth Report*, which I frankly find far more valuable than world poverty reports.

The world's rich – or HNWIs, as Merrill Lynch calls them, short for High Net Worth Individuals – were at the top of their form in 2007, when there were 10.1 million of them. Sometimes the category is further refined to reflect the numbers of UHNWIs, or Ultra High etc., etc. Merrill and Cap Gemini do not measure their wealth in the sense of possessions or total assets, as WIDER, for example, does in its world household wealth survey. Their reports measure primarily liquidity – that is, investable cash and other easily converted assets, which yachts, mansions and Picassos, for example, are not.*

To be an HNWI you need a cool million in liquid assets, whereas to attain the truly dizzying altitudes of the UHNWIs the entry fee is $30 million. Between them, the 10 million and some people at the top of the world wealth pile in 2007 boasted a total of $40,700,000,000,000 – 40,000 billion and a bit, or 40.7 trillion dollars. This means that, in 2007, a shade over 10 million people – less than the population of greater Tokyo or London and about the same as that of greater Paris – together possessed liquid assets equal to more than

---

* They don't count the first residence, but apparently second or third houses, although illiquid, are in the tally.

three times the annual GDP of the United States or of the European Union, six times the GDP of China and thirteen times the GDP of India.

These wealth reports help to clarify the real concentrations of world wealth because the 'top 1 per cent' category of standard publications provides by no means a full picture. They show where the seriously wealthy can be found: more than half still reside in the USA, Germany and Japan, but the share of emerging market wealth is increasing. The reports also document the reasons for which I always refuse to believe official government pronouncements when they announce that 'It would be great to spend more on [health, education, child welfare, scientific research . . .] but we can't afford it.' Well, maybe 'we' can't, but there are some that can, and we have spent the last three decades allowing them to go scot-free and virtually untaxed.

It is true that the poor dears were hard hit by the crisis. The 2008 report, just cited, concerns their wealth in 2007, but the 2009 report contained the sad news that there were now only 8.6 million HNWIs, a drop of 15 per cent, while their collective wealth had dwindled to $32.8 trillion. Twenty per cent had simply evaporated – pfffft – dragging them back to the levels of 2005. Before the crisis, the rich as a group could look forward to wealth gains of over 10 per cent per annum, so losing nearly twice that much in a single year must have hurt. But not to worry: the *World Wealth Report* confidently predicts that, by 2013, this privileged group will enjoy $48.5 trillion. Another 15 trillion or so in five years is not too dismal a prospect.

Now, having paused to shed a tear, let us recall that, despite losses, the post-crisis United States still boasted 2.7 million HNWIs, less than 1 per cent (0.08) of the population, and 30,600 Ultras, more than any other continent. Some proved to be cannier investors than others (thanks to Merrill Lynch?

I doubt it). In Europe, for example, the French proved twice as good at hanging on to their money as the risk-taking Brits: the French lost only 12 per cent of their HNWIs, whereas in the UK their numbers shrunk by 26 per cent. The Germans were the most prudent or foresighted of all – from 2007 to 2008 the number of rich Germans dropped by a mere 2.7 per cent.

If you really like stories about wealth concentration, here is another tasty morsel: in 2008, when the crisis had already bitten hard, the Ultras – those worth $30 million or more in investable assets – saw their numbers dwindle by nearly a quarter, from over 100,000 to 78,000 worldwide, apparently because these people can afford to gamble big time and many lost a lot of money as a result. But this comparatively tiny group of 78,000 risk-takers still owned *35 per cent of all the assets of all the HNWIs – that is, more than $13 trillion, about the size of the annual GDP of the European Union.*

Exuberant neoliberal periods are best of all for the super-rich: in the single year 2005–6, as turbo-capitalism was driving forwards, total wealth accumulation for this minuscule elite grew by an impressive 16.8 per cent. As Merrill Lynch puts it, this was 'another sign that global wealth is rapidly consolidating among this ultra-wealthy segment'.

To sum up, about one person in 800 on the planet shares the world's real spoils, and less than 1 per cent of those – i.e. one in every 80,000 people – are seriously, but seriously, rich. All this is confirmed by *Forbes* magazine's annual list of the world's billionaires, which provides the ultimate figures on quintessential wealth concentration and shows fluctuations similar to those documented in the *World Wealth Report*. Although in 2007 *Forbes* calculated the total wealth of its list of the world's 946 billionaires at $3,500 billion, it appears to have found the task of adding up these fortunes too onerous in 2008, when their numbers rose to 1,125, then in 2009 when the figure dropped precipitously to 793. Since I have no intention of totting up their total wealth myself, I don't know how much the figures went up or down in 2008–9. We can bet, however, that those 332 hardship cases knocked off their perch on the billionaires list in 2009 are now merely multi-millionaires.

It is still fascinating to see how steeply the peaks can rise, how thin the air can become at such altitudes. According to all these sources, at last count we had 8,600,000 happily affluent HNWIs, with more than a million each in investable cash, sharing nearly $33 trillion. Then we had less than 1 per cent of them, 78,000, rising above the level of the herd with more than $30 million in liquid assets and together owning the equivalent of the GDP of the European Union. Finally came 1 per cent of these Ultras, who made it on to the *Forbes* A-list of billionaires.

Now try the following simple calculation. If you have 'only' 1 billion investable dollars, like pages and pages-worth of people at the end of the *Forbes* list, and if you are such an incompetent investor that you make a return of 'only' 5 per cent a year, or $50 million, then every day of the year, Sundays and holidays included, you must spend $137,000 in pure consumption or you will automatically become richer. In other words, once you reach this level, it is virtually impossible ever to be poor or even just affluent.

WHY INEQUALITY MATTERS, AND NOT JUST TO THE WORST OFF

Now let us leave the super-rich behind and move on to mark some of the lesser known impacts of inequality.

If I had been asked a while ago 'Why is it preferable for everyone to live in a more equal society?' I probably would have responded with some truism, for example 'Because they have fewer poor people, so probably less crime, less illness and so on.' I know now that this answer barely scrapes the surface because I've read the work of Richard Wilkinson, a pioneering author who explains 'why more equal societies almost always do better'.[14] In a short book published in 2000, Wilkinson, an epidemiologist, stuck mostly to the health and psycho-social effects of inequality and class differences. He made an enlightened contribution by pointing out that deprivation is not just a matter of people's material conditions, however difficult they may be, but it also has a crucial impact on the overall quality of the social environment. Writing in a series called 'Darwinism Today', he naturally took a Darwinian perspective and pointed out that,

> By virtue of having all the same needs, other members of our own species are our most feared competitors – for housing, jobs, sexual partners, food, clothing and so on. But they are also our only source of help, friendship, assistance, learning, care and protection. This means that the quality of our social relationships has always been vital to our material welfare.

As soon as health researchers grasped this point, they started looking for the less examined causes of ill health and found that factors such as bereavement, lack of control over one's work, and fear of unemployment or of losing one's savings were directly related to health outcomes. Fixing such problems is not just a question of wealth redistribution either; social cohesion matters a lot more. In Britain during the Second World War, for example, people were materially deprived yet had a remarkable sense of solidarity and, to the amazement of many health professionals, the population's health improved markedly.

Numerous studies have shown since then that, in egalitarian societies, more people take part in community, cultural, charitable and sports activities; they belong to all sorts of clubs, associations and networks and their social involvement has a measurable impact on health. Indeed, 'low social status and weak social affiliations are among the most important risk factors affecting the health of modern populations.' And, crucially, within countries, absolute levels of income matter less than relative social status. The words that recur most frequently in studies of health breakdowns and levels of violence are words like respect, pride, status and self-esteem and, on the other side, shame, social inadequacy, embarrassment and humiliation. People of low social status feel disrespected and often take out their anger and frustration on those below them, particularly women and children, but also on vulnerable minorities. They take it out on themselves as well, usually without realizing it, through ill health and various kinds of social dysfunction.

The chain is quite simple when one thinks about it from this perspective: inequalities imply rigid hierarchies; hierarchies imply social distinctions and exclusion, which reinforce low status and give rise to constant, stress-provoking humiliation for large parts of the population. Consequently, unequal, hierarchical societies (and workplaces) will produce worse health outcomes and greater violence than more equal, less hierarchical ones – QED.*

Nine years later, Wilkinson and his co-author Kate Pickett

---

* In *Mind the Gap*, Wilkinson, as a health professional, also supplies information on the physical, biological and medical consequences of low social status not mentioned in this brief account. As I was working on this chapter, the news was full of the twenty-second, twenty-third and twenty-fourth suicides at France-Telecom (thirty-four took place between January 2008 and January 2010). Employees interviewed spoke about the rigid hierarchies and the stress of their jobs, as fewer people were expected to take on more work and were forced to move to another location every three to five years, but the words that kept coming back were 'They treat us like less-than-nothings; we're disposable, we're Kleenex . . .'

expanded their scope to show a great many other social effects attributable to inequality besides health levels. They argue, and their graphs, based on innumerable studies, show, that beyond a certain point, higher income by itself has no influence on health, welfare and happiness: 'Richer people tend, on average, to be healthier and happier than poorer people in the same society.' No surprises there, for sure! 'But [when] comparing rich countries, it makes no difference whether, on average, people in one society are almost twice as rich as people in another.' For instance, Greeks on average are twice as poor as Americans. They spend half as much per person on health care and their hospitals have a lot less hi-tech equipment, but Greeks have a higher life expectancy than Americans and a 40 per cent lower infant mortality rate.

Other indicators show that Greeks ought normally to be happier as well, although austerity measures imposed in 2010 will weigh heavily on the great majority of the population. Happiness has now become a subject of inquiry for economists and can be statistically described despite cultural differences (and, the economists claim, despite the subjects' desire to please the researcher with an optimistic answer or to put a brave face on their discontents). Two economists at the Wharton School (the prestigious business school of the University of Pennsylvania) would disagree with Wilkinson and Pickett: they believe that more money definitely equals more happiness and claim to 'establish a clear positive link between GDP and average levels of subjective well-being across countries with no evidence of a satiation point beyond which wealthier countries have no further increases in subjective well-being'.[15]

So the richer the happier? Well, maybe. But Wilkinson and Pickett, with a massively impressive set of references, show that it's not merely poor health and violence that are more common in more unequal societies: on their list of the problems that proliferate wherever inequalities are most profound are the usual indicators of life expectancy and infant mortality, but also 'levels of trust, mental illness including drug and alcohol addiction, obesity, children's educational performance, teenage births, homicides, imprisonment rates and social mobility'.[16] Their data sets deal only with developed states, so there are no comparisons between wealthy countries and poor ones, or even with 'emerging market' middle-way countries. The contrasts between wealthy states, all members of the OECD, are nonetheless extremely sharp, and this remains true across all the indicators and elements treated.

Japan, Scandinavia and continental Europe consistently fare better than the United States, the United Kingdom and Singapore – precisely the countries where neoliberal values have penetrated most deeply. Australia and New Zealand are never at the extreme edges on the bad side of the graphs, whereas the USA and the UK always are. But Oz and NZ are almost always closer to the high inequality extreme than to the Japan/Scandinavia pole, denoting lower inequality and better quality of life. They also show poorer social outcomes. Portugal, too, lands most of the time on the adverse side of the indicators.

These results have nothing to do with cultural traits – Japan and Norway are no more alike culturally than the UK and Singapore. Nor can the results be attributed to particularly awful numbers in well-defined ethnic groups such as blacks in the United States, who do not notably drag down the averages. Inequality is unequivocally the defining variable. For example, if you take the death rates only of white Americans, they are still worse than those in countries that are more equal. Rates of illness for white, middle-aged men classed according to both income and education are consistently higher in the USA than in Britain. Britain is an unequal society, but not quite so direly unequal as the United States. In Japan, income differences were drastically reduced during the forty years following the Second World War, with the result that Japan is now at the top of the league tables in virtually every category of good social outcomes. The United States, an egalitarian country in the 1950s and 1960s, has since slipped way behind and is now number 30 for life expectancy in the developed world, while Japan is number one.

Poor social results reverberate throughout the whole society to the point that you can predict a poor outcome in one category if you know what it is in another. What other factor, if not inequality, would cause a society with the highest prison population also to have the highest rate of obesity?

As inequality rises, people become increasingly stressed and anxious. In the United States between the early 1950s and the early 1990s, dozens of studies corroborate this observation for men, women and children regardless of race and social class.* A single instance: using the same standardized measures, by the end of the 1980s the *average* American child was found to be more anxious than child *psychiatric patients* in the 1950s. Status, or 'social evaluation anxiety', which causes people to feel they are being constantly judged and found inferior, sets in early and increases with adolescence. Wilkinson and Pickett don't mention it, but I would bet that, just like obesity, anorexia is far more common in more unequal societies, where young women in particular are made to feel that their bodies do not meet certain ideal social norms.

'Most people can be trusted.' Do you agree or disagree with that statement? Statistically speaking, the more unequal the society, the smaller the proportion of people who agree.

---

* Hispanics in the USA seem to escape certain poor outcomes because they practise greater social solidarity.

Trust in others declines as inequality grows. People who trust each other cooperate, give time and money to charities, believe in shared values, obey the laws – not to mention that they live longer and healthier lives. They also do not live in gated communities or drive SUVs, which many seem to buy not just to show that they can afford them but also to look tough and feel safe from others.* All this can be statistically demonstrated.

Do neoliberal societies and their governments actually *want* their people to be more incarcerated, distrustful, stressed, prematurely pregnant, depressed, drug- or alcohol-addicted, fatter, crazier, more homicidal, less educated and shorter-lived than other people? Do governments of the now more equal countries consider the consequences when they seek to reduce social benefits and worker protection and institute neoliberal 'reforms' as they are now doing throughout continental Europe? A more equal society may seem expensive to maintain, but it's a bargain when one thinks of the alternatives: illness, crime, ill health, stress and all the other impacts impose huge costs, including high financial costs.†

Even more surprising, perhaps, is the established fact that less equal societies are less innovative and creative, at least as measured by the number of patents granted per head of population. The explanation is perfectly rational when you think about it: unequal societies make millions of people feel that they are losers, second-rate failures. Unequal societies, like those that refuse to recognize women, squander their best and most abundant resource: the talent of their people. Wilkinson also points out that inequality even has ecological

---

* At similar income levels, Canadians buy minivans; Americans buy SUVs.
† In May 2010, a succinct piece in *Le Monde* announced that delinquency costs France an estimated 115 billion euros a year.

consequences because it encourages consumerism and status competition. A more equal society changes public attitudes and encourages people to see social and environmental problems as problems they themselves, working with others, can solve. In a word, greater equality is the best investment, bar none, that any government can make.

So why don't the governments of the most unequal countries react? There may well be lobbies for obesity – the junk and fast food corporations come to mind – but I can't think of any for the other indicators of inequality, and a losers' lobby isn't on any maps I know. The problem is governments' unwillingness to consider the consequences and to connect the dots. If we allow finance and the economy to rule society; if we ignore the wisdom of Adam Smith's 'vile maxim', we get what we deserve. As the evidence shows that the most unequal societies are also unequivocally the most neoliberal and the most dysfunctional from myriad points of view, isn't it time to draw conclusions and call a spade a spade or, as the French prefer, a cat a cat? Deep inequality is the social equivalent of a thousand Katrinas, a hundred tsunamis, except that it wreaks havoc month after month, year after year, dragging down not just the poor and vulnerable but everyone else as well.

HOW THE CRISIS IS HITTING THE SOUTH

So far we've looked mostly at the better-off countries, but the crisis and the damage it inflicts are worldwide. At first, the pundits practised denial by stages – the collapse would be confined to the financial system and wouldn't hit the real economy; then they said it would touch only certain countries; and, when it hit them all, they said it would be over soon. If you listen to them now, it's already over. The same people who didn't see the crisis coming now pass judgement, on its progress. All their prophecies were disproved virtually as soon as they were made, particularly the claim that the less developed countries could be 'decoupled' from the effects of the crisis. This particularly uninformed conventional wisdom had perhaps the shortest lifespan of all.

The crisis is global, and poor countries are hit harder because they are more vulnerable, have few social cushions and more to lose. If you're eating 3,000 calories a day, you can still get by on 2,000, but if you start from 2,000 the effect of a drop to 1,000 will be far more severe. The consequences of losing your home, even if it was a cramped and poor one, are far more brutal than living in three rooms instead of six – and so on, in every aspect of life. The lower you are on the ladder, the easier it becomes to lose your foothold altogether. This is true for poor countries and especially so for the poor in poor countries. Family solidarity can go only so far to remedy their situation.

Neoliberal policies, particularly those imposed for decades by the World Bank/IMF tandem, created devastating inequalities in the South just as in the North, so the economic slump hitting them today is the crowning blow. But it is not the first. Let me list from my archives a few salient items gleaned from various sources and authorities at the time of the financial crisis in Asia, then Latin America, Russia and elsewhere in the late 1990s.

- For every newly industrializing country (then known as 'NICs'), there were ten countries falling behind; for every beneficiary of rising stock prices, there were ten victims of declining real wages, decreased job security and lost benefits.
- In Korea, job losses for women mounted to more than 7 per cent between April 1997 and April 1998; the hotline for women received seven times as many calls as in the previous year from domestic violence victims; suicides increased by 50 per cent.

- In Indonesia, by 1999, GDP had recovered, but an extra 40 million people, or 20 per cent of the population, had fallen into poverty; unemployment was surging and real wages had declined.
- Growth does not mean redistribution or greater equality: after 1991, growth in India was 6 per cent or more per year, but there were no further reductions in poverty [by the end of the decade]. In contrast, pre-neoliberal era policies between 1974 and 1990 reduced poverty from 53 to 34 per cent.
- Between 1984 and 1990, as Mexico liberalized trade and welcomed foreign investment, white-collar salaries increased by more than 13 per cent, but blue-collar wages dropped by 14 per cent.
- Following the demise of the USSR, life expectancy in Russia fell by five years on average and by seven years for men.

I could go on, but the point is that little progress can be made in reducing poverty so long as inequality is high and rising because of neoliberal policy choices. When these policies reign, as they have done for decades, health and education budgets are slashed, efforts towards land reform cease, small farmers and food-crop agriculture are neglected, privatized companies sack workers and pay the lowest wages they can get away with, and poor consumers are charged the highest prices that can be squeezed out of them.

So, when a devastating global financial crisis is added to previous woes, the picture is black, and our present crisis is no exception. In early 2009, UNESCO estimated that the 390 million poorest Africans would lose a further 20 per cent of their income that year, partly because commodity prices were in freefall. The African Development Bank foresaw a drop in the continent's export revenues of $250 billion in 2009 and expected them to earn even less in 2010. This is not the worst news. As the economy slides deeper into distress, we can look to an increase of 200,000 to 400,000 more infant and child deaths worldwide, many of them caused by grave malnutrition. Lack of proper food will stunt the bodies but also the minds of millions more children who survive but still face a lifetime of cognitive damage.[17]

Countries dependent on manufactured exports, such as China, Korea, India or Malaysia, will suffer as the trade expansion curve goes flat. The ones dependent on tourism are not going to earn anywhere near as much as distant travel becomes a luxury for Americans, Europeans and Japanese: small countries in the Caribbean in particular will feel the pain (so will large developed economies such as France, Spain and Italy). So it goes.

EVAPORATING WORK

When panic struck Wall Street and the City, stock markets all over the world took a nosedive as investors sought safety at all costs and pulled out of emerging markets. In such cases, speculators lose a bit of money, but people on the spot lose their jobs because investments are withdrawn and they have no unemployment benefits to fall back on. A lot of foreign direct investment (up to 85 per cent in some years) used to go into mergers and acquisitions, not new projects, so it could cause unemployment even in good years, when newly merged companies got rid of workers. But in early 2009, the Institute of International Finance forecast that investment in emerging markets would slide to a dismal $165 billion, compared with $466 billion in 2008 and a record $929 billion in 2007.

Sure enough, in January 2009 the International Labour Organization (ILO) published it annual *Global Employment Trends* report full of alarming figures – which it labelled 'realistic, not alarmist'. All the categories to which you don't want to belong – the presently unemployed, the working poor (those earning less than the equivalent of $2 a day), and those in 'vulnerable employment', including family workers and the self-employed, were set to swell dramatically according to ILO projections.

In 2007 there had been 180 million unemployed; the ILO said the crisis could cause their ranks to go up by 18 to 30 million, with a worst-case scenario of an extra 50 million jobless. The numbers of the working poor could, at worst, rise by 200 million, from 1.2 to 1.4 billion. A shocking one-half of the world's workforce – a billion and a half people – was already in the category of 'vulnerable employment' in 2007. Another hundred million people could join them, but again this was the ILO's worst case and, said the organization, not expected. One can see from these numbers that, even in the peak year of 2007, the human race wasn't doing very well work-wise. The 'working poor' and the 'vulnerable employment' categories, along with the unemployed, were, even then, over 90 per cent of the entire global workforce. When you first come upon such ILO figures they bring you up short – that was my reaction, anyway.*

Then, five months later, in May 2009, the ILO published

---

* The ILO doesn't make these comparisons especially easy. One's first question is 'How many people in the global workforce?' It's about 3.1 or 3.2 billion as best I can make out, but you have to derive the number yourself from other data. Their definitions aren't too clear either. Although nobody from the geographical group called 'Developed Economies & European Union' is part of the 'working poor', because nobody makes less than $2 a day, we have plenty of working poor according to our own definitions and the cost of living in our countries. Between 48 and 54 million 'developed & EU' workers are classed as 'vulnerable' – I assume this means in casual, precarious or self-employed jobs, but I can't swear to it. The EU itself admits to having 72 million poor people in the twenty-seven member states. So if I've made mistakes interpreting the ILO numbers, I beg your indulgence and also beg the ILO to make the task of researchers a bit less complicated.

an update: its figures in January had not been nearly 'alarmist' enough. Both the best- and worst-case scenarios for the new jobless had increased by 10 million, with virtually no chance of the best case coming to pass. The worst case would mean that unemployment could reach 239 million people – an increase of nearly a third worldwide.

The latest ILO estimates available to me as of this writing date from January 2010 and show that the worst case did not quite come to pass, but the picture is still one of deep gloom. After four years of steady decreases, the global unemployment rate 'already started increasing in 2008 but the 2009 rate, as well as the number of unemployed persons, shows a much sharper increase'. No relief is in sight for the group of 'Developed economies and EU' – quite the contrary. They will do worst of all the ILO groups in the world, with an overall unemployment rate of 8.4 per cent in 2009 increasing to 8.9 per cent in 2010. Second and third worst will be Central and South-Eastern Europe, followed by Latin America and the Caribbean.[18]

Despite the ILO prognosis, despite the EU's status as world's worst basin of unemployment increases, as of the spring of 2010, EU governments were hell bent on introducing drastic austerity measures guaranteed to reduce economic activity and thus employment even further. Now up to their necks in debt because they have assumed the private debt of the banks, these governments are determined to make their peoples pay once more, instead of, for example, cutting military spending or taxing the banks. Even if Europe is slipping back from a higher standard of living than, say, Latin America, this is going to be a hugely difficult adjustment with untold miseries in store for millions. Eastern and Southern (non-EU) Europe also risk explosion.

One of the many joys of financial globalization is its capacity to reduce the shares of wages in a country's GDP – and thereby increase the share that goes to capital. We saw this mechanism at work in the previous chapter for Europe, where the transfer from labour to capital of total GDP has been around 10 per cent. It's worse in Latin America: there the workers have lost 13 per cent of their previous share.

The ILO explains in another report how, in '51 of the 73 countries for which data are available', the share of wages in total income declined over the past two decades. Meanwhile, over the same twenty-year period, the income gap between the top 10 per cent and bottom 10 per cent in each country increased, meaning that the economic rewards were creeping upwards everywhere. Those years were a period of rapid economic growth, and by 2007 world employment was almost a third higher than it had been in 1990. Workers, however, were not receiving the returns they deserved, because 'the gains from the expansionary period which ended in 2007 benefited high-income groups more than their medium- and low-income counterparts.'[19]

Good point. Remember too that part of the share of 'labour' is in the form of executive salaries. Traders and CEOs are also employees. In the United States of the 1960s, the salary difference between the CEO of a large corporation and his average worker reached 60 or 70 to 1 – already an attention-grabbing differential – but progressive tax brackets, with the highest at 90 per cent, evened things out somewhat. Now the differential is 450 or 500 to 1 and climbing, while the top tax rate is 35 per cent.* The same patterns apply in countries as diverse as Australia, Germany, Hong Kong, the Netherlands and South Africa.

In 2007 in the USA, the top fifty private equity and

---

* It's more complex than that because, above each bracket ceiling up to the next one, there is a surtax (i.e. 28 per cent if one earns between $175,000 and $350,000, then 35 per cent of everything above $350,000) but at that level people have various means of escape – and you see my point anyway.

hedge-fund managers averaged $588 million each. The size of bankers' bonuses often causes normally placid people to foam at the mouth, especially when they are literally taken from our own pockets, i.e. from public bailout money. Bonuses, however, are much less outrageous than the system itself. Everywhere, tax loopholes you could drive a bus through help the rich to rake in ever more loot. A few of them are well-tailored crooks, but if caught will usually do less time in prison than some stupid poor kid arrested for possession of a few grams of coke or marijuana.* When job levels have dropped to such depths in a time of crisis, it takes four or five years for them to recover to pre-crisis levels, if indeed they ever do. But, once more, we can see that we are not living through a crisis for everyone. The costs of the rescue packages for financial institutions will be paid by ordinary taxpayers, but the benefits of financial globalization have gone in only one direction, and capital can on the whole rejoice in its good fortune.

There are other reasons that this very bad patch is not going to disappear any time soon. The national banks in the poorer countries bought only limited amounts of toxic securities from the hotshot financial peddlers, and they do not, for the most part, have a solvency problem as a result of subprimes or other financial derivative products. But a lot of these banks in countries such as Mexico are Mexican in name only – they are in fact subcontractor or branch banks of US financial institutions which have been particularly reckless. This is also the case for many in Eastern Europe. Just like their big brothers in the North, they too are going to reduce lending to try to increase their capital. Lack of credit will further contribute to unemployment.

Migrants from poor countries working in the North have

---

* Again, Bernard Madoff sentenced to 150 years to assuage public anger is the exception, which is why I call him the sacrificial wolf.

for years supplied far more income to their home countries than the foreign aid coming in. Remittances from these workers regularly dwarf official development aid, which is being reduced practically as we speak (Italy has already announced a reduction of 55 per cent of its ODA). In some small impoverished countries such as Haiti, remittances contribute more than 10 per cent of GNP. Since immigrant workers are the first to lose their jobs in the rich countries, their remittances are going to slump automatically and the standards of living will drop accordingly at home. Might there be a silver lining, for example a sense of national solidarity developing in times of hardship, that would link the rich in poor countries to their own poor people? Don't count on it. African elites also subscribe to the vile maxim of 'All for ourselves'.

Two researchers at the University of Massachusetts, James Boyce and Léonce Ndikumana, have painstakingly traced the scale of capital flight from sub-Saharan Africa to Northern havens. Their findings on forty African countries over a thirty-five-year period show that, by 2004, African political and economic elites had stolen fully $420 billion, which, with interest, amounts to $607 billion looted from the public purse. Much of this was simply pocketed from incoming loans: for every dollar of loans theoretically supposed to promote African development, 60 cents left the country and ended up in one of our banks, only too happy to credit it to the individual accounts of the thieves.[20]

Many people already know about the thefts by dictators such as Mobutu of Zaire or Sani Abacha of Nigeria, but what they managed to steal turns out to be just the tip of the iceberg (or one tree from the forest and a bucket of sand from the desert). Comparatively speaking, the sums coming out of Latin America in capital flight were greater, but proportionally the money from Africa constituted a heavier burden for ordinary Africans. Sub-Saharan Africa's 'external assets', meaning money held abroad by Africans, were almost three times as great as the continent's external debts, which in 2004 amounted to $227 billion.

Massive capital flight thereby constitutes a double crime: not only was public money stolen, but the loans from which it was pilfered still remain on the books and still have to be paid back. The interest on these loans – 60 per cent of which exited the country immediately – was paid thanks to slashed health and education budgets, thanks to the unnumbered sacrifices of ordinary people, year after painful year. Boyce and Ndikumana show that this siphoning off of capital from Africa meant that GDP would have been 16 per cent higher if the money had stayed at home; what was stolen represented two-thirds of all capital stock.

Sub-Saharan Africa received very little private money in the form of loans – 90 per cent came from public sources in official development funds from national development aid ministries or from the World Bank and the IMF. Two hypotheses can be considered: *either* these international financial institutions did not know that the loan money, intended for development programmes, was being stolen and sent to foreign accounts, and therefore proved themselves incompetent; *or* they knew it was being stolen, did nothing to prevent it and were therefore criminal accomplices to the thefts. I would be happy to hear from them on this subject, as I see no third possibility.

But even this isn't the worst news. The United States NGO Global Financial Integrity has issued another damning document, a report entitled *Illicit Financial Flows from Developing Countries: 2002–2006*, which shows that Southern elites made a killing during the hottest freewheeling neoliberal years. Who said these countries were 'poor'? The GFI's work shows that total capital flight exiting the developing world may be as much as a trillion dollars a year. 'Illicit financial flows' are defined as money that is 'illegal in origin, transfer or use' and reflects 'the proceeds of corruption, crime and tax evasion'. These flows increased steadily from 2002 to 2006. Development aid flowing into these countries is dwarfed by the outflows – indeed by a factor of $10 going out for every $1 coming in. Increases in capital flight during the period were highest in North Africa and the Middle East. From which country would you think the highest absolute amounts were coming? I wouldn't have guessed myself – it's China.*

Another thorough study by Norwegian experts commissioned by their government confirmed these figures, and in 217 pages tells you everything you can hope to know about tax havens and how to use them. They estimate that probably 20 per cent of inflows to tax havens come from richer people in poorer countries.[21] What can I say? Study the rich, not the poor.

A WAY OUT?

People aren't blind – they know perfectly well that globalization isn't fair. In late 2007, the BBC World Service undertook polls in thirty-four different countries and asked them what they thought about the 'fairness of sharing economic benefits

---

* Dev Kar and Devon Cartwright-Smith, *Illicit Financial Flows from Developing Countries: 2002–2006* (Washington, DC: Global Financial Integrity, 2008). The same organization, Global Financial Integrity, in May 2010 issued a further report (Dev Kar, Devon Cartwright-Smith and Ann Hollingshead, *The Absorption of Illicit Financial Flows from Developing Countries 2002–2006*) after having asked itself the far more difficult question 'Where did the pilfered money actually go?' The authors conclude that a share between 46 and 67 per cent went to developed country banks, whereas the rest landed in offshore centres. However, since their methodology relies on IMF data and the broad IMF definition of 'offshore centres' includes Ireland and Switzerland, that obviously ups the total now in the coffers of developed country banks.

and burdens' in their nation. They had a choice of saying that these were 'very' or 'somewhat' fairly shared, or 'not very' or 'not at all' fairly shared. The representative sample came to 34,500 people, and those answering the questions were, on the whole, not amused.

Only six countries had a majority who believed that benefits and burdens were shared very or somewhat fairly. Among the relatively happy are, rather surprisingly, Chinese and Australians – inequalities have increased enormously in both countries – plus Canadians, Nigerians and a smattering of small Arab country citizens. On the other side, Latin Americans are furious, Europeans (the UK, Spain, Germany, France, Portugal, Italy and especially Russia) are mad as hell, and South Korea, with 85 per cent of 'not very/not at all' and zero 'very fairly', is seething. Altogether, the world's answer was

'very fairly': 5 per cent;
'somewhat': 24 per cent;
'not very': 36 per cent;
'not at all': 28 per cent.

The other 7 per cent didn't know.[22] Note that these results are from December 2007 – that is, before the worst effects of the crisis were felt.

US citizens are generally an optimistic lot but, in the same survey, 74 per cent of them said that economic conditions in their country were a little or much worse. They're right: look at the public, federal expenditures of the USA. In 1980, the beginning of the neoliberal revolution, 38 per cent of these expenditures went to programmes targeted to persons, 41 per cent to the military and 21 per cent to private enterprises. By 2007, expenditures on persons had declined to 32 per cent, military expenditures had increased to 45 per cent, and expenditures in support of private enterprises had increased to 23 per cent.[23] These changes may not appear drastic but, with a federal budget as huge as that of the United States, a single percentage point means tens of billions. These figures of course do not include the massive bailouts more recently handed over to the private financial services industry or the massive, unprecedented military budgets for 2009 and 2010.

If I were an elected official I would look at these figures and, if I had any sense, tremble. We can't go on like this, as I hope this chapter has convinced you. The social impacts are too dire. Who can do something about it besides citizens? States, that's who. Globalization has not wiped out the state, but states have been making terrible policy choices for decades. We still have a little democracy left. Perhaps we can't change globalization directly because, by definition, there's no democracy at the global level, and many of the main actors in this drama escape our reach. But our own governments can and must be told at every opportunity: enough is enough!

3

THE MOST BASIC BASICS

PART 1: FOOD

The third prison wall is the resource crisis that increasingly places the greatest necessities of life beyond the reach of millions, whether physically or economically. If you live in a rich Northern society with good rainfall you may not notice this crisis much, since you have no problem that the local supermarket and the sink tap can't solve. However, for an increasing proportion of humanity, the daily struggle for adequate food and clean water forms the fabric of their lives. Before we are anything else, we are living bodies that must have these essentials – a banal remark, no doubt, but it is still the bedrock of life and thus the most central pillar of human solidarity. We will look at the food and water crises separately, but they are clearly related and intensify each other.

Most people will remember the context of the most recent food crisis because, in the spring of 2008, after a prolonged absence, food and hunger hit the front pages and TV again.

Spectacular price spikes and dramatic riots in over thirty countries drove a sudden revival of interest in how much people did or did not have to eat. Official agencies issued dire predictions concerning the additional numbers of the hungry and the poverty-stricken. As a result of sky-high food prices, at least one prime minister, in Haiti, bit the political dust. Then, as suddenly as it had flowered, prices subsided somewhat, the rioters went home and media interest withered.

A DECEPTIVE CALM

The food scene may appear quieter now, but that is only because hunger has become more entrenched and – one is forced to say – more disgracefully routine. Prices remain high compared with those earlier in this decade. In June 2009, the director of the World Food Programme (WFP) announced that, over the previous two years, an extra 115 million people had been added to the rolls of the hungry. In 2008, the Food and Agriculture Organization of the UN (FAO) estimated their numbers at 963 million. Based on preliminary estimates, six months later FAO feared another 100 million would join them in 2009 because of the financial and economic crisis – approximately 4 million new victims every week. The WFP noted that, in the poor countries, remittances from émigré family members were drying up, while jobs, exports and household incomes were also shrinking drastically on the home front. Before the crisis, the basis for the Millennium Development Goal of cutting hunger in half was 800 million people; in January 2010 FAO published the tally of 1.02 billion people in the world now chronically hungry – 25 per cent more than the MDG base.[1]

Food stands squarely at the crossroads of the ecological, social and financial crises and provides a graphic example of how they reinforce each other. It underscores the new reality of unpredictable, hunger-provoking price volatility that has little or nothing to do with local conditions. In the absence of a genuine, overall solution to this calamity that affects every aspect of human existence, vulnerability and hunger will continue to be the daily reality for hundreds of millions.

Before looking at the events that triggered both the escalating prices and the food riots, it's useful to recall how the stage for the food disaster was set over decades. This disaster, like others examined in these pages, was man-made, a long time growing and the result of shameful neglect.

Sad to say, fashions in disasters exist just as they do in clothes, music or home furnishings. In 1974, because of unusually severe weather events, shortages, famines and high prices for petroleum and staple grains, food was suddenly 'hot'. Thus the Food and Agricultural Organization called an exceptional World Food Conference.[2]

Delegates duly met, speeches were given and promises made, declarations were signed and, for a while, some efforts were made to reduce hunger. Most of them were ill-starred or purely technical, such as the Green Revolution, which did increase production but at huge social and ecological cost. It was the first opportunity for agribusiness corporations to get involved in third world farming in a big way through provision of inputs, and it gave more power and income to larger landholders but ruined small peasants, driving them into city slums and concentrating more and more land and resources in the hands of a few. Today, in water-stressed countries like India or Mexico, this irrigation-dependent technology has reached its outer limits.

DECADES OF INDIFFERENCE AND
DESTRUCTIVE 'SOLUTIONS'

In the 1970s, for those of us in the anti-hunger movement, such technical fixes were always destined to make the overall situation worse. We called for measures that seemed obvious enough to us – paying attention to land reform and tenure, giving pride of place to small farmers, aiming for local and national self-reliance in staple food crops. This would entail giving producers up to a certain limit a guaranteed price for their crops, upgrading research particularly to benefit small-holders, holding stocks to even out the peaks and valleys of good and bad years, and making better technology affordable and credit accessible while resisting agribusiness takeovers and the blandishments of large cereals exporters, particularly the USA. With rare exceptions – one was the hugely success-ful experience in Nicaragua under the Sandinistas starting in 1979 – these policies were scarcely tried. Nor have they been tried since; in succeeding decades they were indeed actively discouraged and rendered impossible.*

Throughout the 1980s, as neoliberal policies became more and more entrenched, food for millions disappeared from the

* By using the farmer-friendly measures listed above and redistributing the holdings of the dictator Somoza – who had appropriated control over almost a quarter of all the farmland in the country – Nicaragua within two years became self-sufficient in basic staples: rice, maize and beans. The government expected surpluses the following year, and at its request I car-ried out a study to determine where Nicaragua could find markets for them. Then Ronald Reagan sent in the Contras. They killed a lot of peasants, and the invasion disrupted the countryside to the point that the harvests suffered grave damage. Once the Sandinistas were defeated, everything went back to 'normal'. According to the FAO *National Food Price Review* of December 2008, rice cost 54 per cent more in Nicaragua than in December 2007. The country has been subjected to repeated hurricane damage, half the population is classed as poor and many families are at risk of severe food deprivation.

table, literally and figuratively. A new and devastating development fashion took over, ushered in by the explosion of the debt time-bomb. In the South, country after country had borrowed heavily throughout the 1970s, usually in order to purchase such goodies as armaments, consumer imports for the middle and upper classes, white elephant 'development' projects or higher-priced oil. Few loans were actually devoted to productive investments which could have generated extra income. A lot of money transited via the books of country X or Y but in fact was siphoned into offshore accounts by local potentates. So when in the early 1980s Washington suddenly slammed the borrowing countries with hugely increased interest rates, many found that they could no longer pay the interest, much less the debt itself.

Enter the International Monetary Fund (IMF) and its faithful sidekick, the World Bank – itself one of the major loan-floggers to begin with. Together they devised one-size-fits-all 'structural adjustment programmes' that indebted countries were forced to follow –otherwise no credit source anywhere would lend them a cent. In the case of agriculture, these programmes invariably stressed cash crops for export. You don't pay off a debt by feeding people and producing basic foods for the local market where they can be bought and sold in local currency. These shillings, pesos and rupees are of no interest to anybody except to those local buyers and sellers whom they happen to prevent from starving.*

---

* The progressive anti-hunger movement had coalesced into an organization we named the World Food Assembly. At its tenth anniversary meeting in Rome in November 1984, called to assess events since the FAO World Food Conference of 1974, Southern NGO and academic colleagues assured me that debt was the greatest new contributing factor to hunger, and they strongly encouraged me to write about it. I protested – I'm not an economist – but I followed their advice, which resulted in the publication of *A Fate Worse than Debt* (London: Penguin, 1988) and *The Debt Boomerang: How Third World Debt Harms Us All* (London: Pluto Press, 1992).

Another standard component of structural adjustment was the systematic privatization and dismantling of virtually all government activities, particularly those related to food and farming. If a country had a lot of pastoralists and the government provided free or low-cost veterinary services, the vaccination programmes were handed over to private vets and became too expensive for the poor. Consequently, if one animal in the herd picked up a disease, all the other, unvaccinated ones were hit as well.

If the government subsidised transport so that all food producers paid the same price to get their crops to market, no matter how far away they lived from the nearest market centre, the subsidies were cancelled and people had to pay for private transport according to distance and what the market would bear. If credit had been available to small farmers at controlled interest rates, this too was scrapped, leaving peasants in the clutches of moneylenders. If food stocks were kept on hand to even out supply shortfalls during poor years, the stocks were sold off and governments were told to discontinue stockholding. Families with a shortfall would have to borrow to cover the period before the next harvest and then pay back from that harvest at exorbitant rates. Under orders from the IMF–World Bank tandem, all this happened even in desperately poor countries. Sometimes they led to outright famine, as in Niger in 2004–5.

Official donor development agencies also made sharp cutbacks in their contributions to agriculture, seen as a far less pressing aid target in a period of comparatively low world food prices. How were the poorer countries to feed themselves? Let them eat imports, was the response, much to the satisfaction of the United States and other food exporters. Donors appeared to believe that low prices and generous food aid would be permanently available. The World Bank both led and followed the fashion in its own lending, and in

2008 its Independent Evaluation Group published a scathing report on the bank's neglect of agriculture in sub-Saharan Africa.[3]

In this chronically underfed region, where almost three-quarters of the population depends on food production for their livelihoods, the Bank's evaluation team noted that the institution over fifteen years had devoted a measly 8 per cent of its loans to farms and farmers and declared that 'a major drag on Africa's development is the underperformance of the critical agricultural sector which has been *neglected by both donors and governments over the past two decades*' (my emphasis). That judgement can stand for the rest of the world as well. This most vital of human needs (along with water) was sidelined. In the year 2000, when governments solemnly proclaimed the Millennium Development Goals, one was the goal of cutting in half the number of chronically hungry people by 2015. Even at the time this seemed wildly optimistic but, with another two hundred-and-some million hungry people added since the MDG was set, it has proven utterly unattainable. The FAO and the World Food Programme have admitted that, at the rate we're going, it will take over a hundred years to reach that milestone.

Surely anyone paying attention, as donor governments and agencies like the Bank are assumed to do, should have known that, given the debt burden, the lack of investment in food crops, the progress of global warming and the chronic neglect of food producers, the onset of a major crisis was only a matter of time. But the question remains, Why now? Why the huge spurt in prices in 2007–8? Why all those new victims? What makes this crisis different from earlier ones?

THE NEW FOOD SCENE: UNPRECEDENTED BUT PREDICTABLE

The initial observation is that this was the first food crisis of the era of neoliberal globalization. Previously, famines and shortages occurred on a comparatively local scale and could be pinpointed on a map. This one happened almost simultaneously across the globe, stretching from Bangladesh to Bolivia, from Egypt to Uzbekistan, from Mexico to Mauritania. Pakistan reintroduced rationing after two decades of open food markets; India banned exports of rice; Russia froze the market prices of staples; Ukraine declared an embargo on exports and innumerable hungry people rioted.

It was also the first mainly urban food crisis. Historically speaking, and paradoxically, food shortages erupt in rural areas. People in the countryside who are or could be agricultural producers are the first to go hungry. This was the case with the Irish peasantry in the Great Hunger, the potato blight famine of 1845–9, during which at least a third of the Irish population starved to death, while better-off city dwellers continued to eat well and food exports from the estates of absentee English landlords, removed under military escort, actually increased. It was subsequently true of any number of localized famines.

In 2007–8, the most spectacular manifestation of hunger was instead the quite sudden deprivation of millions of city dwellers, people eking out a marginal existence on the peripheries of the metropolis. They included innumerable failed former farmers who could no longer afford the skyrocketing prices they were expected to pay for their usual staple food items. The urban poor often spend 70 to 80 per cent of their meagre resources on food, so any increase will hit them hard. The escalation, however, was not bad news for everyone: in the last three months of 2007, the three major transnational cereals companies, Archer Daniels Midland, Cargill and Bunge, increased their profits by 55, 86 and 189 per cent respectively compared with those in the same period the previous year.

Many reasons have been cited for the sudden surge – some accurate, others spurious or at least unexceptional. Let us list them first, then assess them. The generally cited causes are

1 common or garden supply and demand factors;
2 weather and climate events;
3 increased petroleum prices;
4 higher demand from emerging markets such as China and India, where the middle classes are upgrading their diets;
5 diversion of land and food crops to the production of agrofuels;
6 financial speculation;
7 trade liberalization.

FACT VERSUS FICTION

One can certainly identify some genuine and quite banal supply–demand issues such as population growth, a slowdown in food production after many years of gradual increases, and much lower world cereals stocks. Such factors contributed to greater demand or lower supply but had been building up over several years, and should not have taken economic forecasters or governments by surprise.

Cereals production has been steadily levelling off or declining in both China and India since the turn of the twenty-first century, whereas from 1980 to 2000 about half the increase in world grain output came from just those two countries. It is furthermore the case that, over the past few

years, production has not kept pace with population growth
and shortfalls have been met by drawing on stocks. When
worldwide cereal stocks decline, prices increase more or
less mechanically (and vice versa), so, when stocks dropped
below two months' worth of world supplies, alarm bells
rang.

Weather and climate events also contributed to the relative decline in supply, but not dramatically. Yes, the wheat
crop failed in Australia because of prolonged drought, the
American Midwest corn belt was hit by floods and there were
unseasonable blizzards in China, but such events were not
enough to disrupt prices to the extent actually witnessed. To
provide a yardstick for comparison, in 2004–5, total world
production of cereals was approximately 2 billion tonnes
(2,000 million), including 600 million of wheat and 750 million of corn. The drop in the Australian wheat harvest, for
example, was about 10 million tonnes.

Climate change is a different matter. Agricultural production both contributes to and suffers from increasing
global temperatures; some experts say that deforestation
and the decay of agricultural residues (as well as farm animals farting methane) are the greatest contributors to global
warming. Climate alterations are already beginning to have
an effect and can be expected to cause enormous upheavals in food production and consumption patterns as well
as affecting every other aspect of human existence on the
planet.

What about the relations between crude and food? Higher
oil prices automatically contribute to higher costs for farmers, especially for mega-farms in the rich countries that rely
on petroleum-based fertilizers and pesticides, petrol-guzzling
farm machinery and long-distance transport. In Europe,
crude oil prices went up by 89 per cent between 2004 and
2007 and urea for fertilizer by nearly as much. Freight costs

which in 2002 were only $10 a ton had escalated to the point that they were being negotiated at $80 to $100 a ton at the onset of the crisis.*

Let's move on to number 4 on the above list – higher demand driven by the increased wealth among the middle classes in emerging markets, particularly China and India. I am ashamed to admit that I repeated this canard myself a couple of times, mostly because a VIP from IFPRI – the venerable International Food Policy Research Institute, was putting it about. Out of charity, I won't name him, but he either hadn't done his homework or was reciting an ideological lesson. This 'explanation' for mounting food prices actually began with George W. Bush who, at a press conference in Missouri on 2 May 2008, announced with a typical Bushian smirk that the Indians were the culprits. Here is the transcript:

> There are 350 million people in India who are classified as middle class. That's bigger than America. Their middle class is larger than our entire population. And when you start getting wealth, you start demanding better nutrition and better food. So demand is high and that causes the price to go up.

This remark is in the same category as weapons of mass destruction in Iraq: if you repeat a lie often enough, it becomes the truth – and the media endlessly repeated this one, probably because it let the USA off the hook. In India itself the statement became a *cause célèbre* denounced by politicians left, right and centre. The US ambassador had to jump

---

* The multiplication of freight costs by eight or ten was partly because of China's huge imports of metal ores – the same ships are used for these ores and for food transport and were in great demand. See Philippe Chalmain, *Le Monde a faim* ('The world is hungry') (Paris: Bourin, 2009), a useful and concise compendium.

into the fray to calm the uproar, assuring all concerned that Bush was a 'great friend and admirer of India'. Other commentators quickly named the Chinese middle class as another guilty party.

The reality is different. According to the Indian Ministry of Finance, per capita consumption of cereals in India actually declined by 14 per cent between 1990 and 2006. The World Food Programme says that 212 million Indians are still chronically hungry, including nine out of ten pregnant women, who get less than 80 per cent of their food energy requirements. Half of all Indian children are said, again by the WFP, to be severely or moderately malnourished; 800 million people live on less than $2 a day, 300 million on less than $1.

This, of course, says nothing about those greedy middle classes supposedly stuffing themselves with high-end food products, but here again the truth is that India imported a meagre 2 million tonnes of wheat in 2007 and is a surplus producer and net exporter of meat and dairy products. The FAO import curves for India are completely flat, except for a very gradual increase in oilseeds imports since the mid-1990s. The country also stopped all rice exports in 2007 so as to continue to assure its own national needs.

As for China, the country was a surplus food trader from 2000 to 2006. It halted ethanol production from corn in 2007 because the price of pork had gone up locally by 42 per cent. That same year China increased its investment in agriculture by 31 per cent. The FAO import curves for top-end foodstuffs are rising imperceptibly, if at all, although the Chinese do consume more eggs per capita than the average American and will undoubtedly move gradually up the food chain, including higher consumption of meat, though probably not dairy products. Many studies have shown that, in any country, regardless of geography or culture, when per capita incomes rise significantly, consumption of two products – meat and energy – always increases.

China recognizes as well that it could have serious food supply problems in the future as a result of ecological damage. Its soils are rapidly eroding, water pollution and shortages are a growing threat, and mega-projects, particularly dams, are encroaching on farm land on a vast scale. The response to this challenge is both surprising and sobering: China is renting or buying millions of hectares of arable land in countries as varied as Mexico, Tanzania, the Philippines, even Australia, but mostly in Africa. It is also sending battalions of surplus Chinese farmers and sometimes military personnel to work on and manage these farms. The jury is out on the impact. In some cases, as in Zambia, it would appear that the production – at least for now – may go partly to local markets and that Chinese experts sometimes provide technology and research services to local farmers. In others, the pattern seems to be much closer to nineteenth-century Western imperial land-grabs, with the single goal of securing food supplies for the home front. One commentator cites the following: 'Small wonder then that Jacques Diouf, director-general of the Food and Agricultural Organisation has warned that "The race by food importing countries to secure farmland overseas to improve their food security risks creating a neo-colonial system".'[4] Prudently, Diouf does not name names, and South Korea has also leased or bought as much or more farmland as China, with Saudi Arabia following suit. Nonetheless, if anyone is 'overeating' and putting pressure on world food supplies and prices, it's not the Chinese but US citizens, whose high-protein, meat-based diet amounts to over 9,000 calories a day in terms of cereals (it takes over 7 kilos of corn to produce a kilo of beef, 2.5 for a kilo of chicken, and so on). Here are the figures for yearly consumption, including indirect consumption, of all cereals in 2006: India:

175 kg; China: 288 kg; world average: 316 kg; USA: 953 kg.[5]

I rest my case. If Americans consumed the same products at the same rates as the Chinese and the Indians, the world would be awash in food surpluses.

NEW AND ORIGINAL WAYS TO MAKE PEOPLE HUNGRY

So let's move on to more serious arguments, like the sudden shift of land and resources into agrofuels* – that is, to grain (mostly corn or 'maize') and edible oilseeds production devoted to the manufacture of ethanol for vehicles. Brazil has been producing ethanol from sugar cane for decades, often deforesting vast tracts in order to do so, but its production as such is efficient in standard economic terms (that is, terms which don't take into account ecological destruction). Brazil is the only country where agrofuel production is, in this narrow sense, economically efficient – all other producers depend on government support.

The United States and Europe are justifying their switch into agrofuels on ecological grounds. Such claims are fallacious. Many studies have shown that there is no environmental benefit whatsoever in terms of greenhouse gas reduction when all phases of this production (fertilizer, mechanization, etc.) are taken into account. Even worse, according to a study led by a Nobel Prize-winner in chemistry, Paul Crutzen, agrofuels are the source of much higher environmental costs, and this supposed 'cure' for greenhouse gas emissions is far worse than the disease. In a 2007 paper, Crutzen and his

---

* I prefer 'agrofuels' to the term 'biofuels', which could convey the meaning that these are somehow 'organic' or harvested from weeds or other 'free', naturally occurring plants.

colleagues showed that growing and using agrofuels emits far more greenhouse gases than fossil fuels and therefore increase global warming (70 per cent more if they are made from rapeseed, 50 per cent more if made from maize). That's the science.[6]

Besides, the whole agrofuel concept has been roundly denounced by such revolutionary institutions as the OECD, the FAO, and the British House of Commons. *The Economist* notes that ethanol production is responsible for about half the drawdown in world cereal stocks, which, as we have seen, always causes prices to rise automatically. And, aside from the extra greenhouse gases, using food for fuel can be seen as morally indefensible. The grain equivalent of the agrofuel needed to fill the 25 gallon tank (about 100 litres) of a single SUV just once could feed one person for a year. The head of the Trade and Agriculture Department at the OECD (who calls them 'biofuels') summarizes unequivocally their role in food costs:

> As a large part of the [land] use expansion was due to biofuels, there cannot be any doubt that biofuels were a significant element in the rise of food prices. More specifically, in North America and Europe biofuels cannot be produced, and would be very little used, in the absence of government support through subsidies, tax breaks, tariffs, and use mandates. In other words, biofuel support policies have contributed greatly to the rise in global food prices.[7]

Many people have denounced these fuels as anything from 'foolish' to 'a crime against humanity'. So what exactly are agrofuels fuelling? Clearly, they are both speeding climate change and forcing more people to go hungry through higher prices. Furthermore, and without their consent, European and American taxpayers are paying for them.[8]

This is undemocratic, unfair and unacceptable – but not to everyone. The real advantage of agrofuels has nothing to do with preventing climate change or reducing greenhouse gases. It doesn't even relate to finding alternatives to petroleum in order to reduce US dependency on the Middle East. The main reason Congress once more increased public subsidies to agrofuels in 2008 is because US farmers' incomes increased by 48 per cent in 2007, and that important rural constituency is happy, thank you very much.

In the dismal and chronic Unites States trade deficit, agricultural exports stand out as export stars, and 'improved' – read 'higher' – prices caused the surplus of agro-exports versus imports to reach $12 billion in 2007 and an estimated $24 billion in 2008. If agrofuels reduce oil dependency marginally, that can serve as a convenient alibi. In fact, these fuels eat up fully a third of the US corn crop of 300 million tonnes, which means that they are diverting 15 per cent of total world corn production towards fuelling automobiles. Since this reduces the supply of corn for animal feed, there is a knock-on effect on the price of wheat, which can be a substitute, albeit a more expensive one.

Will this situation change under the new Democratic presidency and congressional majority? Don't count on it: many new subsidized ethanol plants have sprung up in the Midwest and Barack Obama was once the junior senator from Illinois, in the heart of the corn belt.

Now we come to factor 6 – financial speculation on commodities markets. As with agrofuels, we find ourselves here in especially fertile terrain for explaining the food crisis. 'Speculation' has come to be a rather dirty word, but on commodities markets it's generally quite innocent – or at least it used to be. These markets deal in real, tangible goods such as cereals, live cattle and hogs, frozen pork bellies, orange juice concentrate, sugar, and so on. Buyers and sellers of these goods need knowledge of prices in advance, which is why the places they trade are known as 'futures' markets.

Farmers want to be sure they can cover next season's planting costs, so they sell their crop at a guaranteed price before it is harvested and deliver the goods later. Cookie manufacturers want to know how much their raw materials will cost them in six months, so they buy grain and sugar in advance at a guaranteed price for future delivery. The people who smooth out these transactions by betting that commodity prices will go up or down, who buy and sell futures contracts for clients or for their own account, are called speculators – they are speculating on the upside or downside risks inherent in any market. Members of a skilled profession, they play a useful role, up to a point. That is why commodities futures markets have existed in the United States for 160 years, ever since the Chicago Board of Trade was set up in 1848. Since those early days, these markets have become infinitely more complex and trade in myriad products, but the goal is always the same: to even out the risk.*

A refinement on such straightforward futures contracts is

* On 31 July 2009, the Chicago Board of Trade was 'decommissioned' and, with the Chicago Mercantile Exchange (CME), the New York Metals Exchange (NYMEX) and the latter's commodity division COMEX, merged to form the CME Group. I encourage readers to visit the website www.cmegroup.com, if only to get an idea of its scope and complexity. It boasts the 'broadest array of futures and options products available': if you are looking for a derivative contract (i.e. one 'derived' from some underlying security or product), this is where you go. You can bet on real-estate or interest-rate products, foreign exchange (currencies of all sorts), energy products, metals, tropical commodities and many other more or less exotic choices, including 'weather products' (risks due to 'temperatures, snowfall, frosts and hurricanes'). The CME Group is also developing its clearing house activities so that, in all product classes, it can act as 'a buyer for every seller and a seller for every buyer' on all contracts. In that way, if a buyer or seller defaults, the risk is contained and does not ripple through and contaminate the entire derivative product-risk system. Here we confine ourselves to cereals markets, where price volatility hit the greatest number of blameless people hardest.

called the index fund, a much more recent invention. Here the investor buys into a fund based on the prices of one or, more often, several commodities; the value of the investment will simply mimic the day-to-day value of the commodities themselves and the investors never actually take delivery of any physical good. Index funds are generally limited to large players with at least $100,000 to invest.

When the subprime housing bubble collapsed, it caused a stampede of investors into various other markets in hopes of saving their marbles and making a quick profit elsewhere. Evidence is now emerging that the huge surge – and subsequent plunge – in oil prices in 2008 was also a result of this sudden speculative activity, but in the case of cereals it's absolutely certain. For example, in 2003, commodities index fund investors had placed $13 billion on these exchanges. In March 2008, five years later, their investments had multiplied twentyfold, to $260 billion. This was not farmer or cookie-manufacturer money. In the course of a single day, 27 March 2008, the price of wheat shot up by 31 per cent. The *New York Times* estimated that, all told, $300 billion had poured in from Wall Street and calculated three-month increases at 35 per cent for corn futures, 42 per cent for soya and 64 per cent for wheat. Cereals – usually quite boring, stable sorts of goods – were suddenly hot! The Commodities Futures Trading Commission (CFTC), supposedly the government watchdog keeping an eye on these exchanges, said that, depending on the commodity concerned, Wall Street controlled 20 to 50 per cent of all contracts on crops and animals. The CFTC could estimate but it couldn't intervene, and here we have another perfectly scripted neoliberal morality play.

Why did a designated regulator not regulate in a time of obvious over-the-top speculation and crisis? The answer is simple. In mid-December of 2000, the 106th United States Congress in its wisdom passed the Commodity Futures

Modernization Act. The 'modernization' involved can be freely rendered as 'total deregulation'. Congress chose to pass this bill while President-elect George W. Bush was waiting to receive the keys to the White House and President Clinton was packing his bags: he was in no position to veto anything. Most of the evidence shows that both Clinton and the Federal Reserve chairman, Alan Greenspan, approved of the new legislation anyway.

This 'modernization' act replaced three venerable New Deal laws that had governed US commodity exchanges since the 1930s. Under the previous legislation, traders were obliged to disclose their holdings in each agricultural product and respect strict position limits. Maximum holdings were specified in each commodity so that no firm, or group of firms, could 'corner the market' and set prices as it pleased. The laws were intended to prevent hoarding and manipulation, and that is precisely what they managed to do for more than sixty years. 'Modernization' in 2000 meant that, henceforward, all trades on 'over the counter' markets would be exempt from any regulation or oversight. 'Over the counter' simply means any trade between two consenting parties and represents the overwhelming majority of exchanges that take place on commodities markets. Regulators were kindly requested to keep their noses out of business which no longer concerned them.

The Modernization Act was later criticized for containing an 'Enron loophole' that allowed the now disgraced and defunct energy firm to hoard kilowatt hours of electricity and boost prices outrageously. This was hardly surprising, as Enron lobbyists had helped to draft the bill. No matter: over the counter markets grew exponentially, reaching $9 trillion ($9,000 million, $9,000,000,000,000) in 2007. The result of this market churning in food commodities over the five years between March 2003 and March 2008 was a price increase of

314 per cent for wheat, 134 per cent for corn and 199 for soya oil. There was even a little something for the South: markets registered plus 34 per cent for cocoa, 167 per cent for coffee and 69 per cent for sugar. No one active in these markets was thinking for a single instant about people half-way around the world who would find themselves unable to pay for the least tortilla, chapatti or bowl of rice. They were not on the same map.

'FREE TRADE' AND THE DREAD P-WORD

We now come to the seventh and final factor identified as contributing to periodic spurts in food prices, which is trade. The subject is particularly vast and won't be done justice here. But, in the whole canon of neoliberal dogma, 'free trade' is probably the most revered virtue and 'protectionism' the most loathsome sin. This seems bizarre. Whereas most people would unhesitatingly agree that it is a sacred duty to protect one's family, one's home, one's natural environment and, if need be, one's country, in the context of trade, protection is anathema. This shift in meaning is a remarkable ideological coup, and the stigma instantly attached to 'protectionism' is not likely to disappear anytime soon.

Let us, nonetheless, reject knee-jerk reactions and think rationally about this question, meanwhile seeking another word to describe what is meant. A quick check suggests possible substitutes for the verb 'to protect' – defend, guard, look after, care for, save from harm, shield, safeguard or watch over. These are mostly nice cosy and warm-sounding words, conveying a sense of welcome security. None of them, unfortunately, takes kindly to an ending in 'ism'. Protectionism in matters of trade is blamed for stifling innovation, rewarding laziness and greed, increasing unemployment, deepening financial crises and leading to war – this last based on memories of the 1930s, when 'beggar thy neigh-bour' policies of competitive protectionism really did build international hostility through 'lose–lose' scenarios.

'Beggar thy neighbour' means seeking to benefit one's own country at the expense of others. Its policy tools include tariff and other barriers against imports or, somewhat more subtly, currency devaluations to favour one's own exports. Had you noticed all those Europeans flush with high-value euros head-ing for New York with empty suitcases to take advantage of prices marked in weak dollars? Or heard the US Treasury demand for the nth time that China revalue its currency to make its exports to the US more expensive and less competi-tive? Governments are not going to admit that they use such policies to favour their own economies at the expense of others, but it happens all the time.

Both the United States and the European Union, despite World Trade Organization (WTO) rules, continue to export their subsidized agricultural products to third world markets, frequently undercutting local farmers and wrecking their chances of selling their harvests at a remunerative price. Dumping – the practice of breaching other people's frontiers in order to sell at below one's costs, usually to open up a market, or simply to earn something rather than nothing – also happens all the time.

Trade rules that apply to food and agriculture, like many rules the rich try to make for the poor, are cases of 'Do as I say, not as I do'. For example, the USA applies low tariffs for food grown in poorer countries if it enters more or less as har-vested, but the moment it is processed, tariffs shoot skywards. Agribusiness likes to keep the more lucrative, 'value-added' activities such as processing for itself, thus depriving poorer countries of both jobs and revenues.

Food trade is fine if it contributes to a more varied diet and does not deprive people, especially poor people, of their livelihoods. But one should also think about its ecological footprint – I nearly wrote 'foodprint'. Our food travels too far before it reaches us and thereby exacerbates the climate crisis. You may have heard the same stories I have – the European 7,000 km yogurt and the frozen French-fried potato that has to travel to at least five distant places for washing, peeling, cutting, frying, freezing – these stories may be apocryphal but not by much. And, as Herman Daly points out, instead of shipping American cookies to Denmark and Danish cookies to the USA, it would be more rational simply to exchange recipes.

In the 1930s the wrath reserved for protectionists was pretty much limited to those who set up high tariff barriers or flooded markets with cut-price merchandise; today the WTO has added many refinements. It specializes in hunting down and trapping the more wily and devious protectionists who use the 3Bs – 'behind borders barriers'. For those who haven't closely followed WTO negotiations or European Union manoeuvres to impose economic partnership agreements (EPAs) on smaller, weaker (mostly African, Caribbean and Pacific) countries, the 3B strategy can be a little difficult to grasp. Most people still think of 'trade' as exchanges occurring between nations with distinct frontiers and of 'trade barriers' as tariffs or quotas erected at those frontiers to keep out other people's goods. In the far broader definitions of the EU or the WTO, however, 'protectionism' is more likely to be disguised and to lurk in government regulations, investment codes, health and safety standards, professional qualification requirements, intellectual property rules, consumer protection measures and the like.

One of the oldest trade stories of modern times is the ongoing USA–EU beef hormone dispute, in which the Americans blame the Europeans for keeping their hormone-fed beef out of the EU on spurious health grounds. The USA, authorized by the WTO Dispute Resolution Body, retaliated by slapping prohibitive tariffs on Roquefort cheese and other EU food products. At the WTO, a bizarre form of 'justice' prevails, under which blameless French sheep-farmers have been made to pay, through a significant loss of their US market, for a decision they had absolutely nothing to do with, before or after the fact. It is worth noting too that these farmers live in the thistle-covered Larzac, an austere and semi-arid part of France where alternative economic activities are simply not available.*

The only time the WTO tribunal has ever ruled in favour of a country refusing certain goods on health grounds was when it agreed that countries outlawing imports of asbestos insulation had a point. The dispute resolution judges could scarcely do otherwise, since a specific lung cancer has been incontrovertibly proven to be caused by inhalation of asbestos fibres. In ten other cases where such relationships were harder to prove, health regulations were struck down as 'disguised barriers to trade'.

Today's big transnational corporate trade players are also trying to obtain total freedom of investment so that they can realize the old dream of producing whatever they want wherever they want and providing services universally. They call for no restrictions on the possible investment targets: health care and education should be opened to investment, for example, just like banks or insurance companies. For production and/or provision of food and water, the same applies.

The corporate sector is aiming for no limits to the number of companies allowed to enter a given sector or on levels of

---

* In May 2009 the USA and the EU agreed to a truce which will suspend WTO litigation for four years while the parties explore settlement of this long-term dispute through a market-opening deal. Under the terms of such a deal, the EU would be required to increase substantially its import quota for non-hormone fed US beef.

investment (for example, a ceiling of 49 per cent on the foreign corporation's share), no requirements concerning local
employment or local content, and so on. The transnational
corporations and the governments that back them, notably
those of the United States and the EU, also demand access
to government procurement contracts, with no preferences
accorded to national firms. All this is in addition to reducing
or, if possible, eliminating altogether border protections such
as tariffs and quotas.

It now appears that the meandering 'Doha Round' of trade
negotiations at the WTO, jump-started in November 2001
in the post-September 11 context, may never be completed.
In the spring of 2010 it was still floundering, yet the head of
the WTO, Pascal Lamy, is doggedly pursuing his agenda and
was chosen to succeed himself, as nobody else was foolhardy
enough to apply for the job. Although few share his opti-
mism, he remains confident that Doha can be brought to a
successful conclusion.*

This absence of movement internationally has given an
extra push to the bilateral and regional negotiations such as
the EPAs, all of which are 'WTO Plus' – meaning that they
go further, usually much further, than anything envisaged
by the world body. Here the EU has had some success, and
several governments of poor and weak countries, including
all the Caribbean governments and several African ones,
have signed up, ensuring greater poverty and job losses for
their people in future. They are threatened with loss of trade
opportunities and dwindling foreign aid if they don't sign,
but that is scant excuse.

The only genuine solution would be to scrap the WTO, the

---

* In May 2009, before an audience of about 1,500 people, I debated with
Pascal Lamy at the two-day 'République des Idées' event in Grenoble; he
expressed confidence in the Doha outcome both publicly and privately.
We'll see.

EPAs and many of the hundreds of bilateral trade agreements and start afresh, for example with the plans for the Havana Charter, proposed in 1947 and based on the ideas of John Maynard Keynes for an International Trade Organization, a special currency, the 'bancor', and an International Clearing Union with rules that would have prevented the accumulation of huge trade deficits on one side (e.g. the United States) and huge surpluses on the other (e.g. China). But that is a story too long to tell here. Suffice it to say that more trade is in no way the solution to the food crisis, or any other crisis for that matter.

SECURITY OR SOVEREIGNTY?

What should be the goal of a decent food policy, assuming that the parties concerned genuinely want to eradicate hunger? This assumption may be far-fetched, given that hungry people are by definition poor people who also by definition contribute little or nothing to markets, either as producers or as consumers. But let us suppose for a moment that a globalized, free-market, capitalist food system can also try to make sure that everyone on earth has access to an adequate diet. How should one then go about doing so?

The FAO has long stressed the concept of 'food security', and the term has become standard parlance in official encounters and policy documents. Most progressive forces, however, aren't satisfied, including the transnational farmers' organization Via Campesina, active in more than fifty countries, which prefers the notion of 'food sovereignty' and criticizes the definition of food security given by the official World Food Summit of 1996: 'Food security exists when all people, at all times, have physical and economic access to sufficient, safe and nutritious food that meets their dietary needs and food preferences for an active and healthy life.'[9]

That seems a pretty good definition on which most people could agree, so why mess with it, as Via Campesina and most food and anti-hunger activists feel called upon to do, in favour of 'food sovereignty'? The reason is that the official definition says nothing about where the food came from, who produced it, what inputs they used, how big their farm was, and so on. It further does not mention where, how and by whom the food was processed and sold, at what cost and at what price. In a word, 'food security' tells us nothing about who actually controls the whole food chain.

'Sovereignty', on the other hand, means popular, not just state, sovereignty, and it stresses democracy and access in one of the most vital areas of human existence. Many countries, for example in North Africa or the Middle East, can ensure food security for their people in the sense that they have abundant incomes from oil and gas exports so they can pay to import whatever food they need. Theoretically at least they can also make sure that all their citizens have access to it. Yet they can lay no claim at all to food sovereignty. Either their small farm sector is virtually non-existent or they are climatically unfit to grow enough. One can also assume, for example, that, if exporters want them to import, say, genetically modified crops or hormone treated meat, they will probably comply.

Food sovereignty would mean, on the contrary, that as much production as possible is localized, consistent with economies of scale, using local seeds and maintaining biodiversity; that farming techniques are sustainable and respect soil and water resources; that research, technology and credit are adapted to the needs of small farmers, are often subsidized and reduce dependency on fossil fuels; and that national food processing companies respecting local tastes supply most of the foodstuffs sold in urban centres without having to compete with transnational agribusiness giants. Sovereignty does not mean autarky and isolation or control over every detail of the food chain, with no exchange or trade. It does mean having a choice, particularly the political choice of deciding which spheres of national life must remain free from vulnerability and dependency on the choices of outsiders.

In other words, the concept includes a kind of built-in checklist specifying who produces, who transforms, who controls the marketing, who benefits, and so on. The world is very far away from achieving anything resembling food sovereignty, although many groups are trying to achieve it locally or regionally, over limited areas and for relatively small numbers of people, particularly through closer producer-to-consumer ties. These are all praiseworthy efforts, but so far the scale is much too small.

Unfortunately, indifference to the key concept of food sovereignty in policy decisions is the main reason that hundreds of millions of people will continue to go hungry. Governments, meanwhile, have to recognize that, if they don't change their ways, if they continue to neglect the agricultural sector in a context of extreme price volatility for vital commodities, they are playing with fire. Food-rich countries, especially in the North, should also think seriously about all those discontented, dispossessed ex-peasants not far away, crowding into urban slums and ready to risk whatever it takes, including their lives, to reach more favourable shores.

We have known for thirty years at least what works and what doesn't – still assuming that getting rid of hunger is the criterion. What doesn't work is collectivization, whether Russian, Chinese, Algerian or any other kind – unless the local community has specifically chosen it after thorough debate. What also doesn't work is agribusiness takeovers of land and food systems in which producers become mere cogs in the agricapital wheel. What does work is the short list of policies with which I began this chapter – the ones the

activists who made up the World Food Assembly were advo-
cating in the 1970s and 1980s. They entail paying attention
to individual family farms and land tenure, the inclusion of
landless agricultural workers, and providing some security in
the form of price guarantees if markets fail. If the consumer
in the concerned country is too poor to take on the risk of a
guaranteed price, then the state or agencies such as the World
Bank should set up a fund to do so. They should also ensure
reserve stockholding. They should stress food crops, research
adapted to local needs and low-cost technologies. Decent
policies would put back in place all the ones dismantled by
the structural adjustment policies of the Bank and the IMF –
everything neoliberalism forced people to abandon. All such
policies have a huge drawback: they don't make money for
international capital – all they do is feed people.

I had almost begun to hope that food policy might be
like what Winston Churchill once said about the USA: 'The
United States invariably does the right thing after having
exhausted every other alternative.' But, alas, neither the USA
nor the other big players and payers have yet exhausted every
damaging alternative. As I write, powerful forces are designing new programmes which will replace their failed policies
of the 1960s and 1970s with the new improved technological
fixes, and they intend to impose them, particularly in Africa.
The usual suspects – the World Bank and the agribusiness
transnational corporations such as Monsanto, but also (as
we saw in the previous chapter) newcomers like the Bill and
Melinda Gates Foundation – are designing interventions
guaranteed to destroy African soils, African farmers and
therefore African food sovereignty and the chances of Africa
emerging from its status as 'the hungry continent'.

As I handed over this text to publishers, the news of highly
probable famine for at least 20 million Africans in Somalia,
Ethiopia, Uganda and Kenya was slowly penetrating Western

media. Rainfall has been erratic or non-existent for three years; the maize was dying in the fields before it could be harvested. I felt transported back to 1974, when I first began to work on the causes and remedies of chronic hunger and famine. It is hard not to despair. Still, countless people are struggling for food sovereignty – some of them because they have no choice. As for Southern governments, they must concentrate on their most valuable natural resource – small farmers – and give them all the help they can.

PART 2: WATER: THE PERFECT CAPITALIST PRODUCT*

We live in a capitalist society, and water is the ideal product for capitalism. The word 'product' is used intentionally, as one of the objectives of capital is to transform everything, including nature, into a commodity that can be turned into money in the marketplace. One need not be a Marxist to see evidence of this tendency everywhere. Water – if the market could capture it completely – would be the ideal product for reasons which illustrate perfectly classical economic theory, from Adam Smith onwards.

Water is rare and scarce Although 70 per cent of the earth's surface is covered by water, virtually all of it is saltwater. Only 1 per cent is available freshwater; a further 2 per cent is also fresh but locked up in the polar ice-caps or glaciers, and therefore unavailable. This resource is also growing scarcer, and scarcity is the condition for putting

* I will deal only with freshwater, although some of the problems for ocean ecosystems (pollution, overfishing, and so on) have obvious similarities with those of freshwater systems. This part of the present chapter is very close to a contribution I made in 2008 to the Zaragoza International Expo, whose central theme was water.

a price on anything – abundant resources are low cost or no cost. Price is a way of rationing scarce resources, so, the scarcer the good, the higher the price – for classical theorists, this is the vital function of the market.

Water is indispensable Nothing alive can do without water because living things are all largely made of it. Most plants are 90 per cent water, and you yourself, depending on how much fat your body carries, are between 45 and 75 per cent water. Women have an extra supply of subcutaneous fat, so the proportion of their water weight is less than that of men. None of us, male or female, could think, see, speak, feel, and so on without water because our brains, like our skins, hearts and other vital organs, are at least three-quarters water. Because their tiny bodies are 80 per cent water, babies are particularly vulnerable to water loss, and in poor countries thousands still die of dehydration. Educating mothers and supplying them with oral rehydration salts packets to combat this particular risk has been one of the longest and strongest campaigns of UNICEF. Courageous politicians and activists such as Gandhi may win major battles by going on hunger strike, but I know of no one who has attempted a thirst strike because they would be dead before they could get their political point across.

The supply of fresh water cannot be increased No human ingenuity can add to the supply; what we have is all we have – in fact, we are reducing our supply in various ways. We can invent techniques to capture more water from the atmosphere, but we cannot increase the total moisture content of that atmosphere or augment the freshwater cycle of evaporation/precipitation – indeed the spread of deserts and of mega-cities is impairing it. The planet may have accumulated a great amount of water underground, but there, too, the supply is finite, and we are constantly 'mining' groundwater and aquifers, many of which will not be replenished by nature for hundreds or thousands of years, if ever. In such a context, greater demand as a result of irrigated agriculture, industrial development, more affluent lifestyles or simply expanding populations will automatically lead to greater scarcity and therefore higher prices – not just for the water itself but for all the foodstuffs, energy supply and industrial products that depend on it.

There are no substitutes for water This trait alone shows how unique water is compared to other goods. Classical economic theory teaches that, when the preferred product X is not available, consumers will fall back on product Y. This remains true for foodstuffs, energy and other vital goods but not for water. Although one can joke that the French, and perhaps the Spaniards and Italians too, would like to believe we can substitute wine for water, this remains only a joke – water is in a class by itself.

Imagine an economist trained in the classical liberal capitalist mode and a capitalist entrepreneur who have no prior knowledge of the good we're discussing here. They would take one look at these different attributes – inbuilt rarity and scarcity, indispensability, no possible additional creation of the resource, no substitutes – and conclude that this 'product', whatever it is, is a goldmine and a dream come true. As soon as they could carry out a marketing study, they would be even more enthusiastic. They would note that, from the commercial point of view as well, no other product has the same characteristics.

- The market for this good is permanent, as the indispensability argument in particular makes clear.
- Demand for this good will increase regularly, even

exponentially, owing to agricultural and industrial development, as well as population growth, no matter what the available supply.

- Price increases will logically follow. The number of 'consumers' is necessarily equal to the number of people on earth, not just for each person's physical survival, but for all kinds of ancillary needs such as cooking, personal hygiene, and keeping one's clothes wearable and one's dwelling liveable.
- Consumers can be charged virtually any price for this product, because life itself is at stake. In the context of necessarily increasing scarcity, consumers will be obliged to reserve a substantial part of their income to secure it.

These economic rules will apply *so long as this product remains in private hands. The only other option for citizens in a society where water is considered a commodity is revolt and peaceful or violent appropriation of the resource* – a question we will have more to say about later.

All these characteristics show that, if humankind were to decide that, from now on, it is our duty to provide a decent and dignified life for everyone on earth, then water would have to be considered a *universal public good under public control, understood as including not only government oversight but also democratic, popular citizen participation.*

It would be foolish to count on the willingness of capitalist entrepreneurs not to take advantage of the incredible characteristics of water as merchandise. If they can gain control over such a resource and dictate the terms of its availability and use, they will avail themselves of their advantage to the fullest extent to secure private profit. In such circumstances, no one should expect anything else. We can't count on all governments either. Some are not elected at all, and even elected ones can be subject to corruption, favouritism, collusion with commercial interests and the like. The European Union negotiates all its trade agreements with the interests of water companies (and other transnational corporations) in mind, with no regard for local populations. The presence of the people in matters regarding the supply and distribution of water is indispensable.

Saying that water should be a universal public good does not mean that it should also be free. I would argue to the contrary that, above a certain basic daily supply for individual consumers, it should cost something and its price should escalate fairly rapidly with consumption levels. Its price, however, should be determined politically, not by purely economic forces of supply and demand. Precisely *because* water can be seen as the capitalist's dream, water capture, management and distribution must be under democratic control that includes robust and enforceable price mechanisms.

A scarce, valuable, indispensable resource must be conserved and carefully managed and allocated, and the question is which groups should pay what for which water needs? Should a rich homeowner pay the same rate per cubic metre to fill his swimming pool that another domestic user pays to fill a kettle or take a shower? Should farmers using notoriously wasteful methods of irrigation be able to pay particularly low prices no matter how much water they use? Should the cost of the huge amounts of freshwater needed for cooling thermal power plants be factored in to the cost of energy coming from that source, say a nuclear power plant, with regard to energy from another source, say wind turbines, or should consumers pay the same price for energy from all sources? These are the kinds of questions any democratic water allocation system would have to be able to answer.

WATER RIGHTS AND WATER WRONGS:
NATURAL, ECONOMIC AND SOCIAL

The first aspect of water inequality is natural. Although it may seem unreasonable to speak of nature as 'unfair', the natural distribution of water on our planet really is shockingly unequal. Some countries are richly endowed; others have almost none. Nine big countries possess 60 per cent of the world's available freshwater supply: Brazil, Russia, China, Canada, Indonesia, the USA, India, Colombia and the Democratic Republic of Congo. As far as global warming is concerned, your CO_2 emissions contribute to it wherever you live, so you should try to reduce them. But there is no way you can help to alleviate water shortages in Algeria, Australia or Atlanta by turning off your taps in Berlin, Barcelona or Belgium.

If you consult the official tables you will find that the cubic metres available per person per year in various countries stand in stark contrast to each other.[10] At the extremes of the supply per capita continuum, every citizen of Iceland is theoretically blessed with an incredible 566,667 m³ of freshwater per year, but the average inhabitant of Kuwait has access to only 7 m³ – so the theoretical Icelander has 81,000 times as much water as the Kuwaiti.

Those are the extremes. As with any bell-curve statistical distribution, most countries lie closer together, towards the middle. The statistics still give a good indicator of where to look for stresses, high prices and conflicts. For example, the high-income developed countries boast an average of 9,245 m³ per person per year; the low-income countries average 5,102, which is quite enough to live on comfortably if properly distributed.

A good rule of thumb says that, under 1,700 m³ per person per year, a region will suffer occasional water 'stress'; less than 1,000 can be defined as water 'scarcity', with an important impact on human health and economic development. Several authoritative sources foresee that, by 2030, two-thirds of the world's population will live in water-stressed countries. An enduring feature of the Israel–Palestine conflict is access to water, because both are badly served by nature; the Israelis have 240 m³ per person per year and the Palestinians only 203. Latin America is exceptionally well off in terms of water endowments: Argentina is at the 'low' end, at 20,500 m³ per person, while Brazil, Chile, Colombia, Ecuador, Paraguay, Peru and Uruguay all have upwards of 40,000.

Many Middle Eastern, North African and Sahelian countries are indeed parched, but Iraq (2,489 m³) has almost the same amount of water per person as Spain (2,558); and Iran (1,930) has more than Germany (1,861). In the Sahel, even Niger, which recently experienced a severe famine, has 2,257 m³. When people lack water in Sahelian countries, it is most often to the result not of absolute shortage or drought but of poorly organized, urban-biased or corrupt distribution.

But even abundant water, properly managed, can be in the wrong place, and droughts can still hit hard locally. They may also have immediate political consequences. Poor Australia theoretically has almost 24,000 m³ of water per person, but its heavily populated east and south have undergone a decade-long drought, the worst in its history. Agricultural production has plummeted and many farmers have given up and left the land. The 2007 election sanctioned the conservative Australian government unwilling to tackle climate change. The United States (which has 6,800 m³ per person, very unevenly distributed) is trying to force Canada (88,000 m³ per person) to export its pristine, underground water, using the US–Canada Free Trade Agreement and the North American Free Trade Agreement (NAFTA) as its attack weapons. Many Canadians are resisting, and this is a subject for permanent conflict over the question of resource sovereignty.

The second aspect of water inequality relates to distribution between sectors of economic activity. However many private swimming pools you may see if you fly over Southern California or the Balearic Islands, comparatively little water goes to private domestic consumption. Individual household consumption varies between only about 8 and 11 per cent of total consumption worldwide. The trade-off between industrial and agricultural water use is usually determined by politics, but, worldwide, agriculture definitely takes the lion's share. Overall, about 70 per cent goes to farming, 22 per cent to industry and only 8 per cent to domestic use. These averages hide vast differences, depending on the level of development and, in some developed countries like the USA or France, the place given to agriculture. The average figures are shown in table 3.1.

Table 3.1 Average percentages of water use

	World	*High income*	*Low/mid income*
Domestic	8%	11%	8%
Industry	22%	59%	10%
Agriculture	70%	30%	82%

Source: UNESCO, 'Water for People, Water for Life', United Nations World Water Development Report, 2003

The United States, which now devotes 80 per cent of its water nationally to agriculture, will not be able to continue in the same profligate style. Irrigated agriculture represents just 16 per cent of the cultivated farmland in the country but produces half the total harvests, and land is irrigated even in such semi-desert states as Arizona. The aquifers are shortly going to disappear but, faced with powerful farm lobbies, Congress does not intervene and environmentalists have little influence.

At 22 per cent worldwide, industry is way behind agriculture, but that figure too conceals sharp contrasts. Some industries are especially thirsty. The cooling of electric power plants, especially nuclear plants, is second only to irrigation in water use and causes damage to marine or freshwater aquatic ecosystems because the water rejected after cooling operations is substantially warmer than the ambient temperature. The microchip industry uses untold tons of pristine water. Every tiny computer chip requires 32 kilos of water (plus 1.5 kilos of fossil fuels). A single silicon wafer producer in the US state of Washington, where Microsoft is headquartered, uses 7.6 m^3 of water every *minute*, drawn from a pristine aquifer 300 metres below the surface.

Other instances of water use we rarely think about are 2.5 litres to produce a litre of petroleum; 2,700 litres for a cotton T-shirt, 4,000 for a kilo of beef and *1,000 for the cereals needed to produce a single litre of agrofuels* – this alone should be enough to disqualify agrofuels as an alternative to petroleum. Well-off people probably 'consume' indirectly about 3,000 litres of water a day.

The third water aspect of water inequality is social and does the most harm. Once more we find the familiar disparity between rich and poor. Over a billion people still lack access to clean drinking water, and consequently millions die of water-borne, preventable diseases every year. As we have known since the nineteenth century, anywhere on earth, infant and child mortality rates only begin to fall, and life-expectancy rates to rise, when a community can provide people with clean water.

For example, a safe water supply and personal hygiene are the only ways to combat cholera. In the 1980s, a cholera outbreak struck a poor suburb of Lima, Peru. The Lima area is notoriously dry and the stricken community depended on cistern trucks to bring in its water supply. Structural adjustment privatization programmes enforced by the World Bank and the International Monetary Fund had raised the price of water and of its transport largely beyond the reach of the poor, who purchased as little as possible and never 'wasted' it for washing their hands. Any public health worker could predict the results.

When poor mothers mix commercial baby-milk formula with dirty water, their babies are almost always condemned to death by diarrhoea (2 million deaths a year minimum), but the World Health Organization (WHO) lists over twenty water-related diseases, most of them completely unknown in the rich countries. The distance a poor woman has to travel to collect water will have a measurable impact on her family's health. Less than 20 litres per person per day in the WHO vocabulary constitutes 'basic' or 'no' access, with a 'very high' (negative) health impact – over a billion people are still in this category. Fifty litres per person per day constitutes 'intermediate access', with a 'low' impact on human health. Only slightly over half the world's households have a household connection to tap water, guaranteeing 'optimal' access of 100 litres per person per day and thereby a 'very low' health impact.[11]

HUMAN INTERFERENCE: NEW AND NEWLY RECOGNIZED DANGERS

Most governments of emerging, newly industrializing countries still do not see pollution as important so long as industry thrives: they want giant dams for energy and water management; irrigation, however wasteful, is equivalent to 'development'. Pollution of rivers in China is a major problem (as is the exhaustion of its aquifers), and in heavily industrial districts rivers are used as chemical dumps. Over the past three decades, China has devastated its water resources, and scarcity is a growing threat, with a quarter of its agricultural land now desert. Dried-up river systems, massive schemes for river diversion and gigantic dam construction have created millions of environmental refugees. Sanitation systems in some large cities are under serious stress. Although China has four times the population of the United States, its central bureaucracy for environmental management is one-twentieth the size of that of the USA. China is beginning to make some feeble attempts to curb energy and water use, but it may be too little too late.

The country's water problems also pose dramatic economic threats. To alert its corporate clients who are thinking about investing in China, Deutsche Bank runs seminars to explain the water problems they are likely to encounter. For starters, China uses at least seven times as much water to produce a single unit of GDP as more developed economies, and its water prices are also completely unrealistic. They do not reflect real scarcity, so they encourage further waste and depletion. Deutsche Bank warns brokers who sell clients a financial stake in Chinese projects that they should make sure to disclose whether or not the project has proven access to renewable water supplies – otherwise, they could face litigation later on.

Scarier still, more than half the Chinese population, 700 million people, has no access to clean drinking water.* Their supply is below WHO quality standards and is often contaminated by both industrial and human or animal waste. Lack of clean water for animals is a source of now all too

---

* If we accept the UN figure of 1 billion people lacking access to clean water worldwide, and if 700 million people in China alone, according to the WHO, lack such access, this leaves roughly 'only' 300 million people lacking access elsewhere, which seems far too few. However, if you search the internet for 'access clean drinking water', you will find all sources giving 'a billion' (or 'over a billion') without access to clean drinking water and 2.4 or 2.5 billion without access to proper sanitation. I cannot by myself resolve the contradictions of the United Nations information systems and statistics.

familiar viruses that can pass from poultry to pigs to people
and provoke the flu pandemic that WHO experts say is not a
question of 'if, but when'. Water shortages and pollution on
such scales can have disastrous impacts everywhere. This is
a huge problem well beyond China. In the Northern 'developed' countries our water is also being massively polluted
by large farms discharging irrigation water loaded with pesticides and fertilizers, or animal wastes and antibiotics from
industrial animal-raising enterprises. Aside from plant-cool-
ing destruction of river and marine systems, the chemical and
paper industries also make us environmentally poor. Water-
pollution control and waste-water recycling have become
multi-billion dollar industries in themselves.

Human beings change the climate for the worse and
create a cycle of man-made droughts by misusing the water
cycle. Over half the world's population now lives in cities,
often mega-metropolises of 10 to 20 million people which
act like deserts made of cement. To encourage rainfall, we
need much less concrete and much more greenery – parks,
green roofs and green belts around urban areas. Many cities
are mining groundwater so fast that one hears stories of
overpumping that has caused sink-holes to open up in parts
of Florida and swallow houses, even entire streets. This phenomenon is called subsidence: it is already affecting Mexico
City and Beijing because the water under the city has been
pumped out. The US–Canadian Great Lakes are being
drained because, every year, four times as much water is taken
out of them as nature can put back in.

Not nearly enough people – not even enough scientists –
see global warming as a water problem as well as a fossil fuel
problem, but in fact the two are intimately linked. The more
deserts we create, whether those deserts are made of sand
or concrete, the more heat will be reflected back from the
earth's surface into the atmosphere, heating it up. Preserving

freshwater where it is, in lakes, rivers and watersheds, would be an enormous contribution to reducing global warming because it is the hydrological cycle that cools the temperature. Furthermore, as the *New Scientist* reported in July 2007, 'for the first time we have proof that greenhouse gas emissions have already begun to alter how much rain falls around the world, and the effect will become more extreme over the coming decades.' The unwelcome message of this research is that dry regions will become even dryer and some tropical areas – plus Canada, Northern Europe and Russia – will get wetter. In places where agriculture is already marginal, it could well become impossible. As the scientists who collected the evidence of this phenomenon point out, people are more immediately and drastically affected by the absence of water than they are by temperature, and the deleterious effects of changing rainfall patterns are likely to cause major upheavals and massive migrations.[12]

Although it does not take a genius to predict trouble on the horizon, governmental authorities do not seem to have devised any plans for what happens if the taps in, say, a major US city such as Atlanta, which has experienced serious water shortages, actually do run dry. The data are well known, and US federal officials have declared that 43 per cent of the country is in a state of 'moderate to extreme drought' – but they seem to have no contingency plans. What would happen to agriculture, ranches, tourism, hospitals? In Georgia, even religion has been affected – not only does the governor pray in public for rain, but full-immersion baptisms have been suspended – this in a state where evangelical Christians are the majority.

We can ask the same questions about any number of places in Europe, including Eastern Europe, Greece, parts of Spain, and places further away such as Ankara – not to mention Australia. Every summer the consequences are on television:

out-of-control wildfires, soaring death rates among elderly people, crop failure, animals dying of thirst ... We can imagine other impacts, however little we may like to think about them: new 'dust-bowls', as witnessed during the Great Depression in the United States, mass migrations, epidemics, and the collapse of certain economies in several regions.

What about the drastically falling water tables in India, where some land is already turning into desert? How will China continue to feed itself when the stressed Yellow River basin is effectively exhausted? Is all this simply too awful to contemplate, with the result that public officials refuse to do so and hope, in some sort of 'magical thinking', that the drying-up will conveniently go away?

WATER RIGHTS AND WATER FIGHTS

Contrary to officialdom, some people are thinking very hard indeed about water and water shortages, among them corporations and the military. We, too, should think about corporate and military control over water and its future impact. The only way to avoid them is to manage water as a universal public good and to promote democratic control over its supply, treatment and distribution. Fortunately, there is also some remarkably hopeful news about victorious popular struggles for control over water, of exactly the kind recommended here. The more public awareness of the problem and of these success stories, the more they are likely to spread.

Given what we know about water as the ideal capitalist product, it is no surprise that influential, business-oriented bodies do not agree that it should be a universal public good. Their tactics have changed somewhat over the past two decades and they now stress much more skilful public relations, particularly corporate social responsibility (CSR). They do not want to be regulated in any way, so they also stress 'voluntary measures' and 'self-regulation'. Where water is publicly managed, they often hope to privatize it, as has been accomplished in other former public service areas such as telecoms, transport or utilities. To accomplish their goals, they use both public and private bodies as mouthpieces.

The World Business Council for Sustainable Development is one private-sector endeavour that specializes in pushing for PPPs, or public–private partnerships. The siren song they sing over and over to the public authorities is 'private enterprise can provide you with better technology, better service, greater efficiency and lower costs'. The song – as in the Greek myth – actually leads to disaster: one can find stacks of evidence, starting with the water privatizations of Margaret Thatcher's Britain which almost always resulted in lower quality, higher prices and little or no service to neighbourhoods inhabited by people unable to pay the new, inflated rates. And how would you like to find rats in your toilet, as certain customers of Yorkshire Water did after it was privatized?

Privatization means nothing more than handing over the results of the work of thousands of people over decades with virtually no guarantees. The word itself is a lie, and the phenomenon should be called, rather, 'alienation', or simply a 'sell-out' or a 'give-away'.

The World Water Council (WWC) is an international public–private think tank and event organizer founded in 1996, with headquarters in Marseilles. It claims to be 'dedicated to strengthening the world water movement for an improved management of the world's water resources'. It is, however, well on its way to being a quasi-official international organization, although it has no mandate from the UN – or from anyone else for that matter. The WWC is also clearly biased towards industry, which provides a good part of its funding, and is another strong advocate of PPPs. Since 1997 it has organized the triennial World Water Forum, with both governmental and strong corporate presence. In 2000, the forum in The Hague attracted 5,700 participants, while both those in Kyoto (2003) and Mexico City (2006) boasted more than 20,000. The organizers claimed that 33,000 people turned up at the fifth one in Istanbul in March 2009. The ministerial declarations that emerge from these forums have become in many ways the official international water agenda. In between its forums, the WWC promotes neoliberal 'solutions' to the crisis.

The World Economic Forum, better known by the name of the Swiss Alpine village where it meets, in Davos, Switzerland, came out with another plea for water PPPs in its 2008 meeting, co-signed by its founder and chairman, Klaus Schwab, and by the president of Nestlé, Peter Brabeck. They call for 'new forms of cooperation between governments and corporations' in order to respond to the coming crisis and to 'improve the political and economic image of water'. I was not aware that the 'image of water' was in need of improvement; in any case, the Davos objective for 2008 was to set up an 'unprecedented and powerful public–private coalition which will help to find solutions so that we can together manage future water needs . . .'.

However one looks at it, water is big business, even beyond supplying it or treating it. Financial analysts are quick to point out that some thirteen Arab countries, many of them rich oil producers, are officially 'water-stressed'. A conference held in November 2007 by the Saudi Water and Power Forum brought together energy and water specialists from all over the world, including corporations, to whom the Saudi government announced its intention to spend $100 billion over the next twenty years on desalinization plants and other water treatment facilities – all this for a country which will still have a population of fewer than 40 million in 2020. Drought or deserts, plus mountains of cash, seem to many industrialists to be a marriage made in heaven.

These semi-public or private international bodies have been set up in order to create an intellectual and media climate favourable to private enterprise and to public–private, or simply private, water management. They would not be so successful, however, were it not for the political, ideological and financial support of major international, intergovernmental, entirely *public* institutions that push the neoliberal line on water, with all the considerable power and prestige at their disposal.

Alas, even the United Nations fits this description: it has set up an in-house structure called the Global Compact, which corporations can join simply by signing up to a set of principles concerning the environment, human rights and labour relations. Coca-Cola is a member, and some NGOs in India have complained bitterly, accusing the company of draining precious water resources as well as polluting their land and water. One of Coca-Cola's largest bottling plants in India has been shut down since March 2004 as a result of their activism, and one notes that it only joined the Global Compact in 2006 as its reputation was plummeting. The UN does not seem to have asked the company any embarrassing questions; meanwhile an international campaign has succeeded in removing its products from over twenty colleges and universities in the USA, the UK and Canada. Coca-Cola has also been dropped from the socially responsible investment fund of TIAA–CREF, the largest pension fund in the United States.

Let us mention the World Bank and the International Monetary Fund *pour mémoire*, given that they have insisted on privatization for years and made it a condition for their loans to over a hundred indebted countries. They forced these

captive customers to become more 'market oriented' and regularly interfered with water management. The public–private
partnerships promoted by the Bank in particular were invariably controlled by the private partner, because that partner
needed to make a profit, and the public 'regulators' lost
control over corporate behaviour. Even so, the companies
did not always find the financial returns up to their expecta-
tions, and since 2003 some of the largest, including Veolia,
Suez and Thames Water, have withdrawn from some major
contracts – but not without making legal claims demanding
tens of millions of dollars in 'anticipated profits' they never
collected.

To place water privatization and corporate control in
perspective, it is important to note that, despite all the
pressures, public systems are still the norm, although not
in France, Britain and parts of Spain – this is why these
countries are home to the major transnational water corporations. Privatization did not become a global threat until
the 1980s and 1990s. Companies have often seen water as a
kind of final frontier, and one executive, quoted by Maude
Barlow, was heard to say: 'We're going to do for water in this
decade what we did for telecoms in the 1990s – get complete
deregulation.'[13]

The European Union has proven particularly corpo-
rate-friendly, going out of its way to place the interests of
European transnationals above the public good under all
circumstances. The Trade Directorate is perhaps the most
flagrant example of devotion to business interests. The action
of successive EU trade commissioners (Leon Brittain, Pascal
Lamy, Peter Mandelson) in the negotiations concerning the
General Agreement on Trade in Services (GATS) provides
a vivid illustration. The GATS is one of many agreements
under the auspices of the World Trade Organization, and,
since services now make up about 80 per cent of the European

Union's GNP, they are an important vehicle through which the Commission tries to make all countries, rich or poor, open their service sectors, including water, to the investments and penetration of EU companies. The Commission negotiates for all the member states, and in the case of water it does so on behalf of corporations such as Veolia, Suez, Générale des Eaux, Thames Water and Aquamundo.

The European NGO Corporate Europe Observatory (CEO) obtained correspondence sent by the Commission to these European water TNCs in which the former asked the latter to provide detailed requests for the GATS negotiations: Which countries does your company want opened up as a priority? Which aspects of the water business in these countries interest you most? Treatment? Distribution? Bottling? (CEO did not have access to the replies of the companies.) As a result, the EU placed on the negotiating table requests to seventy-three countries, including some very poor ones, to open the sectors most important to the TNCs.

As noted, the 'Doha Round' of WTO negotiations has been at a standstill for years, largely because of agriculture, not services, and the Commission is consequently putting great efforts into bilateral and plurilateral free trade agreements, hoping to obtain equal or superior results to those available through the GATS. These deals are called economic partnership agreements, already briefly described in relation to food and the 3Bs, or 'behind borders barriers'. Among these 'barriers' are any measures a government might take to regulate foreign direct investment or prevent the commercialization of its water.

MONOPOLIES, GOOD AND BAD

Why should the privatization of water have particularly negative outcomes? Classical economics explains clearly why poor results are to be expected, especially when the private service provider enjoys a *monopoly*, as is almost always the case with water. If, until recently, water has generally been a public monopoly even in capitalist, free-market countries, it is for good reason. Water treatment and distribution do not benefit from competition as ordinary manufacturing or service businesses would, and therefore do not conform to the capitalist principle that competition is healthy because it generates innovation, greater efficiency and lower prices. In the case of water, it is logical to have a single authority overseeing the whole of the network and in command of its various components because, in cases that economists call *'natural monopolies'*, a single authority is the best way to arrive at the greatest efficiency, the best quality of service, optimum fairness in price, and so on.

A 'natural monopoly' means that one firm can produce the given, desired output at a lower cost than two or more firms could do, because a single firm can create more 'economies of scale'. This is why most market economies have opted for water networks managed by public authorities – at least, this was the case until neoliberalism became economic religion. The choice of public management had nothing to do with 'socialism' or with a bias towards public over private. It merely showed concern with efficiency and maximum cost–benefit advantages.

However, when a private, profit-oriented corporation gets its hands on a 'natural monopoly', it behaves exactly as one would expect. It goes after profit, the higher the better, and it cuts costs, first by massive lay-offs of personnel but sometimes by neglecting maintenance and infrastructure. Poorer neighbourhoods get worse service or none at all. More money must be spent on high salaries and benefits for the managers, often foreigners in the case of TNC management. Under private management water is never subsidized or free. The World

Bank and the IMF, both chock-full of economists, are apparently unaware of these first-year economics course facts about natural monopolies.

None of this is to say that public water provision is perfect and has never encountered any problems anywhere. Of course it isn't; of course it has. Sometimes public administrations are inefficient, unaccountable and corrupt. Sometimes the infrastructure is deficient or not maintained. If a public entity truly needs help in improving its water distribution and treatment, instead of looking to the private sector it should seek out a public–public partnership, as has been successfully done, for instance, in South Africa and Malaysia. And when the public sector fails, popular struggles should be directed at fixing the problems, not at destroying a public service in favour of privatization.

ANOTHER WATER WORLD REALLY IS POSSIBLE

We know now who the adversary is and what he wants. The targets of social movements should also include the improvement of public regimes in order to make them more responsible and more responsive to public needs, so that people will defend them. The best contemporary collection of hopeful stories about water is to be found in *Reclaiming Public Water: Achievements, Struggles and Visions from around the World*, first published by the Transnational Institute and the Corporate Europe Observatory in 2005 and updated since.[14] The book, which now exists in about twenty languages, contains more than twenty cases of water battles – from developed and less developed countries on every continent, from large cities and small villages – with valuable documentation showing how privatization schemes can be defeated and public control over water re-established.

There are many ways to keep water under public control.

The 'participatory budget' of Porto Alegre, Brazil, well known as a pioneering exercise in popular control over municipal money, also applies to the publicly owned municipal water company. The health results have been outstanding (zero cases of cholera when the rest of Brazil was undergoing an epidemic). The pricing system is exemplary; it escalates exponentially so that rich people filling their swimming pools effectively subsidize the basic consumption of the poor.

The most famous Latin American story is probably the fight in Cochabamba, Bolivia, against another World Bank privatization project. The Bank, in secret, handed over the public water company to a subsidiary of the US Bechtel corporation (of Vietnam War fame), which instantly increased prices way beyond the capacity of the poor to pay. The people quickly formed a broad coalition and called a week-long general strike. They were met with military and police violence; the water war was not won without hundreds of people injured and at least one person, a seventeen-year-old boy, killed. But they did win, and in stages re-established a public water facility with high popular participation.

In the state of Penang, Malaysia, the Penang Water Authority adopted a 'commercial outlook with a social obligations strategy', which has resulted in universal access to water but also high efficiency and profitability, which covers investments and also allows the company to make interest-free loans to poor communities for improved connections. The Penang Water Authority offers the lowest water prices in the country and its employees are imbued with the 'ethos of public service'.

The success stories (and some failures, from which one can also learn) of many other communities are included in the TNI–CEO book: the main thing to remember is that public–private arrangements mean 'profits for the companies, risks for the public sector and costs for the people'. That is a motto in Grenoble, France, which has remunicipalized its water regime and improved maintenance, and now supplies water that, even without treatment, is pure, at the lowest cost of all French cities with a population over 100,000.

People willingly come together in coalitions to protect water. In example after example, broad fronts of interest groups that have never worked together on any other issue can be found fighting water battles; they include farmers, environmentalists, trade unions, political parties, women, indigenous communities, human rights advocates, and so on. Sometimes consumers can become members of the water authority body with voting rights. Sometimes the citizens control the budget (Brazil is champion in this league). In some poor communities in Ghana or India, local people participate in construction and maintenance, thereby reducing costs and providing employment and income within their own community. In Argentina and parts of Dhaka, Bangladesh, the water workers and their union manage the company as well. At the very top of the list of spectacular achievements is the passage of a constitutional amendment in Uruguay making the privatization of water unconstitutional. Water struggles have often succeeded because water is a local issue and coalitions are also local. People understand instinctively what clean water means for their health and their families. It's also easier to win these struggles locally. At the international level, problems are more difficult to solve because of the lack of democracy, but even on the international scale, water activists can make their points.

For example, one can focus on taking water out of World Trade Organization/GATS jurisdiction. In France, Attac campaigned for 'GATS-free zones', resulting in more than 800 French municipal, departmental and regional governments declaring themselves symbolically GATS-free. The local officials were often convinced by arguments concerning

the water sector. This was doubtless because, under the
GATS, once a service sector is 'opened' by a country (or, in
this case, by the whole of Europe) the law applies at every
level of government, from top to bottom.

In Europe, activists can also concentrate on the European
Commission to make it stop serving the interests of EU
transnational corporations above the needs of poor people in
poor countries. Nor can we afford to forget that the World
Bank and the IMF still make privatization, including water
privatization, a condition for their loans. These are all long-
term goals.

Whether one is a believer or not, water should be seen not
merely as a strategic resource but as sacred because it is the
source of all life. It is not by chance that all religions include
rituals founded on the physical presence and the symbolism
of water. Baptism is a rite of initiation and of inclusion in the
community of the faithful. The ritual ablutions of Muslims
before participating in worship signify respect and the desire
for purity before Allah. Water can be a symbol of love and
service, as when Christ washed the feet of his disciples.
Bathing in the Ganges links the Hindu to 'Mother India'
and to the whole of creation. We need to recover our sense
of awe and wonder in the presence of the clear, fresh, life-
giving miracle of water and refuse to allow it to be degraded,
polluted and reduced to the vulgar level of the marketplace.

4

THE WALL OF CONFLICT

A traditional and tempting way to exit an economic crisis was often war. True, wars cost money, but they allowed rulers to raise taxes and to spend the revenue on ships and cannon, stimulating the economy, usually with the support of a patriotic population. It was a gamble but, if victorious, the winner could capture extra resources. Although Roosevelt's Keynesian New Deal policies went part way to pulling the United States out of the Great Depression, it was the Second World War that finished the job and opened history to what media magnate Henry Luce called the American Century.*

So far, that century has lasted about sixty years, but it

* For those who may be new to all this, 'Keynesian' refers to the British economist John Maynard Keynes (1883–1946), who, among myriad other contributions, revolutionized the way governments had previously dealt with economic and financial crises – mainly by doing nothing and hoping for the best – with his insistence on government intervention and job-creating stimulus for the economy. President Roosevelt's 'New Deal' in the 1930s was directly inspired by Keynes's ideas.

seems less and less true that large-scale warfare still helps to prolong the reign of dominant powers, including the United States. When President Reagan elevated Cold War spending to undreamed-of heights, the Soviet empire, trying to keep up with the military outlays of its rival, collapsed. Now that rival may lose its own pre-eminent place because of the ongoing costs of Iraq (even post-pullout) and Afghanistan, now familiarly known as 'Afpak', as Pakistan too sinks into the mire of conflict. The Pentagon's budget now amounts to nearly 5 per cent of United States GDP and shows no signs of falling despite the US government's huge indebtedness.

It used to be that states bankrupted banks: banks made loans for war, states didn't pay them back, and bang! There went the Medici. Now banks bankrupt states: 14 trillion spent by the USA, the UK and Europe to save the financial system is about a quarter of world GDP. If these outlays convinced governments that states can no longer afford wars, it might have been worth it, and yet they go on waging them, as President Obama has again shown.

The more than $515 billion in the 2009 United States defence budget and the $636 billion Congress voted for 2010 naturally create jobs, while US armaments exports serve to reduce slightly the disastrous US trade deficit, but, otherwise, arms production is nothing but pure consumption. It's true that military technology has spin-offs in the civilian economy –the internet and radar are the most famous – but wouldn't it be preferable to spend those funds directly and more productively on the relevant research rather than passing via the Pentagon?

What follows is not about achieving classical hegemony through military might, about large-scale resource capture or about the big, famous wars that demand huge financing and spectacular logistics. We will attempt, rather, to explore what the present crisis may change in the area of conflict and violence and ask whether nations and peoples will have greater recourse to them in today's stressful times than before.

THE GOOD NEWS: NOT IN OUR GENES

In times of economic crisis, when populations are under severe pressure, the search for scapegoats can become a convenient refuge – a tendency Hitler and his propaganda henchmen exploited with terrifying skill, against Jews, gays, gypsies and leftists. Today, working people losing their jobs and houses are victims of distant and unaccountable forces and may seek consolation in blaming immigrants or others closer to home. You can see this tendency at work in France and Italy, where right-wing governments court popularity by harassing and expelling paperless immigrants. In France, this has included shipping Afghans back to Afghanistan regardless of the fate that awaits them there.

Awful stories are published in the US press about disaffected youth hunting down and attacking the homeless for no other reason than that they are homeless. One of these reports featured a homeless couple presently living in a flood-control tunnel in Nevada – they know they are at risk of drowning if there's a flash flood, but they feel safer in the tunnel than outside. The relevant question for our purposes here remains whether or not we are somehow predetermined to respond to strains and tensions with violence. John Gray, the British philosopher who enjoys a good paradox, believes that our society requires doses of madness to keep ourselves sane, now supplied mostly by new virtual technologies of sex and violence. But what will happen when we run out of new vices? How will satiety and idleness be staved off when designer sex, drugs and violence no longer sell? At that point, we may be sure, morality will come back into fashion.[1]

Gray's point has apparently not yet reached the pop culture scene in the United States, where the millionaire owner-promoters of the Ultimate Fighting Championship, who believe that humans are genetically programmed for violence, are making stacks of money betting on that belief. In US sports arenas these promoters have now staged over a hundred 'mixed martial arts' events that have proved hugely popular, bringing in far more spectators and dollars than boxing and wrestling matches. The violence entrepreneurs plan to take their formula – which they confidently predict will become 'the biggest sport in the world' – to Europe and beyond; it's already broadcast on cable or satellite TV in a hundred countries. Pay-per-view TV receipts were heading for $300 million in 2009, and fans are quite prepared to pay hundreds if not thousands of dollars to watch these ultra-violent combats from a ringside seat.[2]

There are a few rules – no head-butting, hair-pulling, clawing, pinching or twisting flesh, sticking fingers into any of an opponent's orifices, or striking the spine or back of the head, and no groin attacks of any kind; anything else is pretty much OK. Although the mats in the Octagon – the cage within which the fights take place – are often spattered with blood, the organizers point out that no one has ever been killed in one of their bouts. It may sound like the late Roman empire scenario minus the emperor with thumb up or down, but does it mean that violence in terms of organized group conflict is really in our DNA? Might not the Ultimate Fighting Championship be one way to ritualize combat for those who enjoy watching bloodshed? The neo-gladiators are not actually slaughtered, but the spectators still feel gratified. This might be progress of a sort.

If such increasingly ritualized and spectacular violence can be considered from that point of view as encouraging, here is some more good news concerning collective fighting – that is, organized conflict of one group against another that causes significant fatalities.* Ask any group of any age, sex or political views whether human beings will ever stop fighting wars, and more than 90 per cent will answer no. However, a growing number of primatologists and anthropologists disagree.[3]

Although down the ages they have undoubtedly engaged in lethal group conflict, it is 'statistically much more common for humans to be cooperative and to attempt to get along', says anthropologist Robert Sussman of Washington University, Saint Louis. His colleagues at Yale, Carolyn and Melvin Ember, oversee the Human Relations Area Files, covering some 360 past or present cultures. Their breakdown of the data shows that, depending on the culture, the frequency of intergroup warfare can range from 'all the time' to 'not very often' and, in some cases, 'never'; consequently waging war is not a biological but a cultural trait. Douglas Fry, an anthropologist working in Finland, has identified seventy-four present-day cultures that never fight. When people can walk away from conflict, they generally do. Our real problems as warring humans began with settlement, agriculture and the higher stakes of having a lot to lose, especially food stocks.

Archaeologist Brian Ferguson of Rutgers University has found that the first clear-cut evidence of organized battles between rival groups occurred only 14,000 years ago – another way of indicating that war emerges not from our genes but from our lifestyles. A crucial lesson for our own time is that, historically speaking, *environmental factors always play a key role*, particularly drought or floods that reduce food supplies and threaten to cause famine. Stephen LeBlanc of Harvard has shown that such factors are particularly closely

* Many 'peace and conflict' NGOs as well as peace research institutes define 'war' broadly as organized group conflict that causes a thousand or more deaths.

correlated with conflict, but war, he says, 'is not so hard-wired that it can't stop'.

Another hopeful sign is that, whatever the appearances, people today are fighting less and are much less likely to die in warfare than they were in previous centuries. No wars have taken place between developed countries since 1945. Whatever else one may think of the policies of the EU, the absence of war in Europe is a huge achievement. Some argue that globalization may also decrease the likelihood of warfare because improved communications give people an opportunity to feel empathy with those who are not members of their own 'tribe'; I would reply that those it leaves out – and they are innumerable – may fight more than ever just to maintain a foothold.

Genetic arguments for the persistence of group fighting have often called on primatology, the study of human beings' closest simian cousins. Lethal fights among apes do occur, but they do not prove that humans, despite sharing at least 98 per cent of their genes with these animals, carry a penchant for warfare in their DNA. The well-known primatologist Frans de Waal has found that it is possible to reduce conflict among apes in several ways – by ensuring that the young of aggressive rhesus monkeys are raised by more peaceful monkey caregivers, by obliging the animals to cooperate in order to obtain food, or simply by giving them fair and equal access to food. Another trait to watch out for in groups of both apes and humans is the tendency to be more belligerent towards others when they think they can get away with it. Bullies are not confined to the schoolyard.

AN EXIT FROM WAR?

Although it would be a very long shot to predict that war can one day be eliminated entirely, these scientific findings do point to concrete ways to keep the tendency towards bellicose behaviour in steady decline. People fight when they perceive that the distribution of vital necessities is unfair. They and their governments fight over resources: oil has figured prominently over past decades and, as we shall shortly see, water is now competing for top honours in this department.

Abundant energy, less subject to wild price swings and less unevenly distributed than today, would help a great deal to reduce warfare. If we put an end to dependency on fossil fuels, whose increasing scarcity and volatile prices can cause such hardship and destabilization that governments are prepared to resort ot arms to prevent them, we would eliminate a major cause of war in our own time. A question I have asked myself since 1974, when OPEC first increased the price of oil, is why governments are collectively intent on remaining dependent primarily on one of the most fragile, volatile regions of the world. That they are voluntarily nurturing insecurity is more obvious than ever now that we have proof positive that some of the same governments and wealthy individuals from whom we purchase black gold also finance terrorist activities directed against us. National security, if nothing else, should incite our leadership to swear off the black stuff and go for the gold, like sunbeams.

The dramatic failure of the Copenhagen climate conference in December 2009 was a disaster for more than just the climate. Reducing conflict depends directly on developing plenty of cheap, stable and fairly allotted alternative energy sources and making them readily available throughout the world. The sun and the wind are free resources, although investment in the corresponding technologies is necessary to capture the unlimited energy they can provide. Western governments' refusal to subsidize these technologies for the less developed countries is tantamount to gathering the tinder for future flare-ups.

Alternative energies, in turn, would reduce global warming, which restricts access to fresh water, increases the frequency of extreme weather events and is already making large areas either too dry or too wet for successful farming. All these factors will contribute to conflict as people compete for space and survival. As we saw earlier, the simultaneous food riots in more than thirty countries in which people were killed pointed to weather events but also to external causes such as agrofuel production and speculation that caused the prices of staple foods to escalate to unaffordable levels.*

Since humans fight when too many people are competing for scarce resources, this suggests the hardly original observation that a stable population would be another major contribution to a stable world. How does one achieve such stability and eventually gradual population decline? The single most tested, reliable method is the empowerment and education of women. Plenty of proof exists that better-educated women have fewer children and can even, within one or two generations, attain the birthrates of the now developed societies.† The religious fanatics who refuse to educate women and to make contraceptives easily available are generally the same ones who sponsor what one scholar refers to as 'the remnants of war' – namely, insurgencies, guerrilla warfare and terrorism.

---

* I was chided by a young French anthropologist especially familiar with West Africa for referring to 'food (or hunger) riots', which in the places they occur are referred to by those concerned as '*le movement contre la vie chère*' ('the movement against the high cost of living'). Whatever they're called, these demonstrations assume that the government can do something about food prices. About all a poor-country government can do is to acquire buffer foodstocks and release them as appropriate. It can also practise policies that provide land and protect and nurture its own small agricultural producers. The other price factors, particularly speculation and diversion of land for agrofuels in rich countries, are beyond its control.

† The same is true for the daughters of immigrant families who have been brought up in Europe.

More equal, fairer, more democratic societies are the human equivalent of monkeys cooperating to obtain food and having equal access to it; both are less aggressive. Monkeys don't legislate or organize tax regimes and redistributive welfare societies, but humans have proved that they can do so, even if neoliberalism has encouraged gross inequalities and selfishness over the past several decades. As for the importance of the female factor, women are statistically less prone to violence than men, so, the more educated they become and the more active they are in economic and political life, the better off everyone will be. Societies that believe, like troops of apes, that 'they can get away with it' are the most dangerous to others, whether they be North Koreans or the Americans under George W. Bush.

So what are our prospects? Unfortunately, despite this good news, the current crises, particularly the ecological one, do make the threat of serious and intensified conflict a lot more plausible than it was even a decade ago. If fairness and a measure of equality in the distribution of vital resources are preconditions for peace, then an increasingly unfair, unequal world will by definition be a more violent place. If climate change gets out of hand and causes further scarcities affecting the most basic basics of food, water and energy, bloodshed will be the inevitable result.

NAYSAYERS AND DENIERS: STILL WITH US

Granted, it happened almost twenty years ago, but the man who is now top economist in Barack Obama's team, Larry Summers, placed himself firmly in the global warming and resource shortages denial camp in 1991, when he declared that

> There are no limits to the carrying capacity of the earth that are likely to bind any time in the foreseeable future. There

isn't a risk of an apocalypse due to global warming or anything else. The idea that the world is headed over an abyss
is profoundly wrong. The idea that we should put limits on
growth, because of some natural limit, is a profound error
and one that, were it ever to prove influential, would have
staggering social costs.[4]

A few months later, Summers wrote a long letter to *The
Economist*, in which he argued that, even assuming the most
pessimistic scenario, 'global warming reduces growth over
the next two centuries by less than 0.1 percent a year. . . .
Raising the spectre of our impoverished grandchildren if we
fail to address global environmental problems is demagogu-
ery.'[5] This is exactly the kind of blinkered thinking that is
steadily increasing the probability of conflict – nature is just a
place to grab raw materials as we go about pursuing growth;
the biosphere is subservient to our needs and we needn't
worry about 'an apocalypse due to global warming or anything else', as Summers put it. So let's not worry about the
security issues either.

Climate sceptics had a field day in Copenhagen, and there
are still people like Summers lurking out there. Some of them
are the climate change deniers who tell us that 'nobody knows
– maybe we'll even have an ice age'. This is generally followed
by some statement couched in pseudo-economic terms, supposedly explaining that it is too costly to prepare for such
an eventuality and we would do better to spend our limited
resources on more immediate needs.

So might we have an ice age? Yes – and it would still be
the consequence of global warming, as the relevant literature
shows. The Pentagon was worried enough about this prospect a few years ago to commission a report which detailed
the impacts, including those for US national security, if
an abrupt slowing of the oceans' 'thermohaline conveyor'

were to take place.[6] I won't go into the details of the science here, but if warm ocean currents such as the Gulf Stream, which is the North Atlantic arm of the 'global thermohaline ocean conveyor', were to flip towards the cold side, we could quickly find ourselves faced with much lower temperatures, specifically in Northern Europe and the East Coast of the USA, but with grave consequences everywhere. Among these impacts would be reduced human carrying capacity for the entire earth and security threats causing the development of 'fortress states' intent on safeguarding their own resources. 'Less fortunate nations, especially those with ancient enmities with their neighbours, may initiate struggles for access to food, clean water or energy', say the authors of the Pentagon report, and these states will make 'unlikely alliances' in order to do so. Resource access, 'not religion, ideology or national honour', will become the prime mover of war. No wonder the Pentagon is concerned.

These authors note that the geological record shows eight abrupt changes in the thermohaline conveyor, including one 8,200 years ago that is strikingly similar to what they see happening now. For them, the relevant question is not 'Will this really happen?' but 'When? With what impacts? How should we prepare?' Their scenario is plausible even though it has been much less discussed in the past few years than previously. The conveyor can make this flip because rapidly increasing global warming is melting glaciers everywhere and sending torrents of freezing water into the oceans, making them not only colder but less saline in the process. The science is complex and the outcome uncertain, but, once the phenomenon is triggered, it takes hold with unbelievable speed. A few years is enough to alter the climate for a millennium or more.

So whether we lose the human carrying capacity of the planet directly because of global warming making the world hotter or lose it indirectly through glacial meltdown does not matter much, although it will matter enormously to the victims. The geographical distribution of those who suffer most would change, but more wars and serious conflicts would be the outcome in both cases. With direct global warming, the tropics will be hardest hit; if it is indirect and leads to the cold flip, northern latitudes in Europe and the USA would be hardest hit. Perhaps it is time to revive the discussion about the ice age to make the rich countries sit up and take notice.

WATER WARS, PAST, PRESENT, FUTURE

Strategic battles over water are as old as history, even though the issue takes on a particular urgency in the context of climate change and conflict. The enterprising scholar Dr Peter Gleick of the Pacific Institute for Studies in Development, Environment and Security has established a detailed chronology of water conflicts, beginning with the biblical flood – a conflict between God and man – and the border dispute between Lagash and Umma in 2500 BC, in which the King of Lagash diverts water from the canals to deprive Umma of its water supply.[7]

There is even one incident in Gleick's chronology that pits apes against humans. In the year 2000 in rural Kenya, tankers deliver water to a drought-stricken area and thirst-crazed apes attack the villagers to get their share. Score: eight dead apes, ten injured villagers. His continually updated timeline also mentions the events of 2006 when Hezbollah rockets damaged a wastewater treatment plant in Israel and Israel retaliated, attacking water systems throughout southern Lebanon, 'including tanks, pipes, pumping stations and facilities along the Litani river'. Entries for 2007 and 2008 evoke social conflicts: for example, the Indian farmers who stormed a dam to prevent allocation of water exclusively to industry and clashes over water in Africa pitting cultivators against animal herders. More worrisome for geopolitical stability were terrorist actions by the Taliban – one in Afghanistan, the other in Pakistan – the first carried out against NATO forces to prevent dam construction, the second to destroy a dam that ensures the main water supply for Peshawar.

In warfare, water can be a target or a weapon; the opponent tries to gain control over supply and waterways or to use it as a political tool by flooding, diverting, poisoning, or threatening to do all this and more. Some water conflicts can be solved non-violently through law, as in the United States where two or more states contest the use of water: Kansas threatened to take Nebraska to court for using more than its allotted share of water from the Republican River (yes, that's its name) and demanded tens of millions of dollars in compensation. Since the Second World War, some 400 water agreements have been signed throughout the world, whereas during the same period thirty-seven violent clashes between states over water were also recorded.[8] Such violence is widely expected to become more frequent and severe as both water scarcity and populations increase, especially in poor countries.

As early as 1991, the then secretary general of the United Nations, Boutros Boutros-Ghali, warned that future wars would be not about oil but about water. In 2008, the present secretary general, Ban Ki-moon, spoke both to the participants in the World Economic Forum in Davos and in the UN General Assembly about current water wars, laying particular stress on the crises in Kenya, Chad and, especially, Darfur, which some have begun to call the 'first climate change war'.

The Nobel Peace Prize committee took a quantum leap in recognizing global warming as a prime cause of warfare by giving the 2007 Peace Prize to Al Gore and the Intergovernmental Panel on Climate Change. So the environment–conflict and, especially, the water–conflict link are now boldly, almost routinely asserted. What further evidence do we have?

One scholar who is making the case scientifically in order to demonstrate the link between water and conflict is Marc Levy, of the Center for International Earth Science Information Network (CIESIN) at Columbia University. In his work with the International Crisis Group, he is combining databases on civil wars and water availability to show that, 'when rainfall is significantly below normal, the risk of a low-level conflict escalating to a full-scale civil war approximately doubles the following year'. Among other cases, he cites certain areas of Nepal where, after severe droughts, there was heavy fighting during the Maoist insurgency of 2002, whereas there was no fighting in other parts of the country that had not suffered drought. Levy's case studies indicate that drought causes food shortages and promotes anger against the government. Sometimes, in these cases, 'semi-retired' armed groups re-emerge and start fighting again.

The International Crisis Group has placed seventy locations on its 'watch list' for present or latent conflicts, and Levy is in process of compiling rainfall data for all of them to see if this evidence can help predict increased conflict. So far, he believes his approach is likely to flag the Ivory Coast, among others, as a renewed conflict hotspot. Later on, it may be possible to add other water data to the conflict-prediction database, for example by factoring in flooding and storms. For the moment, Levy says that the data strongly support the finding that, for intrastate conflict, 'severe, prolonged droughts are the strongest indicator of high-intensity conflict' (defined as conflict involving more than 1,000 battle deaths). 'I was surprised', he adds, 'at how strong the correlation is.'[9]

Military strategists are also acutely interested in the probability of water conflicts.[10] Outside of the larger democratic countries, the world possesses too few laws concerning water, and those that do exist are fragile. Where rivers are concerned, de facto usage favours the upstream country, and many downstream countries are unhappy with this situation. However, since there is no enforcement mechanism, no recognized arbitrator and no competent international jurisdiction, conflicts that arise can fester or explode.

A large portion of the world's population is supported by the 200 largest river systems – a great many shared by two nations and fifty of them shared by up to nine. More dangerous still, many countries depend on some particularly important river systems in especially conflict-prone regions: the Nile (9), the Congo (9), the Zambese (8), the Amazon (7), the Mekong (6) and the Tigris–Euphrates (3). But these places are not even the scariest items on the water danger list. That distinction goes to Asia, specifically to the Tibetan plateau, the region's main source of water, where the Himalayan glaciers feed ten major rivers and are said to provide water for 47 per cent – nearly half – of humanity.[11] Like glaciers everywhere, these are melting, although no one knows for sure how fast. In 2007, the Intergovernmental Panel on Climate Change predicted that 80 per cent of their mass could disappear within twenty-five years. It has since recognized that this claim was based on insufficient evidence – after all, we're talking about 1,300 glaciers in eight countries covering thousands of square kilometres with varying climatic conditions. The error nonetheless triggered a media frenzy as climate-change deniers went after the IPCC with a hatchet and a tooth-comb and found a few other minor mistakes in the 1,000-page report. Some experts noted that, on other questions, the IPCC had been too cautious, for example when it fixed the limits of biodiversity loss at '20 to 30 percent'.*

In any event, considering how quickly we, and the IPCC itself, are being constantly obliged by facts to revise our timelines, past experience says warming and melting could accelerate. Geopolitically this is bad news. Pakistan, for example, depends on the Tibetan plateau glaciers for its water, but also for its food – all its irrigated agriculture is fed by them. Pakistan is also rapidly becoming a vulnerable, not-quite-failed state which could soon rival Afghanistan for complexity, instability and ethnic–religious–tribal conflict. In June 2008 the Pakistanis told their energy supplier, Saudi Arabia, that they couldn't pay that month's oil bill, and the country is rife with all kinds of tensions. But ethnicity, religion and even energy supply pale beside the potential for water fights. The India–Pakistan conflict over Kashmir has everything to do with water. Although the River Indus flows through Pakistani territory on both its banks, and although the Indus Waters Treaty between India and Pakistan has survived so far for fifty years, the situation could rapidly degenerate as the glaciers melt and a large part of the Pakistani water supply disappears. Further south in Asia, Thailand and Vietnam are increasingly displeased with China's unilateralist moves to dam the Mekong River.

The NGO International Alert has compiled a list of fragile states at risk of armed conflict because of climate change; it includes places where fighting is ongoing or latent, such as Somalia, Nigeria, Iran, Colombia, Indonesia, Algeria and Peru.[12]

---

* The media rarely – and the climate deniers never – mention that there is no doubt whatsoever that glaciers are melting or that global warming exists and is largely a result of human activities. See Fred Pearce, 'Don't forget the big picture: special report on climate impacts', *New Scientist*, 27 February 2010.

Another sampling of serious future instabilities and conflict zones would have to begin with the Middle East, an especially vulnerable zone because of its climate, rapid population growth and several longstanding, unresolved water disputes. This region depends on three rivers – the Nile, the Tigris–Euphrates and the Jordan – plus the West Bank groundwater aquifer. Any or all of them could blow up. Turkey controls less than 20 per cent of the Tigris–Euphrates basin's landmass but claims that it holds 'absolute state sovereignty over the river waters because it is the upstream state'. However, Iraq and Syria together cover two-thirds of the basin's landmass downstream, and they demand an equal share of the water. In response, the former Turkish president, Süleyman Demirel, said, 'We do not ask them to share their oil. Why should they ask us to share our water? We can do anything we like.'

That they did. The Turks have completed their network of twenty-two dams, nineteen hydroelectric plants and a vast array of irrigation works to transform Anatolia into a breadbasket. The impact was not long in coming. In June of 2009,

> Iraq accuses Turkey, and to a lesser extent Syria, of choking the Euphrates with hydroelectric dams that have restricted the flow, damaging the farm sector already suffering from decades of war, sanctions and neglect. The dispute is a delicate diplomatic issue for Iraq as it seeks to improve ties with its neighbours ... 'We are passing through an emergency and the country is threatened with an environmental and humanitarian catastrophe', said [a parliamentarian] ... Farmers faced with the start of the planting season between the Tigris and Euphrates south of Baghdad were in dire trouble because they did not have enough water for rrigation, he added.[13]

The River Jordan lies at the heart of the Israel–Jordan–Syria –Lebanon–Palestine impasse; all are water stressed to varying degrees. Thanks to the territory it took over in the 1967 war, Israel is the upstream state for most of the river basin; it also exploits the Yarquon–Taninim aquifer, counting on it for a substantial part of its water supply, to which it simultaneously restricts Palestinian access. One need not point out the importance of control over this aquifer to any future peace agreement. Indeed, as one anonymous military observer noted, 'Israeli strategists always name control over water sources as one critical factor making necessary, in their view, retention of at least a part of the occupied Arab territories.' As for Egypt, the last nation downstream on the Nile, it has made quite clear that it is prepared to go to war against any of the eight upstream states to preserve its access to the river on which it depends for 97 per cent of its water.

Even when recognizing that conflict can never be ascribed to a single cause, there seems no doubt that water figures as an increasingly exacerbating factor, especially when one takes into account its intimate links with food production.

The combination of water scarcity and nuclear weapons does nothing to ease the minds of military strategists in these fragile regions or elsewhere. We are now living in a world where already conflict-prone states will become more so; in which nuclear states such as the sworn enemies India and Pakistan could have a water showdown; where China, faced with extended and spreading desertification could turn ugly. Since the future also depends on the Tibetan plateau glaciers, it makes any relaxation of Chinese control over Tibet utterly improbable.

Meanwhile, water issues are generally dealt with in a fragmented way, with no authority in charge. International law on freshwater among less-developed countries is absent or ineffectual, so conflicts will escalate as food and water scarcity and population pressures grow. Despite all these unfavourable trends, water should not become a convenient excuse for despotic governments like that of Sudan. As a *New Scientist* journalist pointed out, 'President Bashir's administration, with its huge oil wealth, had the responsibility and the means to offset drought [in Darfur] through serious investment in hydrology, climate forecasting, irrigation, drought-resistant crops ... It was politics that caused the rift between the "Arab" and the "African" communities in Darfur, not climate change.'[14]

Indeed, Kansas did not take up arms against Nebraska and, on the other side of the Atlantic, the Rhine Commission quite adequately settles any water disputes arising between France and Germany. Water conflicts have a different face and severity depending on whether the river in question flows through democratic, stable countries or through poor nations already torn by ethnic or other tensions. Better distribution of wealth and technology plus less waste of precious resources are the best ways to reduce the number of water wars. The best way of all of dealing with conflict is, first, to conserve water, second, to seek negotiated agreements on its use and, third, and most important, to prevent it from disappearing in the first place. Promoting international peace and security goes hand in hand with eliminating man-made global warming factors, particularly in the rich countries, not in 2020 or 2050, but now. We need no further proof that poor water quality and water scarcity simultaneously threaten economic well-being, social stability and human security. The only way forward is through cooperation.

Let us only mention *pour mémoire* the extreme weather events, the hurricanes and floods and droughts that will ravage more and more poor communities – as well as some of ours in the North. As Hurricane Katrina showed the world, even when they happen in richer states, it is still the poor who suffer most. Diseases, too, are going to thrive in warmer weather, their vectors spreading them further and faster, affecting primarily the South but also people in the North. Cold winters will no longer kill off the viruses. Devastation of species which are our life-support systems is proceeding at a rate which scientists tell us is about 1,000 times the normal background rate of species extinction. Multiply by seven the number of hours it takes you to read this book: that is how many species will have disappeared forever by the time you finish.

This is what global warming promises to transform: personal safety and health, access to food, water and medicine, geopolitical and strategic balance, social cohesion and peace itself. This being the case, can we please stop talking about 'future generations'? With accelerating climate change, we are talking about our own generation, right here and right now. We also need to stop talking and shout. So far, the leaders still can't hear us.

'IF YOU WANT PEACE, PREPARE FOR WAR':* STILL TRUE?

This Latin dictum may have worked for the Caesars. However, in preparing for war today, powerful nations will get not peace but more war. They are not focusing on the real sources of future conflict and are consequently spending their military budgets in the wrong way and on the wrong things. The most important international institutions where the rich nations hold all the cards – the World Bank and the IMF – are exacerbating the stresses that contribute to outbreaks of violence and war. Defence budgets are more a part of the problem than of the solution. This is obvious in the case of monster US budgets but also in that of the European Union.

* Si vis pacem, para bellum.

The sources of future conflicts are already clear. Here we can name five.

1 Growing inequalities

It may sound like political heresy, but one can look back on the Cold War with a certain nostalgia. Those times, although terrifying in their own way, also provided a strange kind of stability. The superpowers had to consider every place on earth seriously; none could be treated as unimportant because any place could become a base, a staging area, a strategic pawn for the other side.

Today the situation is radically changed. There are a great many places that aren't worth bothering about; they are full of losers, of the excluded, the hundreds of millions that the elites see as 'rubbish people', both disposable and dispensable. There are quite a few loser states as well; our ministries of foreign affairs now call them 'failed' or 'rogue' states. What about these 'losers' and their relation to conflict? Such people and groups are far more conscious of their situation than they used to be. Recall chapter 2: many studies have shown that the sense of injustice relates less to the absolute level of one's purchasing power and status in life than it does to the comparison with others. Inequalities are increasingly visible everywhere. Lots of ordinary people in Europe are furious about bankers' bonuses and the tax havens scandal and lots of people in the United States are being thrown out of their homes by the subprime scandal – it's quite obvious to them all that there are big winners and big losers. This goes for poorer societies as well: nearly everyone has at least some access to television; half the human race now lives in cities, many of them made up largely of slums.

Resentment is growing. People don't ask themselves 'What have we done wrong?' but 'Who has done this to us?' Because they cannot usually touch the people responsible, whom they may see on television, they can vent their fury and take out their grievances on neighbours of a different ethnic group – think of Rwanda and more recently Kenya. You don't need nukes – machetes and matches will do as well to murder thousands, if not hundreds of thousands. Think too of the Somali pirates – perhaps more a nuisance than a threat today – who could make many converts.

All the elements of the systemic crisis – casino economy, massive inequality, the environment, resource shortage, 'failed states', and so on – increase the dangers of military response. In the poor world, the poor will mostly fight against the poor as social exclusion and environmental disasters create more and more struggles for mere survival. Poor people already live in the most threatened areas; the elites have become quite good at creating their local enclaves and fortresses, but their gated bastions cannot protect them forever. To prevent their collapse, they will increasingly employ the military or private mercenaries to control populations perceived as troublesome, superfluous and irrelevant.

2 Environmental refugees

Among the most visible future sources of international tension are the millions of environmental refugees already virtually on our doorsteps. Beyond the stresses noted above, these people will be responding to insurmountable pressures – rising sea levels, dwindling food production, disappearing water. If women are already walking 10 kilometres a day to reach the nearest well, what happens when they must walk 15 or 20? There are limits to the conditions of life that can be borne. In the summer of 2007, floods in India, Pakistan, Bangladesh and Nepal caused 20 million people to flee their homes or to become trapped in villages at risk from landslides, snakebites and disease. Bangladeshi health workers were overwhelmed as more than 50,000 people with life-threatening diarrhoea sought treatment. UNICEF reported that 'hundreds of thousands have lost their homes, their possessions, livestock and fields and will have to begin their lives from scratch when flood waters recede'.

When the next floods strike in Southeast Asia or elsewhere, do we expect those remaining simply to stay put and hope for the best? The United Nations High Commission for Refugees foresees 200 to 250 million environmental refugees by 2050 – but since we now know that global warming is accelerating much faster than scientists, much less high commissions, believed possible, we should automatically revise the date. The ecological impact is already visible. The most fragile zones will be coastal lowlands – Bangladesh, of course, but also many other coastal areas in Asia, the Pacific Islands, the Maldives, around the Mediterranean, in the Caribbean and in Latin America. Many others will be in Africa.

Although most of these climate refugees will either try to go somewhere else in their own countries or to migrate into neighbouring states which are just as poor and fragile as their own, a great many who have the means to do so will attempt to reach Europe or the United States. That they will risk the journey is clear: no one knows the true numbers of those already dying at sea between Africa and EU member states or on the US–Mexican border, but they are at least in the high hundreds if not thousands every year.

Such migrants are not recognized by any kind of international law. The Geneva Conventions of 1951 are limited to refugees forced out of their countries for political and/or ethnic reasons. They will not be considered legitimate entrants into Europe, where refugee/immigration policy is geared entirely to considerations of public order and dealt with exclusively through police and security measures.

3 Risk-increasing European responses

The European Union's reaction to perceived threats is strictly limited to military-security type responses. The EU agency FRONTEX, founded in October 2004 and charged with overseeing Europe's borders to prevent illegal migration, saw its budget shoot up thirteenfold in five years – from €6,280,000 for 2005 to €83,250,000 for 2009. When the long-predicted, ever stronger human tide begins to flow northwards, what will European governments do? Line up their armies at the borders with machine guns and mow down the innumerable climate refugees as they try to cross? No one in the EU seems to be planning for such emergencies, although they lie only a few miles down the road.

Europe's policies regrettably contribute nothing to alleviating the causes of migration. To the contrary, the EU systematically blocks the avenues to economic success in poor countries through its agricultural policies, subsidies and dumping, which ruin southern hemisphere farmers; its industrial fishing fleets that rake the sea beds and leave no catch for local fisher-folk; and its trade policies, which have often destroyed infant industries in developing countries. Although the EU pretends to be taking a leading role in the climate negotiations, it is still far too timid considering that it is one of the most technologically sophisticated areas on earth and could well afford profound and rapid change in its energy policies, including putting an end to agrofuels.

Javier Solana, the European 'high representative', at the time the closest thing the EU had to a foreign minister, issued a report in 2008 in which he recognized the many challenges climate change poses to European security, including that of environmental refugees. His recommendations were, however, curiously meek and mild, consisting mostly of 'monitoring', 'studies' or 'early warning' concerning 'state fragility and political radicalisation, tensions over resources and energy supplies, environmental and socio-economic stresses, threats to critical infrastructure and economic assets, border disputes, impact on human rights and potential migratory movements.'[15] Yes, fine – but then what? Maybe Solana couldn't say in a public report what radical responses Europe must actually envisage. At least he pointed attention in the right direction, calling for a 'multilateral response' and declaring that climate change is a problem for today, not for the future; it is 'one which will stay with us'. He was also correct to define global warming as a 'threat multiplier' that will make all existing tensions and instabilities worse.

Climate change and the problems it provokes will also wipe out decades of development efforts, and the hardest-hit countries will be the ones that are already overburdened and conflict prone. Anything beyond a temperature rise of 2 degrees Celsius, said Solana, will 'lead to unprecedented security scenarios as it is likely to trigger a number of tipping points that would lead to further accelerated, irreversible and largely unpredictable climate changes'. The failure of Copenhagen now virtually guarantees a rise of *at least* 2 degrees Celsius.

Although Solana said almost nothing about how Europe will be forced to react concretely, he did list various areas of the globe where trouble can be expected. Some of these are places ordinary European citizens rarely think about – for example, Central Asia, where Kyrgyzstan has lost 1,000 glaciers in the last four decades, or the Andes, where glaciers are also melting, gravely threatening the water supply. He noted that '2 billion Asians live within 60 km of a coastline' where sea levels are going to rise. Changes in monsoon patterns

will have a tremendous impact on agriculture. This is already
the case in India, where the 2010 harvests will be drastically
reduced because of the failure of the monsoon.

Solana was less specific on the possibility of conflict
between Europe and its own neighbours in the Arctic, where
melting will soon offer immense hydrocarbon reserves to the
appetites of several Northern states. Solana's colleague, the
European energy commissioner Andris Piebalgs, nonetheless
announced that Europe is going to go after all that oil and
gas – whereas Russia has literally planted its flag at the North
Pole. Since a new Arctic shipping passage will soon be open
for at least three months of the year, will it be free for all to
use – or simply a free-for-all? If we expect to avoid interstate
conflict, who is going to control the Arctic using what legal
instruments?

And how does Europe intend to react to the hugely exac-
erbated climate threats in North Africa and the Middle East,
in particular the endless Israel–Palestine conflict, knowing
that water supply in Israel might fall by 60 per cent over this
century – from already perilously low levels?

4 Risk-promoting international financial institution policies

Not generally placed anywhere in the neighbourhood of
future sources of conflict, the IFIs (the World Bank and the
International Monetary Fund) are still destabilizing the world
as they have done for decades, particularly through their
structural adjustment programmes in poor indebted countries. The World Bank Group is made up of the bank proper,
formally known as the International Bank for Reconstruction
and Development; the International Finance Corporation,
its agency for public–private loans; and the International
Development Association, which is the ultra-low interest
loan window for the poorest countries. The first two, in

particular, contribute massively to fanning the flames of global warming.

Research by a team at the Institute for Policy Studies in Washington, DC, provides excellent evidence showing that the Bank is completely disqualified for pretending to do anything at all about climate change. Its own lending activities are enough to discredit its rhetoric.[16] Yet this is the institution that the major powers have entrusted with international environmental supervision, the one to which the G-20 is allocating responsibility in matters of climate change.

In 2008, the World Bank Group increased its lending to coal, oil and gas projects by 94 per cent above 2007 levels, reaching over $3 billion. Coal project lending alone increased by an astonishing 256 per cent during the same period. The Bank would reply that it has also increased its loans to renewable and energy efficiency, but these concern above all large hydropower projects which many experts say are net greenhouse gas emitters.

The Bank Information Center, also an independent NGO source in the USA, suggests that, if one excludes hydropower, Bank Group funding for renewable energy in 2008 actually dropped by 42 per cent from 2007 to 2008. Even worse, the UK World Wildlife Fund has calculated that over the decade 1997–2007, the World Bank financed 26 gigatons of carbon dioxide emissions. This is about forty-five times the annual emissions of the entire UK.[17] Its own Independent Evaluation Group seems to agree that the Bank is a dire threat to the planet, although it says so in much less forceful language than the NGOs. The group examined some of the $400 billion in investments in nearly 7,000 projects from 1990 to 2007 and found that 'Recent commitments to environmental sustainability by the bank and sister institutions, including the International Finance Corporation, were often not matched by changes within the lenders' bureaucracies or on the ground where dollars were turned into dams, pipelines, palm plantations and the like.'[18]

An institution so heavily invested in fossil fuels cannot claim expertise on how to prevent climate change and provide alternatives for the poor. It is also a public broker for carbon trading with a portfolio of over a billion dollars on which it makes up to 10 per cent in commissions, so it pushes carbon trading as the best way forward on climate change.*

Public institutions such as the EU and the Bank are woefully unequal to the task of helping the rest of the world to move towards renewable energy. There are many ways to do this, but for the moment, because of their heedlessness, they can be seen as contributing to future conflict scenarios.

Fortunately, a few people in official positions are paying attention to the resource scarcity issues guaranteed to provoke conflict. The problem is that they have far less political clout than the IFIs. After the food riots of 2008 in over thirty countries, the director of the World Food Programme, Josette Sheeran, called them 'stark reminders that food insecurity threatens not only the hungry but peace and stability itself', adding the colourful image that 'civilization is only seven meals from anarchy'.†

---

* From the mid-1990s, when the Bank first set up an environment department, I had my serious doubts. I remember one debate about fifteen years ago with its then head, Andrew Steer (now an official in the British Department for International Development), about solar power. Why, I asked Steer, was the bank financing one coal-fired power plant after another in a country such as India which had more sun than it knew what to do with? His answer was that coal was cheaper per unit of energy than solar – to which the obvious reply was, OK, maybe now, but if the bank were to invest in solar technology and guarantee a market for it, economies of scale and innovations in improved technology would soon kick in and the environment would be served. I mistakenly assumed that serving the environment might be the purpose of the bank's environment department. This language was utterly foreign both to Steer and to the bank, and, as far as I can judge, it still is.

† Andrew Simms of the New Economics Foundation in London has also

5 Defence budgets for what?

Where defence budgets are concerned, the world really does seem to be in a deep rut. Generals and legislators are not just fighting previous wars but are showing themselves to be constitutionally unfit to understand the changes in security policies that global warming implies. Developed country governments have, as noted above, every interest in reducing their dependency on fossil fuels, but, even assuming they were to undertake a massive conversion to clean energy, new security threats would simultaneously arise.

Try the following thought experiment. Imagine that the developed world suddenly understood how dire climate change will inevitably prove and stopped buying oil and gas. As the bottom dropped out of their economies and the present purveyors of petroleum discovered that their oil was no longer black gold, what would happen if they were to become not just politically downgraded but poor, with a lot of very unhappy citizens? Such countries, even when rich, were already incubators for terrorists – what might they become if deprived? And if a lot of conversion projects were to turn to nuclear energy, would they not offer that many more attractive new targets for terrorists?

The quasi-sacred status of military budgets should also be seen in terms of wasted funds better spent on green conversion. Armaments already absorb about $1,500 billion a year worldwide, with the huge greenhouse gas emitter the USA, as usual, ahead of everyone else. Recall the 2009 defence budget

used this image (whether before or after Sheeran I don't know), putting the number of meals at nine and making a convincing case for anarchy in Britain if, for example, a truckers' strike or other event prevented food deliveries to all urban supermarkets for three days. This was Simms's 'Nine Meals from Anarchy' Schumacher Lecture in Leeds in 2008, and it contains much other useful information and reflection.

of $515 billion, followed by 2010's $636 billion, which does not include the discretionary funding that various emergencies will require.

Various estimates exist for the military budget of China, the other top greenhouse gas producer; the consensus number seems to be about $70 billion for 2009, but it spends much less of its GDP than the USA on war preparation and execution. The third highest military budget no longer belongs to the UK but to France, at €32 billion ($44.8 billion) for 2009, an increase of more than 5 per cent over 2008. Since France has rationalized military personnel and closed a number of bases, it plans to use the money saved to more than double armaments production. In 2008 the French arms industry produced €9.4 billion worth of military hardware; the figure was expected to rise to €20.3 billion in 2009. Arms exports will also expand: the country expected to sell €6.7 billion worth of armaments, a 5 per cent increase over 2008. The €32 billion defence budget does not include military nuclear components of about €4 billion, which come out of the energy budget.

Well, I like the Bastille Day parade down the Champs-Elysées as much as anyone, especially watching the paratroopers jump high above the city, hover over the great monuments and float down to land *exactly* on the spot on the Place de la Concorde in front of the presidential reviewing stand. I'm a French citizen and, believe me, it's great theatre. The French know how to put on a dazzling show. And unless you have won the Flint-Hearted Championship Award this year, I defy you not to shed a tear when the orchestra of the Garde républicaine plays the *Marseillaise* in the Berlioz orchestration, with full choir and a solo tenor like Roberto Alagna hitting the high notes. But €32 billion? An increase of 5.4 per cent in peacetime? May I please ask why?

The best 'reason' I ever found was stated in the 2004

annual report of the French Conseil économique de la défense (Economic Defence Council), made up of nine high-level French 'wise men', top-ranking corporate civilian or military brass, plus a conventional and unimaginative but well-connected economist. Their brief is to reflect on the defence of Europe, not just that of France, which makes their replies even more relevant.

Let us assume that citizens do have the right to ask certain obvious questions such as Why? What for? Who is the enemy? What threats do we face? Is the military spending you recommend really likely to reduce these threats? How have these threats escalated to the point that you are calling on both French and European taxpayers to make an unprecedented financial effort and put the continent on a virtual war footing? Almost no one seems to be asking such questions. Yet, if we're going to buy all that military hardware, it might be nice to know against whom, or what, it could eventually be used. What do the wise men of the Economic Defence Council reply?

> The threats are evolving and diffuse, they are internal and external . . .; they call for innovative and varied responses whilst not abandoning traditional defence needs and our interest in [maintaining] interoperability with the United States.

Or, more poetically:

> There are no longer threats at our frontiers; but nor are there frontiers to our threats.

France only returned to full NATO membership in March 2009, but the accent on 'interoperability with the US' shows this step had been planned for a long time. Designating threats as 'internal' or 'diffuse' – and thus by definition shifting and elusive – can justify just about any expense one cares to set.

Europeans must insist on more control over the military spending undertaken in their name. As things now stand, it will buy not more security, but less. Rather than spending more, Europe needs to rationalize its forces and stop the extremely wasteful duplication of effort and materiel. Undoubtedly there are some threats and consequently some use for the military (other than fighting poor and unarmed immigrants at the borders), but citizens have a right to be told what those threats are, based on a proper analysis, not rhetoric. I still believe that energy security would afford Europeans far more personal and national security than any other single measure, and that leads us, once again, to the green conversion.

CITIZENS' RESPONSIBILITY

Security threats are not going to disappear, and many of them are related directly to the systemic crisis through which we're now living. This crisis offers a specific task in the realm of peace-building that is a great opportunity for citizens and for social movements. That task is to bring together the peace and conflict NGOs – the peace movement – into greater and more fruitful contact with other citizens groups concerned primarily with environmental and social justice issues – often called the global justice movement or, in French and other languages, the alter-globalization movement.

Strangely, at least in my experience, these two movements see very little of each other and live on completely different activist planets. I travel in a lot of activist circles, but once several years ago I went to a huge international peace conclave in The Hague, Holland, where literally hundreds of peace organizations were meeting. All had their stands, their publications, their platforms. *I scarcely knew, or even knew about, any of them.* This does not mean that they are not doing good work, and I took my ignorance as a lesson: we, and that definitely includes me – have failed to make the crucial links between peace and global justice both in theory and in practice, and it's high time to rectify this error. I hope to have given ammunition – if I may use such a word in this context – in this chapter to convince environmental, social and peace movements that they have everything in common, that their separate struggles are one and the same.

Were you on the streets on 15 February 2003? It was a magnificent, history-making day, when all over the world millions came out to protest against the US invasion of Iraq. The tragedy is that we did not manage to remain allies and fight common adversaries together in the longer term. Those millions in the streets somehow evaporated; the thrilling momentum of that day was lost. Now because of the crisis we all find ourselves imprisoned, and we must recognize that our movements will either succeed together or fail separately. It should not require a new invasion of some poor country to bring us together again. Failure is unthinkable; the stakes are too high. Climate change threatens us as it threatens civilization itself. We must choose to win. We must choose each other.

5

OUR FUTURE

Fear is the discipline of a capitalist society, and today many people are afraid – afraid things will get worse; afraid, if they have a job, that they will lose it and, if they have none, that they will never find one; afraid that their children will be worse off than they are. In some countries they fear losing their health care, retirement or unemployment benefits. Many, especially in the United States, are living day to day, month to month, afraid they may become homeless at any time.

At the same time, and for much the same reasons, people are also angry, conscious that we are living under a grossly immoral rule in which the guilty are rewarded and the innocent punished. The banks have received trillions and the top bankers have used public money to continue to pay themselves immoderate salaries and bonuses. Those who had nothing to do with the crisis have been robbed twice – once of the relative economic security which the casino crash has destroyed for years to come; once again because their own taxes and those of their children's children will be spent not on public goods and a better life for all but to restore a thoroughly rotten system.

Fear and anger are a powerful combination; together they equal frustration and a sense of powerlessness. Perhaps we don't know how to proceed, or we're not yet angry enough; perhaps we fear that action could make things even worse, that there is still too much to lose. Imagine a huge anonymous crowd of the kind you can find in any large city on any day. Each individual in it is silently thinking 'But what can one person do?' If they could see the thought bubbles above each other's heads, they would understand that the answer is not 'Nothing', but 'Join together'. This final chapter is an attempt to overcome some of these obstacles with concrete suggestions.

In the alter-globalization movement we carry brave banners that say 'We Won't Pay for their Crisis', but that, so far, is exactly what we are doing. The injustice is flagrant. We have seen how huge inequalities – particularly in the distribution of food, water and incomes – can encourage conflict which in our day can mean terrorism – the poor person's weapon of choice. And we have also seen how all the crises – finance, food, water, climate change, conflict, inequality and poverty – conspire to reinforce each other and to build a prison, thereby compounding the sense of rank unfairness. We have committed no crime, yet we are all held there against our will.

Scientists have shown that even animals have an innate sense of fairness. This trait was undoubtedly developed through natural selection because it confers an advantage on the individual animal and on the group to which it belongs. Governments and elites apparently do not share

far too vague & general: unhelpful! the contrary ...

this characteristic, and thus they endanger our common survival.*

So many outrageous arrangements have been made in total contempt for hapless citizens that one scarcely knows where to begin; let us note simply that, in a normal society operating under normal market or capitalist rules, the banks would belong to the taxpayers, who are entirely responsible for their salvation. We have all been raised to believe that, when one opens one's wallet or chequebook, it is in the expectation of receiving some good, service or benefit in return. In the case of paying one's taxes, one expects to benefit from a functioning society.

It is further usually a matter of public morality, if only to save the politicians from opprobrium, to protect the innocent and punish the guilty. None of these principles holds true any longer. The guilty are rewarded a hundredfold and the innocent are told to shut up and fork over. They receive absolutely nothing in exchange for their contributions – those of today and of many, many tomorrows. They are given instead unemployment, reduced pensions, gutted public services and lower standards for themselves and their children. Profits are privatized whereas losses are socialized, as is customary

---

* '[Among wolves, coyotes and dogs] players often use self-imposed handicaps to limit the force they use against a weaker playmate when body slamming or biting. And role reversal is common, so that during play a dominant animal will often allow a subordinate to have the upper hand. Such behaviours reduce inequalities in size, strength and dominance between playmates, fostering the cooperation and reciprocity that are essential for play to occur. Indeed, on the rare occasions when a canid says "let's play" and then beats up an unsuspecting animal, the cheat usually finds itself ostracised by its erstwhile playmates . . . . *a sense of fairness is common to many animals*, because there could be no social play without it, and without social play individual animals and entire groups would be at a disadvantage . . . *morality evolved because it is adaptive. It helps many animals, including humans, to survive and flourish in their particular social environment.*' (Marc Bekoff [professor of biology at the University of Colorado, Boulder], 'Virtuous nature', *New Scientist*, 13 July 2002; my emphasis)

in societies based on neoliberal, market-fundamentalist ⟩⟩
ideology.

The recent extreme events, unprecedented since the 1930s,
should lead us to examine carefully the place we are living
right now and what might happen to alter the landscape – for
better or for worse. One might class the possibilities nega-
tively and positively. On the negative side are many fears,
but on the positive side also a great many hopes and rational
proposals, which could ripen into reality if popular forces
began to organize into alliances with political weight and
clear purpose.

First the fears: in short order, things could indeed become
worse. The crisis isn't over just because financial markets
and governments want it to be or because stock markets have
begun to show signs of life. In the 1930s, officialdom made
the same mistake by stopping too early the application of
Keynesian remedies through government intervention. This
hiatus resulted in a relapse, and it finally took the Second
World War to pull everyone free. We risk something similar.

Plenty of financial products are still out there waiting to
blow up – for example, it is becoming clearer that the commercial real-estate bubble, as opposed to the housing one,
hasn't yet fully burst. A lot of banks have made huge loans
to countries of Eastern or Southern Europe in deep trouble,
and the European Union package of 'aid' to Greece and
others is in large part a disguised bailout for big French and
German banks in particular. Meanwhile, the United States
is cranking out Treasury bonds as if they were newspapers.
Imagine that a bubble in US government paper inflates and,
like all bubbles, is punctured. In this scenario, the US dollar
can no longer play the role of universal currency; stopgap
measures are put in place to little avail; millions, and not just
Americans, lose their savings, pensions, insurance, and so on.

The climate begins to flip. The American poet Robert

Frost wrote, 'Some say the world will end in fire; some say in ice . . .' For Europeans and North Americans, it could go either way – towards ice as a result of melting glaciers pouring billions of tonnes of freezing water into the oceans, creating havoc with the Gulf Stream and other ocean currents; towards fire as CO^2 and methane emissions cause runaway temperature rises accompanied by drought and rapidly rising sea levels. Millions of climate refugees are on the move and no army on earth can stop them. Epidemic diseases are spreading much faster and conflicts aimed at securing such basics as food and water are proliferating. Soon all our fine monuments and trappings of civilization resemble the statue of Ozymandias in the limitless desert.*

Unsurprisingly, humans are loath to envisage such calamities, preferring to believe that somehow 'they' – those in positions of authority – know what they are doing and will take care of things so that no one need confront a horror-film scenario. Facing such a possibility for the first time in the history of humanity, much less that of Western (or, for that matter, Eastern) civilization, is exhausting, scary and gives rise to the Scarlett O'Hara syndrome: 'I won't think about that today. I'll think about that tomorrow.'

The performance 'they' have given so far with regard to the crisis is hardly conducive to confidence. But alternative scenarios exist and many remedies are staring us in the face.

* I met a traveller from an antique land / Who said: Two vast and trunkless legs of stone / Stand in the desert . . . Near them, on the sand, / Half sunk, a shattered visage lies, whose frown / And wrinkled lip and sneer of cold command / Tell that its sculptor well those passions read / Which yet survive, stamped on these lifeless things, / The hand that mocked them and the heart that fed. / And on the pedestal these words appear: / 'My name is Ozymandias, King of Kings: / Look on my works, ye mighty, and despair!' / Nothing beside remains. Round the decay / Of that colossal wreck, boundless and bare, / The lone and level sands stretch far away. (Percy Bysshe Shelley, 'Ozymandias', 1817)

When our leaders lack all vision and boldness, everything is up to the people. The people's task will be daunting. Part of the multiple crisis is the assault against democracy. Citizens are being gradually deprived of their voice, perhaps most obviously in the European Union, where democratic practice is held in open contempt, as the French, the Dutch and the Irish learned when they did not vote 'correctly' on the decision made by their betters to impose a new treaty.

Downgrading popular sovereignty is only one aspect of the attack on democracy. The concept of 'stakeholders' has nearly replaced the simpler and more straightforward notion of 'the people'. 'We the stakeholders of the United States' – or, as the French Constitution says, 'Sovereignty resides essentially in the stakeholders' – sounds really inspiring, no? We owe this shift to British Third Way theoreticians; let us recall that having a 'stake' always refers to property or bets, never to political rights or political power.

Contempt for the ordinary person, assumed to be politically incompetent, is accompanied by the unbridled and privileged access given to private-sector interests. Lobbyists in the United States are at least obliged to register, but in Brussels they can exercise vast influence with impunity. The recently established EU 'voluntary register' is a bad joke, encouraging further undermining of democracy.

The ordinary person, who used to be considered a 'citizen' – how quaint! – is now reduced to the status of consumer. Even the goals of the EU are now expressed in terms of the market (the 'free movement of goods, services, capital and people'), with 'free and undistorted competition' the cardinal rule. 'Consultation' and 'consensus-building' similarly replace the far healthier confrontations and differences of opinion that democracy entails. We are 'consulted' on decisions the powerful have already made and are unlikely to alter on grounds that those consulted do not accept them.

As we confront the crisis, the enormous task before us is to restore both representative and participatory democracy in order to regain and exercise political control over our own affairs. Who might do such things, or, more bluntly, who has a genuine interest, material and moral, in doing such things? The answer is simple: footloose finance capital has proven itself the enemy of all – of working men and women, pensioners, farmers, trade unionists, small business entrepreneurs, environmentalists, public service employees and users – the list goes on. Finance capital has become at once more remote from the concerns and activities of real people living in the real economy and more damaging to their lives. All it can do is create bubbles, and virtually everyone's wellbeing depends on changing a world in which finance capital rules.*

It is clear that national governments and the embryonic 'world government' of the G-20, World Bank, IMF, WTO, et al., have chosen to serve the narrowest possible private minority interests of transnational financial and industrial corporations. Despite the odds, however, interests opposing their choices are legion, the motivation for collective action exists and the raw materials with which to build powerful new social and political alliances are before us. We have the numbers, the ideas and, collectively, even the money. What we lack is sufficient self-confidence, rooted in the collective consciousness of our own strength and our great, historically proven capacity for creating positive change.

Hope is fragile. But look at the historical record. Although

---

* In the 1950s, outstanding loans in the United States were evenly divided between the financial sector and the real economy. By 2007, over 80 per cent of loans from US banks were going to the US financial sector. See Dirk Bezemer (fellow at the Research School, Economics and Business Department, University of Groningen), 'Lending must support the real economy', *Financial Times*, 5 November 2009.

'they' may win much of the time, inertia, ignorance, injustice and violence do not always triumph. The story of human emancipation is not over. A stubborn and dangerous reality can give rise to fear, frustration and a sense of futility, but also grounds for hope.

Throughout this book, I've tried to suggest avenues of escape from crisis prison, and here I propose to put forward others that could rid us of these plagues and chart a rational path to a better future. To me and, I am convinced, to thousands, millions of others, it is blindingly obvious that we must use the occasion of the financial crisis to tackle the environmental and social crises, including poverty, inequality, scarcity of basic resources and climate change. This is the only genuine exit – it is our own historical alternative to the Second World War and a clear and present duty. A fantastic opportunity is there to be seized.

Our opponents are the financial interests that were utterly unprepared for the mess they got us into and now refuse the smallest sacrifice, however reasonable, to get us out of it. They want once more to be left alone so that they can continue to apply the law of 'All for ourselves'. National governments either can't see the many paths that could lead to a greener, fairer future or refuse to take them. The de facto world government, the self-appointed and self-legitimized G-20 that has replaced the G-7 or G-8 seems to be made up either of ostriches with their heads in the sand or of generals fighting the last war, busy solving the crisis of 1929. Sometimes our governments seem simply to be stumbling along from day to day, hoping that next month, next quarter, next year the skies will have cleared. That's one possibility.

The other is that these leaders know exactly what they're doing, and what they're doing is refounding neoliberal financial capitalism in all its splendour. This includes the 'emerging' countries and nominally communist China. What really counts is 'business as usual', as soon as the 'usual' can be supplied. This system has for decades handed over unprecedented riches and innumerable privileges to capital, and governments apparently see no reason it should not do so again, once more at our expense. So they are tweaking the system a bit around the edges, while trying to appease public outrage and acknowledging, for example, that exorbitant bonuses are very naughty indeed. They know perfectly well that, although bonuses infuriate people, they are merely the cherry on top of the cake, not the cake itself. That's the second possibility.

I believe this second possibility is more plausible. The bailouts, TARPs and other grand stimulus packages do not reflect mere timidity and a dearth of ideas, although both play a part. They reflect above all the triumph of the Davos class and of neoliberal ideology, deeply ingrained in the heads and hearts not just of those who run our affairs but of much of the general population. It governs their behaviour, but also to some degree our own.

In 2009, Goldman Sachs, rarely mentioned today without Matt Taibbi's colourful qualifier ('a great vampire squid wrapped around the face of humanity, relentlessly jamming its blood funnel into anything that smells like money') ,[1] on 131 business days, made $100 million *a day* and posted $6 billion in profits for the third quarter alone. This, as the *Financial Times* notes, 'suggests the authorities' drive to revive markets after the crisis is yielding huge windfalls for some financial institutions.'[2] 'Suggests'? It proves, rather, that the politicians operate on the basis of some variant of 'What's good for the banks is good for the country and the world economy'. If Goldman's in heaven, all's right with the world.

Particularly in the United States, politicians are also indebted for campaign contributions to the powerful financial industry. Yes, they will regulate with seemly moderation;

they will provide guarantees and capital injections for a while longer – at least as long as the value of their currencies holds up. This they can do only by borrowing even more from the future, and sometimes that works; countries have carried heavy debts before and emerged stronger and healthier. If, however, the titanic debt of the USA collides with the iceberg of inflation and the dollar becomes about as valuable as paper towels, all bets are off. Along with violence, runaway climate change, widespread unemployment and misery; dramatic inflation is another terrible misfortune I hope we can avoid. These worries lie behind the recommendations to be found in the following pages. The origin of our word 'crisis' is the Greek *krisis*, meaning 'decision'. It is high time to take some.

INCENTIVES, COMPENSATION AND CAPS

Wrong economic incentives send wrong signals and cause harmful behaviour – that's a truism. Smart people acting rationally on these incentives as individuals, mostly within the law, can collectively lead society into black holes. I have no intention of explaining in technical detail how to regulate the financial industry. Clearly common sense and a bit of willpower on the part of regulators have been in short supply for two or three decades and deserve a comeback.

One should start by checking out all the regulations that the financial industry spent $5 billion lobbying out of existence, particularly over the past fifteen years. They should almost all be put back in place. The European model is that of the 'universal' bank allowed to deal in all financial activities. Re-enacting everywhere the equivalent of the Glass–Steagall Act separating commercial and investment banks is the first order of business. Too big to fail is just plain too big, end of story.

Banks should never again be given the insane permission

to keep their losses secret and their risks off-balance sheet; therefore all 'shadow banking' has to be made illegal. The rules about capital adequacy and permitted risks must be seriously tightened. I also think derivatives, including credit default swaps, particularly when they are allowed on securities that the buyer neither owns nor has agreed to borrow, should be dropped because they have no relationship whatsoever to the real economy. However, some reasonable people argue that some derivative products can play a positive role. The point is to favour activity in the real economy and put finance back in its place. Ratings agencies cannot continue to be paid by the people whose securities they rate. This job should be done by public rather than private companies, particularly for government bonds. These unremarkable recommendations have been utterly ignored by the G-20. There are many other proposals I shall make in a moment.

But, before that, let me address one issue that has attracted attention, even that of the G-20, because it is so visible and turns normally placid people into raging bulls: bankers' pay. Yes, their remuneration is often unjustifiable and their bonuses obscene, but, whatever the appearances, this is not the immediate problem. The real danger that ought to be recognized and fought is that the whole system feeding their greed is based on debt. It's rather like the cartoon character running on air between two cliffs – so long as he believes he is still on solid ground, he keeps moving, but the moment he looks down into the abyss he panics and plummets.

Unsustainable debt has resulted from more and more money being ploughed into the financial sector rather than being invested in the real economy – as noted above, more than 80 per cent of all bank loans are now devoted to purely financial pursuits. The financial sector was also more than three times bigger in 2007 than it was in 1980. Industrial corporations too have often been making more profits out of their in-house financial departments than from producing widgets.

The real economy uses credit, of course; it takes on debt but pays back its loans out of real value created by real investments. On the other hand, if the same house, or the same structured investment vehicle based on subprime or commercial real estate mortgages, is sold six times, each time at a profit, it's still the same house, office or financial package – nothing has been added to the economy through these transactions except more debt. On the contrary, much has been taken away from it, because indebted people (and even indebted bankers) must spend more money paying back their loans and less on real goods or real investments.

This said, and despite my contention that bankers' pay and bonuses are really side issues compared with the enormous debt overhang, there is still a regulatory issue I want to put on the table immediately without pretending to have the answer. As we saw in chapter 2, inequalities pushed to extremes are poisonous for humans and for the societies in which they live. They have huge and costly effects for everyone, rich and poor. Both economists and psychologists have shown that most people, above a certain level of material well-being, are content with what they have, so long as they don't see themselves as way down the social and economic ladder from others in the same society. The criterion is comparison with others, not absolute levels of wealth and possessions. Gaping inequalities are nothing but a sign of primitive or out-of-control social evolution. They destroy solidarity and prevent people from trusting each other and cooperating; they can eventually demolish the very notion of citizenship when everything in the society becomes a monetized, marketable commodity and people become mere consumers – a lot of them unable to consume even the basics.

After the Second World War most people, at least in the

more developed countries, assumed humanity had got beyond that primitive phase, except perhaps for some backward sheikdoms; they believed that the welfare state would work its magic in the North, while decolonization and national liberation movements in the 'third world' (as we called it then, in reference to the two poles of the 'free world' and the 'communist world') would make societies in the South more equal as well.

We were dead wrong. Adam Smith's vile maxim has never been so true. For the past three decades we've let the masters of mankind loose again, and they have behaved more shamelessly than ever. This isn't just a moral argument – it's a security issue: the degree of social cohesion and the success of societies themselves are going to depend on how it's resolved. At some point, financial compensation has got to be limited and outrageous multiples of wealth outlawed because they will stretch societies and the environment to the breaking point – that point where the only way to deal with the have-nots is with tear gas and bullets.

If the lowest-paid, worst-off people in a given society have, say, a thousand a month, what should be the multiple at the top? Five thousand? Ten? Twenty? Fifty? A hundred? Personally I think some figure between ten and twenty would be more than adequate, but that's only my view. What I'm sure of is that it's a debate we neglect at our peril. The 'international community' has identified poverty lines, or floors, under which people should not have to live, of a dollar or two a day. The numbers of people 'below the poverty line' are closely monitored. What we need now are ceilings. Citizens' movements have got to put the issue of limits on the table no matter how loud the Davos class screams. It will undoubtedly take years to get action – all the more reason to start right away.

THE GREEN NEW DEAL

At the Attac Summer University of August 2007 in Toulouse, the economist Gérard Duménil was giving one of his brilliant lectures about the casino crisis we had all long expected and which now seemed truly ready to pounce upon a still largely unsuspecting world. These summer universities are for a non-specialist audience, and Duménil went back to the basics, describing the standard tools governments can use to stave off a recession or a depression: they can (1) reduce interest rates to encourage households and firms to borrow for consumption or investment; (2) stimulate the economy through government spending, as Keynes recommended in the 1930s, even when it leads to greater indebtedness; and (3) devalue their currency openly or surreptitiously to make imports from other countries more expensive and their own exports more attractive. Then he explained the limits to each of these strategies and how quickly we could reach those limits. He concluded that the tools of economic salvation really did seem to be lacking this time around and the traditional remedies were out of date for facing a challenge of such magnitude. Events have proved Duménil correct.

Even in the 1930s these measures were not applied for long enough or hard enough, and what really 'solved' the long-drawn-out crisis then, as we noted earlier, was the Second World War. A repeat of such a military Keynesian strategy didn't bear contemplating for our own time so, given that history has moved on, I started asking myself what else might be possible when the standard tool kit was inadequate and war unthinkable. The same idea surely occurred to many others around the same time; I developed it for my contribution to the mass 'teach-in' held a month after the Attac event, in September 2007 at the George Washington University in Washington, DC.[3] The message, briefly stated, is that it is time to undertake and finance a green conversion on a par with the effort the Allies deployed in order to win the Second World War. This is our only chance of escape from a crisis prison, which, as we know, is not just financial but also social and ecological. To do so we must mobilize the whole of society, just as happened in the early 1940s. This makes our time a moment of tremendous hope and possibility – but such moments have a way of not lasting.

The idea of a 'Green New Deal' had been simultaneously invented or was being elaborated elsewhere, notably in Britain, where a working group at the New Economics Foundation has published an excellent and thorough report which I fully recommend.[4] Many others, however, may mean quite different things from what I include in the notion of a Green New Deal.

Here is the gist of my proposal. Individual solutions ('change your lifestyle and your light bulbs') are never going to be sufficient to meet the challenge ahead. Such action is still valid, even vital – I continue at every opportunity to encourage it – but we must recognize simultaneously that, by itself, it is completely inadequate to the scope of the task. What is required is a change of scale by several orders of magnitude. The question I wrestle with is this: Can we save the planet while international capitalism remains the dominant system, with its focus on profit, shareholder value and predatory resource-capture worldwide, and with no-holds-barred finance capital making more and more decisions? Can we save the planet when faced with a powerful caste that wants only one thing – which is everything?

Sometimes I answer 'No: we cannot. We can't reverse the ecological and climate crises under capitalism.' But that is a despairing answer and, if true, it means there is virtually no hope – no hope, because I do not see how even the most convinced, most determined people could replace, much less overthrow, capitalism fast enough to carry out the necessary systemic change before a runaway climate-change effect takes hold. It's no good waiting for the revolution to solve the problem for us, and we're going to be living under capitalism for a while longer, so we may as well accept that and try to think of something else. And, to do so, we must confront both governments and the economic system itself.

People are generally way ahead of their governments. The political problem is not simply to 'throw the rascals out', because they would be replaced by other rascals just as bad, just as beholden to the corporations, their lobbies and the financial markets. The problem is to convince politicians that ecological transformation can pay off politically.

Activists and experts have got to work with local, regional, state and national politicians and governments, help them to find like-minded partners and formulate ambitious projects they can undertake on the broadest scale possible. They must, furthermore, help these politicians and governments to become brilliant, well-known ecological examples with the electorate by publicizing their efforts and their successes. We must shine a light on the best public-sector initiatives, preferably *large* initiatives, because best ecological practice is still too small scale and often closer to folklore than to believable political undertakings. Schemes that work should be publicized and replicated; those in charge should get credit for them.

As for the economic system as a whole, perhaps the most difficult and crucial issue was well described by Jared Diamond in his book *Collapse*, in which he examines several cases of previous societal extinctions as a result of overexploitation of the environment and identifies several common characteristics. One of these is the isolation of the elites, giving them the capacity to keep on consuming far above the ecologically sustainable level long after the crisis has already struck the poorer, more vulnerable members of society. That is where I think we are now, not just in isolated places like Easter Island or Greenland but globally. Our global financial, corporate and political elites are all busy grabbing what they can today, and too bad about tomorrow – their motto remains *Après moi le déluge*.

So how can we *realistically* combat the ecological footprints of these dinosaur elites, recognizing that we don't have the option of shouting 'Off with their heads' in some imagined, worldwide revolution? We can't force them to change both themselves and the system that has served them so well, whereas we know that we *must* change that system because it is raping the planet, and its inherent logic is to keep on doing so. The answer isn't easy, but I believe that what citizens must insist upon and provoke is the *coming together of business, government and citizens in a new incarnation of the Keynesian war economy*. I was born in 1934, and I remember very well when the USA switched massively to a war economy, converting all the rubber plants in my native city (Akron, Ohio) to production not for private cars and trucks but for the military. There was huge popular involvement and support – even from children.

In our own historical moment, we have a similar opportunity to bring all these sectors together. The fallout of the economic crisis for ordinary people in terms of jobs, housing, consumption and future welfare is growing more serious daily. I am convinced, alas, that, without comparable action, the world's economic problems are going to fester and get worse. This means that some new economic tools have to be picked up and used to combat them, simply because the old tools have already been pushed to their limits and have little or nothing left to give.

If these traditional tools won't work, the new one that can pull not just the USA but every other country out of the economic doldrums is a new and far broader environmental

Keynesianism, a push for massive investment in conversion and eco-friendly industry, in alternative energies, in the manufacture of lightweight materials for use in new vehicles and airplanes, in clean, efficient public transport, in the green construction industry and retrofitting, in research and development. All these new, eco-friendly industries and products would have huge export value and could quickly become the world standard. The Chinese are already aware of this and are investing massively in solar and wind power. I am trying to describe a scenario that can be sold to the elites, because I don't think they will embrace genuine environmental values and conversion if there's nothing in it for them.

Of course in the 1940s there were some snags, some conflicts, but on the whole minorities and women made progress and the country came together as never before or, indeed, since. There was also an elite group of businessmen called 'dollar-a-year men', on loan from their companies to the government, who were charged with making sure that military production and quality targets were met. They had enormous prestige – I was undoubtedly insufferable bragging to my little schoolfriends that my godfather was a dollar-a-year man. He had the cheques from the Treasury for $1.00 framed in his study.

Taking that period as an example for today is not merely a cynical attempt to get our present elites to move in their own interests. There are also plenty of advantages in such an economy for working people. A huge ecological conversion is a job for a high-tech, high-skills, high-productivity, high-employment society. It would be supported, I believe, by the entire population because it would mean not just a better, cleaner, healthier, more climate-friendly environment, but also full employment, better wages and new skills, as well as a humanitarian purpose and an ethical justification – just like the Second World War. In other words, it's a public relations dream. Political parties that understand this can win on such a programme. Economic solutions can come from a massive Keynesian-type commitment bringing together government, companies and citizens, but such an effort would also have a vital role in renewing social cohesion. It would bring many constituencies together in a common cause and should reward people for their efforts.

Is it possible, politically speaking, to put such a programme into place? Yes, but it will mean hard work and coalition building. Today, no single interest group can solve the problem that concerns it most – that is, ecologists alone can't save the environment, farmers alone can't save family farms, trade unions alone can't save good jobs in industry, and so on. Broad alliances are the only way to go, the only strategy that pays. Social movements have begun to be successful in working democratically and making alliance partners of people who come from different constituencies but are basically on the same wavelength.

Now we must go beyond this stage and try to forge alliances *also* with people we don't necessarily agree with on quite major questions – for example, with business, particularly, I believe, small and medium-sized business. This can only be accomplished by recognizing that disagreement, even conflict, can be positive so long as the areas where it *is* possible to agree are sought out, identified and built upon. We must find where the circles of our concerns overlap. At least one of those overlaps ought to be saving the planet. I don't see any other way of generating citizen enthusiasm, involvement and the qualitative and quantitative leap in scale that is now required. None of this precludes the possibility of keeping the ambitions of business under control through legal limits. Nor should one forget that small and medium enterprise usually has radically different interests from transnational corporations.

One could also try to extend these alliances to the South, aiming at a complete overhaul of the present international financial and trade institutions, which are by nature anti-environmental. I will suggest ways to finance such an overhaul, but let me make clear now that the conversion to an ecological economy is technically feasible. The schemes for new taxes have been thought through; the industrial prototypes already exist; the machinery is ready to hum into action the moment people can make their politicians accept the challenge. Capitalism is not sane in the sense that most people understand sanity – we humans normally think about our future, that of our children and that of our country and the world. The market, on the contrary, operates in the eternal present, which, by definition, cannot even entertain the notion of the future and therefore excludes safeguards against the looming destruction it contains unless these safeguards are imposed upon it by law.

We need law, for sure, and political forces with the backbone to propose and to vote that law into existence and to enforce it; but we also need to think about human motivation. Remember the prestige of the dollar-a-year men of the 1940s and imagine what might happen if we could transpose such rewards into the twenty-first-century world. A significant number of contemporary captains of capitalism, with bloated, unimaginable salaries, might come to believe that money is all very well – but is there nothing more?

Why not found an extremely exclusive International Order of the Earth Defenders, or the Environmental Knights or the Carbon Conquerors, who alone, in recognition of their special contributions to the national and international environmental conversion effort, would have the right to display a highly visible emblem – on a banner in front of their homes, on their cars, on a green-and-golden rosette in their buttonholes

like the French *Légion d'honneur*; a Congressional Medal of
Ecological Honour, the sign of belonging to the small assembly of the anointed, those who have decided to save the earth
in a big way. It would also appeal to their competitive spirit
and desire to stand out from the common herd. I can hear all
the hard-line Marxists laughing – I'm only asking that they
examine the full range of human motivation before rejecting
the idea.

Finally, *myth* has always been the driving force of every
great human achievement, from Greek democracy to the
Renaissance to the Enlightenment and the American and
French revolutions. So it must be in the coming age of ecological stewardship. To save the planet and ourselves, we
must change – and change quickly and profoundly – the way
the majority thinks and feels and acts, and we must start with
the social forces we have right here and right now, and no
others. We must play the hand history deals us.

For such a change, we will need six 'Ms', starting with
money, management and media. but even more important
than these, we must try to create a new sense of mission and
motivation and myth at the noblest level. 'Myth', the *mythos*
in Greek, in this sense has nothing to do with story-telling
or lies. It is the grand narrative that empowers us to believe
that we *can* accomplish what we *must* accomplish. It speaks to
the deepest motivations of human behaviour and inspires the
desire for honour and for a life's work which transcends death.
The elites already have money, management and media. On
our side, we have mission, motivation and myth. If we can
bring together all these, the future will take care of itself.

We still need to identify in more detail our proposals and
the chief strategic problems they present. But an enormous
amount of both theoretical and practical work has already
been done, if not brought together under any single roof,
and Barack Obama, whatever disappointments he may have

caused subsequently, has made the theme of 'Yes we can' universal. We can accomplish what we must accomplish. Here, now, are some practical ways to do it.

PUT THE BANKS UNDER CITIZEN CONTROL, NOW

Nationalize the banks or, better still, socialize them, so that they become citizen-governed, public institutions and credit becomes a common or public good to be used in the service of society. Banks could be local, regional, national or even international in scope, but they should be considered as public utilities. It would doubtless be impossible to take over the entire banking system in a single swoop, but surely the banks that have received enormous dollops of public money could and should be put under public control now.*

Suggesting bank takeovers even at the end of 2008 would have made one a target for horrid accusations of godless communism or heresy, if not a candidate for the asylum; today the idea is sinking in and is actually professed by some perfectly respectable people, including Nobel Prize winners such as Joseph Stiglitz. As the reader knows, Alan Greenspan is not one of my favourite references, but even he has said that nationalization may be needed. James Baker, who served as Treasury secretary under President Ronald Reagan, concurs.

'Socialization' is preferable to 'nationalization' because

---

* Too late to incorporate in this text I learned of a report with alternative proposals for banking prepared by finance practitioners and academics at Manchester University. They show how, since Thatcher, and increasingly under Blair and Brown, finance professionals determine government policy, are included in all the important committees and study groups, and themselves write supposedly 'government' reports. This has got to stop! See www.cresc.ac.uk/publications/documents/Alternativereportonbanking V2.pdf.

some use the latter term to describe the so-called Swedish solution. This technique consists in taking over the banks until they can be rid of their toxic assets at public expense and then handing them back to the shareholders after a period of months or years, fresh and clean. The British Northern Rock and similar nationalizations are cut out to do this – the rotten bits are socialized and the healthy ones left in private hands. You could argue, too, that the USA has already 'nationalized' some financial enterprises such as Fannie Mae and Freddie Mac, which were semi-public to begin with, or the huge insurer AIG, which got $60 billion in a single day and then came back twice for the same amount after the executives had paid themselves large bonuses.* No: I mean socializing them permanently for the common good.

Credit should be a public good. This doesn't mean throwing baskets of money out of airplanes or distributing it randomly in the street; it does recognize the needs of responsible individuals and businesses to plan for the mid- and longer term. Loans would be interest-free, or bear interest equivalent only to the rate of inflation with a small additional service charge to cover operating expenses. Prudential rules would naturally govern the choice of eligible borrowers and the amounts they could borrow.

Credit is a great invention. Before it existed, no one except the privileged could own their own home or, probably, even their own horse. When you own something, you take better care of it and its surroundings, and it contributes to your personal security. The subprime crisis is largely a result of the shameful exploitation of millions of poor Americans who simply wanted their own tiny share in such security, thanks

---

* In addition to its own direct bailouts, the financial powerhouse Goldman Sachs also got $12.5 billion of the bailout the government awarded to the financial insurance firm AIG. Shortly before the bailout, Goldman had said its exposure to AIG's debts was 'immaterial'. Well played, gentlemen.

to credit. The result was 2.8 million families thrown out of their homes in 2008 and 3.5 million in 2009. In other words, in 2009, every hour, 400 families became homeless and totally lost their security.

In poorer, rural countries, particularly in the South, where small farmers are dependent on moneylenders and have no access to regulated credit, they are easy prey. In India, about 200,000 such farmers have committed suicide over the past decade because of heavy debts – many taken on to buy genetically modified cotton seed and the necessary inputs to grow it, believing erroneously they would become better off. In the extremely poor African country Niger, the IMF made the government abandon institutional credit, leaving farmers at the mercy of rapacious moneylenders. The exorbitant sums they had to pay back in cash or in kind increased food shortages and contributed to the famine of 2004–5.

In the USA and Europe, small businesses are dropping by the wayside, not because they are poorly managed but because they are starved of credit. Since small business supplies 90 per cent of all jobs, this contributes to the knock-on effects of unemployment leading to less money in the economy and lower tax revenues, accompanied by more unsustainable expenditure for the state, more failing businesses, and so on.

Because the goal is to use the financial crisis to solve the environmental and social crises, *top priority for socialized banks would go to lending to businesses and individuals with a green project*, for example the provision of alternative energy or construction of energy-neutral buildings. Householders who want to retrofit their homes, install double-glazing, solar panels, insulation or other energy-creating or -saving devices should get loans to do so. Companies working on lightweight materials, fuel cells, novel batteries, energy-saving appliances, and so on should be funded as well, as should public or private research and development agencies and basic research in academia. Every bank would be required to devote X per cent of its portfolio to such loans.

We already know that a green economy can be a formidable job-creating machine. A comprehensive study by the World Wide Fund for Nature (WWF) shows that, already in Europe, renewable energy, green transport and energy-efficient goods and services employ at least 3.4 million people, compared with 2.8 million in traditional polluting industries such as cement, mining, iron and steel, gas and electricity. The potential for clean green jobs growth is significant, particularly in green transport and construction. In the United States as well, the green jobs sector, between 1998 and 2007, was growing much faster than job opportunities in the overall economy. Unfortunately both the United States and the EU are missing the boat on a big public investment push to fast-forward these developments, and their green stimulus efforts are far too puny to make much difference, particularly given the urgency of the task.[5]

The other lending priority for socialized banks would be social enterprises – that is, companies that are democratically run with worker participation and in which a fair distribution of added value takes place. A great range of self-management, social, 'mutualist' and/or cooperative models are available to choose from, and the one that fits each firm, large or small, should be chosen by the people concerned.

France, Spain and Italy, for example, have a long tradition of credit unions, co-ops and 'mutualist' enterprise to the point that, in France, 10 per cent of GDP comes from the social enterprise sector, which provides 2 million jobs that can't be off-shored. Half of all the insurance provided in France (and 30 per cent in Europe) comes from '*mutuelles*'. Unfortunately, also in France, the 'popular' banks pretty much succumbed to the financial-frenzy model of the past twenty years, but in Italy the much more recent Banca Etica already has some €700 million in deposits.

Some form of social enterprise exists on every continent, including the USA. These are private companies, but ownership is collective, decisions are made democratically and they are organized around principles of social solidarity and fair distribution of financial results to participants rather than to non-participant shareholders. Fair-trade companies buying and marketing the products of Southern producers are also often in this category, and the environmental component of social enterprise is growing rapidly as well. Such social-ecological enterprises are the natural clients of banks and credit unions organized along similar lines.[6]

Such models can but need not necessarily include workers' financial participation in the company's capital: the point is that nothing whatsoever, except ideology, dictates that democracy must be confined to the political sphere. Why can't one elect the people who govern a company (for longer or shorter periods, it depends) the same way we elect the people who govern a city or a nation? As far as I can tell, every society needs to organize its investment, production and distribution, and any producer of anything needs investors, workers and customers. Why can't all three find their place somewhere in the management? I know some progressives whose ideal society is one in which everyone rotates, doing every job in a business producing goods or providing services, so that the brain surgeon also collects the bed-pans part of the time. Personally I find this model far too rigid, and I don't believe it makes the best or most efficient use of everyone's aptitudes and time, particularly neglecting the long-slog years spent learning one's craft. I especially don't believe that the usual bed-pan nurse should do brain surgery or the person with little talent for accounting (like me . . .) the accounts.*

Why not instead give vouchers to everyone for life-long learning and leave them free to retrain and find the place that best suits them at each phase of their existence as a guarantee against monotony and dead-end jobs? I also think that salary differences would and in many cases should remain, because these companies would have to be able to attract well-pre-pared employees, but these differences would be kept within socially agreed compensation limits (see above).

That's why I'm not any more specific on how social businesses could operate. 'It depends' – on the size, loca-tion and nature of the production and distribution of goods and services; it depends above all on democratic debate among those concerned. I've already made clear that I hate the overworked, bureaucratic, democracy-diminishing word 'stakeholders', but you see what I mean. I also give a wide berth to those who know exactly what the perfect economy in the service of the perfect society will look like and how it must be organized – and are consequently not interested in listening to anyone else's ideas. Providing blueprints in such matters is neither their job nor mine, and here, as elsewhere, diversity should be the key.

As soon as several social enterprises exist in relative geo-graphic proximity, they can form networks, linking to each other as suppliers and outlets, the way some companies in industrial parks have already been organized physically (for example in Kalundborg, Denmark) to use each other's wastes as inputs and keep production in a closed-circuit loop of energy streams.

---

* Here I'm exaggerating unfairly to make a point: those proposing such systems generally have much lower-skilled tasks and smaller, more basic co-op companies in mind.

TELL THE POLITICIANS HOW WE FEEL

On the Saturday just before the April Fools G-20 meeting in London in 2009, our British friends organized a big, enthusiastic march from Big Ben to Hyde Park for 'Jobs, Justice, Climate' and to tell the G-20 leaders to 'Put People First'. The unions were out in force, and representatives of just about every NGO in the UK except the Pigeon Protection League joined the cortège. The police count of the demonstrators was 35,000 people. It was a great day that ended under intermittent downpours at a big bandstand in the park with music and short speeches. In my own three minutes' worth, I got this huge crowd to chant with me 'The banks are ours'. It sounded great, and let me say it 'rang true'. They *are* ours; we've paid and are still paying for them, and we have got absolutely nothing in return except more demands for our money.

Next day this march was front-page news in every Sunday paper and had Prime Minister Gordon Brown scurrying to proclaim how much he agreed with us. What's happening isn't hard to understand; governments can't hide it or shove it back under the rug, and they know that people are justifiably angry. Given that a political party which firmly placed the banks under public ownership for public, green and social purposes would get re-elected for the rest of its natural life, what's stopping them? Whatever it is, it's up to citizens to tell our governments that they are responsible not just to the banks but also to us, and demand that they act.

Another reason to get the banks under control is that it isn't just the huge bailouts they've collected – it's that they're still collecting piles of taxpayers' money in the course of every normal business day and doing so altogether legally. Take, once more, the case of our favourite giant vampire squid Goldman Sachs, now easily the most powerful financial firm in the world. The squid, as we saw a few pages ago, is doing extremely well, often raking in $100 million daily, and, although I can't manage purplish prose like Matt Taibbi's, I can tell you that, in 2009, despite still owing the US government at least $10 billion, it paid its 28,000 staff worldwide the largest bonuses of its 140-year history – having already in 2008 paid each of 973 bankers $1 million or more. How could this be possible in the midst of the greatest financial debacle in history? How can G S (Giant Squid) be earning such colossal sums with impunity? Easy. And taxpayers should take heed.

The Observer observed that, in pre-crisis 2006, the financial sector's earnings were £186 billion. In 2009 they were expected to be about £160 billion but, because of multiple bankruptcies such as Lehman's, these takings would be shared by a smaller number of firms. Goldman nowadays has far less competition, so it can also charge higher fees. The revenues providing the record earnings and bonuses are indeed entirely legal and will come in large part from . . . the US government – that is, from US taxpayers. *The Observer* quotes an analyst who points out that those firms that have escaped relatively unscathed from the crisis are big intermediaries on the bond markets, where governments are raising billions in fresh cash: 'President Barack Obama's government could issue $3,250 billion of debt before September [2009], almost four times the total issued in 2008. Goldman, a prime broker of US government bonds is expected to make hundreds of millions of dollars in profits from selling and dealing in the bonds.'[7]

And all this at no risk to themselves – it's a dream job. My question is: Why can't a government agency market government debt? Why does the intermediary have to be private and paid huge fees with our money? The same holds true in Europe, where governments borrow from private banks.

The European Central Bank lends to banks at about 1 per cent interest; the banks then lend to governments at whatever rate they can negotiate – a rather simple way to make money. When the European sovereign debt crisis struck Greece in the spring of 2010 a bailout was quickly arranged, partly because European banks, especially in France and Germany, held vast amounts of Greek government bonds and were thus indirectly bailed out. The world's banks are not now doing their primary job and are not lending as they used to do, not even to each other. Interbank lending is the lifeblood of the system, and when its circulation clogs or freezes it's as if your blood had stopped irrigating your body. Like humans, the banks have remained in a kind of cardiac arrest, and long after the fall of the house of Lehman loans were still sluggish or frozen. They thawed somewhat, then seized up once more as soon as the European sovereign debt crisis erupted.

Small and medium-sized businesses in particular which are well managed should not normally fail. The credit freeze is causing enormous hardship, needless lay-offs, lost economic activity, foregone investment and therefore lost tax revenues – all the signs of serious recession. Banks, as the old refrain has it, will only lend to people who don't need loans, and all the corporate-welfare dollars, pounds and euros have bought citizens nothing but more pain.

Meanwhile, as far as I know, no governments have applied any conditions to the money already handed over to the banks, presumably to clean up their balance sheets, although most are asking to be paid back. Consequently the banks are lying low and not lending; some have even confessed – as if it were quite normal – that rather than lending they are hoarding their bailout cash in order to buy up smaller, weaker rivals when the time is ripe. Under our present system, you can hardly blame them. They are capitalist enterprises answering to their shareholders, not to potential customers for loans. Since they refuse to do so spontaneously, they must be forced by law to lend and, if those loans require government guarantees, these should be forthcoming. That is partly what nationalization or socialization means and why it is entirely justifiable. Without the bailouts, many banks today would be worthless, and if they were still listed on the stock markets their shares would be quoted in pennies.

By mid-2009, over 400 banks in the United States were still under serious threat and, as the *New York Times* reported, 'US banking regulators are bracing for hundreds of small and mid-size banks to collapse in the coming months'. It doesn't seem, yet, to be quite that bad. As of early November 2009, 'only' 111 US banks had failed that year – compared with twenty-five in 2008, three in 2007 and none in 2006. But the failures of 2009 hardly seem to signal something one could call a recovery.

The Federal Deposit Insurance Corporation (FDIC), another New Deal innovation, is the agency that guarantees depositors will get their money back (up to certain limits, generally $100,000) even if their bank goes bust. In mid-2009, only a shade over $10 billion remained in the rescue fund, down from $45 billion a year earlier. So the FDIC may have to go back to the Federal Reserve and ask for more money. Without governments, scores of large, medium and small banks would be effectively bankrupt already.

What the giant banks want, and what governments are helping them to do, is to enjoy less competition (as in the case of Goldman Sachs), to concentrate and merge so as to become once again too big to fail, and stage the Financial Follies show all over again – it was such fun last time, wasn't it? One can feel sorry for the more than 110,000 lower-level employees who lost their jobs in eleven big banks between

mid-2007 and the end of 2008 alone, but whose fault is that?*
This situation is intolerable, no? The question is: Will it be
allowed to continue?

One can feel even sorrier for the hundreds of thousands of
ordinary people who were trapped in a personal debt crisis
when housing values plummeted. The rescue efforts now
deployed are for corporations, not for people. A member of
the US House of Representatives, Raul Grijalva, proposed a
bill in 2008 called the Save Family Homes Act, which would
have allowed bankrupt subprime borrowers to continue
living in their homes indefinitely, paying rents based on the
going market rate to the owners of their mortgages. The
banks and financial houses would thus get something other
than an often worthless house in a depressed neighbourhood
overwhelmed by foreclosures. The US banks and mortgage
outfits wouldn't hear of it, and the bill got nowhere.

One of the US cities hardest hit by the subprime crisis
is Cleveland, Ohio. I used to know it rather well, since it's
not far from Akron where I grew up – Cleveland was where
we went for the museum, concerts and Really Important
Shopping. The pictures of its now blighted, vandalized
neighbourhoods with entire blocks of foreclosed houses make
you want to cry. The city government also tried to get the
banks to renegotiate the outstanding loans on the basis of the
current, actual market value of the house: the banks again said
nyet. 'Deutsche Bank was one of the worst', according to the
Cleveland municipal official interviewed on an excellent TV
programme shown on the Franco-German channel Arte.†

---

* Job losses for Citigroup, Bank of America, Royal Bank of Scotland,
Washington Mutual, Morgan Stanley, UBS, Commerzbank, Credit Suisse,
JPMorgan, BayernLB, Merrill Lynch, with Citigroup accounting for
almost a third of the total (*Financial Times*, 5 December 2008).
† Since Grijalva proposed his ill-fated bill in 2008, it appears that banks
and other mortgage owners are in fact selling many of the houses that were

It's not just the US and British banks that are up to the hilt in debts and bailouts: this is a worldwide issue and a blot on the social landscape. It can only be repaired through legally mandated takeovers or, as *Financial Times* columnist John Authers puts it, the 'n-word', 'the economic solution that dare not speak its name'.[8]

Well, let's not be afraid to speak it, loud and clear: the word is nationalization.

SWORDS INTO PLOUGHSHARES, NOT CORPORATE BAILOUTS

While we're on the subject of the proper use of bailouts, let's talk about the bailouts of the great traditional firms such as the automobile companies that have received large public (read 'our') handouts in grants or loans. In the case of loans, the mere fact that governments should have to do the lending, because the banks can't or won't, is another argument for nationalization. I believe these companies should be saved, but not to do the same things in the same way as before. They should be part of the clean green social effort. We have a historical example we could return to, dust off and put into practice immediately: the Lucas Aerospace workers' Alternative Corporate Plan.

Here is a brief account of this inspiring and hopeful though ultimately defeated experiment. In the early 1970s, Lucas Aerospace had fifteen factories and 18,000 employees

Footnote (*continued*)
seized. Thus they can keep the initial mortgage payments of the former occupants and can also sell a proportion of the foreclosed homes at the going market rates. Particularly since the crisis has hit not just poor but also mid-level homeowners and forced them to abandon their dwellings, the houses are not all 'worthless', nor are they all in undesirable, vandalized neighbourhoods – far from it. That applies only to some neighbourhoods in some cities.

in Britain, devoted largely to supplying the military with articles such as Sting Ray missiles, although they also produced
high-tech medical equipment. The workers, technicians, sec-
retaries and engineers at Lucas belonged to thirteen different
trade unions, so it had become clear that they needed a single
voice that could negotiate with management for everyone.

This gave rise to the Shop Stewards Combine Committee
(SSCC). Shop stewards are elected by the workers from
among their own number. This committee was spectacularly
successful in comparison with the national full-time union
officials. For example, in 1972, after a thirteen-week strike
in one factory, the SSCC negotiated a company-wide wage
increase that was 167 per cent higher than the one negotiated nationally by union brass – this after repeated warnings
by Lucas management that the workers would not get a
penny more. The SSCC won not only because they spoke
for everyone but also because they could organize support in
any Lucas plant at any time they chose – strikes, slowdowns,
occupations or other industrial actions that wore down management resistance. So, when the SSCC learned that Lucas
intended to streamline production, close down several factories and lay off at least 20 per cent of the workforce, it quickly
organized the employees to develop an Alternative Corporate
Plan.

The idea was to move to producing 'socially useful' goods
instead of weapons and do it without job losses, using the
existing machinery, equipment and skills inside the company.
Everyone could understand that a Sting Ray missile was profitable for Lucas's owners but brought no advantage whatever
either to the workers or to society, and the Lucas employees
wanted to change the social content of their work as well as to
preserve their jobs. In the 1970s, trade unions still had considerable power in Britain, but the union officials took a dim
view of this initiative and saw the SSCC as rising above its

station. The unions were comfortable with their traditional role of negotiating wages and working conditions (although they hadn't done it very well a couple of years previously)– but an overall corporate plan? Their support was decidedly lukewarm, and the SSCC was on its own.

The workers, engineers and technicians knew their plants and machinery better than anyone and, over a two-year period filled with intense debate and their own market research, they developed an alternative plan for manufacturing an astonishing range of genuinely useful products which – had they been supported rather than suppressed by the official unions and the Labour Party – would have placed Britain in the forefront of late twentieth- and twenty-first-century industry. Their plan was ready in 1976, and already at that early date they were proto-environmentalists. Recognizing that coal and oil would only last so long and that 60 per cent of energy was wasted before doing any work, they concentrated on renewable energy, energy-saving technologies and efficiency, including alternatives to nuclear power. In the early 1970s they had already designed heat pumps for housing developments, solar and hydrogen fuel cells, power packs for small-scale generation of electricity which could be particularly useful in developing countries and, since their experience in aerodynamics at Lucas was second to none, windmills.

In the area of transport, they concentrated on lightweight road–rail systems, notably the rail–road carriage that could run on rails with pneumatic tyres and switch to roads whenever necessary, thus serving areas where the railways were closing down. They designed a hybrid car powered by an internal combustion engine and a battery that achieved a 50 per cent reduction of fuel consumption and toxic emissions. New medical technology included portable kidney dialysis machines, artificial limb control systems, sight aids for the blind developed from their experience with radar, 'hobcarts' for disabled children and improved life-support systems for ambulances.

Wouldn't a person have to be not just unfeeling but completely mad to oppose such creativity and such innovative products? Alas, no. The profit margins for weapons were much higher than for the goods the SSCC proposed, and the goal of the alternative plan was to phase out all military production. The socially useful products it put forward were also much more labour intensive and would have kept the entire 18,000 person workforce busy. Lucas management wanted no part of the plan and announced they would continue with the streamlining, plant closures and layoffs. This is one of the saddest, stupidest stories I know in the long and copious annals of 'capitalists and capitalism always know best'.

But nor did unions and the Labour government know best. The union officials were way out of their depth and possibly jealous; moreover, they had signed a pact with the Labour government aimed at moderating union demands. SSCC members also committed a major strategic error by getting sucked into a long series of fruitless discussions with the full-time union officials, Labour ministers and bureaucrats in London, while simultaneously neglecting their responsibilities in keeping the Lucas workforce united and determined and continuing to build strength at the base. In time, the whole effort withered away and the company won. One can apportion blame. I wasn't there, and perhaps someone who was would tell a different story, but my point here is to propose that, instead of bailouts, governments pay the workforces in the companies that need public funds, say, eighteen months to two years of wages to come up with Lucas-type alternative corporate plans. They could simultaneously continue to produce the smaller number of, say, automobiles, that could actually be sold, while trying to improve their environmental performance. It's true that Lucas had experience with small-batch, small-team production as opposed to assembly lines, but this should not be an insuperable obstacle.

For centuries we neglected the creative possibilities of half the human race, namely women, and many countries still do. The capitalist system has rarely, if ever, acknowledged the creativity of workers. Why not seize the opportunity of the crisis to change this wasteful practice and put worker creativity to work?

HELLO? REMEMBER THE DEBT OF THE SOUTH?

My book *A Fate Worse than Debt* was published in 1987 and I continued to work on the subject of Southern debt for more than a decade after that. I was proud to be one of 70,000 plus people who formed the 'human chain to break the chains of debt' organized by Jubilee 2000 in parallel to the 1998 G-8 summit meeting in Birmingham. These leaders had to notice us, and they replied to the hundreds of thousands who had signed the Jubilee petition:

> Our ambition, reaffirmed by all G8 leaders today, is to ensure the speedy and determined implementation of the [Highly Indebted Poor Countries, or 'HIPC', debt] initiative and encourage all eligible countries to take the policy measures needed to embark on the process as soon as possible, so that all can be in the process by the year 2000. We will work with the others concerned to ensure that all eligible countries get the relief they need to secure a lasting exit from their debt problems. We are keenly aware of the importance of making progress. For the sake of our citizens in our own and all other countries, we must not fail.[9]

Fine words; but what's the state of play a decade later? The Highly Indebted Poor Countries (HIPC) initiative didn't consist in writing off their debts but rather obliged these very poor countries to apply another three to six years of IMF shock treatment ('structural adjustment' policies) before they could become 'eligible' according to IMF criteria for debt relief. Out of forty-nine countries officially classed as HIPCs at the beginning of the process, four said thanks, but no thanks. Some had no government to speak of or were in a state of total chaos or war, so finally the list of the highly indebted poor was reduced to thirty-one countries.

In 1997, the year before the G-8's brave new words in Birmingham, the full complement of thirty-one HIPCs owed their creditors $102 billion. Eight years later, after further structural adjustment austerity and pain, they owed them $100.6 billion. As a group, their reward was a puny reduction of 1.4 per cent. Who did the G-8 think they were kidding? As for the interest payments, in 2001 the same group was handing their creditors $2.87 billion in debt service. In 2006, when several more countries had become nominally eligible for relief, their creditors received $3.29 billion worth of interest payments, nearly 15 per cent *more* than five years earlier. What kind of 'relief' is it when the extremely poor were still reimbursing the extremely rich with over $9 million a day, $375,000 an hour, $6,250 a minute?

We can make the same calculations for the whole of sub-Saharan Africa, where many countries overlap with the HIPC list. In 2007, the region paid back $17 billion in debt service, which comes to $46.6 million a day, $1.94 million an hour and more than $32,000 a minute.[10] One could build and supply a good many schools and hospitals with $32,000 a minute. I rest my case.

The 'Paris Club' is the informal group made up of rich creditor country and international institution civil servants who meet periodically at the French Finance Ministry to deal with public debt relief negotiations. The creditors, gathered in this semi-tribunal, face individual debtors, hear their story, look at their accounts and their IMF compliance reports, and set the relief packages. The least one can say is that they are not the soul of generosity.

They are also secretive. I once asked them for some specific information and in response was insultingly sent a copy of the first, extremely general page of the thick World Bank Debt Tables volume, which at the time I knew at least as well as did the Paris Club. As I recall, I sent back their letter with the simple addendum of Article XV of the Declaration of the Rights of Man and the Citizens (1789), which proclaims 'Society has the right to demand accountability from every public servant for his administration'.*

The HIPC countries have not exactly received the deal of the century – any century. For reasons too complex to go into here, the big Jubilee movement that had brought off the Birmingham Chain more or less closed down a couple of years later, although small and valiant Jubilee organizations continue to do good work in some Northern countries, including the USA and the UK, and a network called Jubilee South soldiers on in the indebted countries that unfortunately have no clout at all. But the debt is still there and it's still deadly. Only a small proportion has been cancelled. Countries that have received some relief have generally used it productively. For example, Tanzania was able to eliminate the school fees imposed by the IMF as a measure called 'cost recovery'. School enrolments, especially of girls, immediately shot up by two-thirds.

Now we have a dazzling opportunity to reduce the social

---

* 'La société a le droit de demander compte à tout agent public de son administration.'

hardships of the South, provide gainful employment for its people and simultaneously strike a very large blow for the environment. Here's how: *Cancel all the public debt of the HIPCs, better still of all sub-Saharan Africa, best of all for every country prepared to comply with certain conditions.* The rich governments and international institutions don't need those annual $3 or $17 or however many billion, and they could instead do a prodigious amount of good for this relatively tiny amount of money – $17 billion, for example, is only 14 per cent of official development aid in 2008 and $3 billion is insignificant (though not for the debtors). *In exchange for debt write-offs, for at least X per cent of the debt relief granted, these countries would undertake important reforestation and biodiversity conservation works.*

Forests are the most efficient tool to absorb CO^2 from the atmosphere, and such programmes could provide large numbers of jobs to people *where they already live*. The IMF and the World Bank could earn their keep by doing something useful for a change, monitoring the accounts and the progress on the ground – you don't just hand over the debt relief to the governments and hope for the best. Nor do you allow the usual World Bank trick of planting fast-growing eucalyptus forests instead of the far more useful and diverse local species. You pay people to grow their own saplings from the seeds of their own indigenous trees and replant them. You make sure the whole plan remains under local community control with popular participation so that the crony landholders don't make off with all the benefits. Reforestation has the added advantage of fixing the soil and water, thus favouring local smallholder agriculture.

You also make it worth people's while to conserve biodiversity, from small medicinal plants to large wild animals. People will uproot and poach so long as they can make money from uprooting and poaching and none from protecting and

nurturing. Well-paid forest and game rangers and conservation workers can and will prevent damage to plants and
animals if their livelihoods depend on it, and we can have the
satisfaction of saving not just future disease cures for ourselves but also gorillas, rhinos, elephants and other friends.
What's not to like? We could have all this at a single stroke
for a small amount of direct green investment in the form of
debt relief that our own governments don't need, with zero
cost to citizens in the North and immeasurable improvement
in our reputations and relations with the South.

Such measures in favour of the climate and of biodiversity
conservation would not exclude investments in health, education, clean water and so on, but they do need to be mandated
and monitored, since local people may not see them as priorities – at least not right away. I know some will object to this
proposal on the grounds that it would 'impose conditionali-
ties', just like the Bank and the IMF. Well, yes, but not just
like the Bank and the Fund. I have been recommending con-
ditionalities since *A Fate Worse than Debt* twenty years ago,
when I recommended helping governments to finance development projects out of local currency rather than paying debt
service in hard currency. One or two creditor governments
did this, including Switzerland. While I'm at it, I would add
an obligation for every government to allow and facilitate the
election of local councils that would work alongside governments in determining debt relief priorities. The councils
would represent the countries' citizens both geographically
and by sector, so that farmers, women, pastoralists, trade
unions, entrepreneurs, teachers, health professionals, and so
on would be heard. My critics are free to trust the governments acting alone; I am free not to.

I also recommend similar programmes of 'debt cancel-
lation for climate' in other, somewhat richer countries that
are not on the HIPC or sub-Saharan Africa list, but we need

to start somewhere, and the poorest countries are the most obvious and most urgent places to do that so as to reduce simultaneously both CO^2 and also poverty and inequality.

HOW TO BECOME CLEAN, GREEN AND . . . RICH!

What should Europe's economy look like in future? Do we want to be merely a destination for throngs of Chinese and Indian tourists? It's good that people should be able to travel, and Europeans are not complaining that Spain, France and Italy are already second, third and fourth in the world for income from foreign tourists.* But how dependent do we want to be on beautiful scenery, mountains, beaches and monuments? Shall we stay stuck in the past, however glorious, counting on the achievements of the kings and cathedral builders, the painters, sculptors and architects of yesterday to keep our economies ticking over in the twenty-first century? It is hardly an inspiring prospect.

Meanwhile, industrial jobs are flowing away on the tide of globalization, smaller innovative companies are suffocating for want of credit, and Europe, despite some notable exceptions, has barely begun to invest in clean green technology. Even Germany, supposed to be the great green model, is building more coal-fired, carbon-spewing power plants, whereas the Americans and the Chinese are gearing up for the ecological revolution.

The Americans are doing it largely through common or

---

* The USA has the highest income from foreign tourists. The top ten are USA, Spain, France, Italy, China, the UK, Germany, Australia, Turkey and Austria; other European countries in the top twenty-five are Greece, the Netherlands, Belgium, Sweden, Portugal and Croatia. If total income from tourism is counted, including spending by citizens of the concerned country, France was first in 2007, with €82 billion.

garden capitalism of the more exuberant variety. Venture capitalist John Doerr, a famous Silicon Valley presence who bet on the best (and much less often the worst) 'dotcom' companies at the turn of the twenty-first century, has clear ideas about the matter. He has already collected a cool billion, partly his own money, partly from fellow venture capitalists, and is going all out for clean green tech – the 'biggest economic opportunity of the twenty-first century'. These people are unlikely to let the credit crunch stand in their way. Their investments in environment-related firms nearly doubled between 2006 and 2007 and have quadrupled since 2005. Here is Doerr at a California high tech-energy conference in 2008: 'Remember the internet? Green tech is bigger. . . . This could be the biggest economic opportunity of the 21st century.' He tantalized his audience with the mouth-watering fact that the global energy business is worth \$6 trillion per year. That puts in the shade anything measured in mere billions, such as the market for computers. 'Energy is the mother of all markets.'[11]

Europe on the whole doesn't even have real venture capitalists. Are all European business people or fortune-holders unimaginative and timid souls? Should we be glad or sorry? Recall, in any case, the Merrill Lynch and Cap Gemini 2009 edition of the *World Wealth Report* indicating that, while the crisis has hit both the numbers of 'High Net Worth Individuals' and the cash they possess, the wealth that belongs to these people is still staggering. Although there may now be 'only' 8.6 million people worldwide with a million dollars or more of investable funds, they still collectively boast a tidy \$32.8 trillion – or \$32,800,000,000,000. Why wouldn't at least 10 per cent of them take a plunge into clean green investments? Plenty of them are in Europe and Japan as well as the USA.

I'm not trying to help Doerr and his fellows, whether American, European or Japanese, make more money. I do believe that a green conversion on the necessary scale will require an all-out effort from both the public sector and private entrepreneurs willing to bet on smart people with new clean green ideas. It will also determine the future for everyone's economy. Maybe private investors willing to gamble big bucks on good new ideas should get recognition like the dollar-a-year men did. If they want to invest only in the likes of Goldman Sachs, then tax their dividends twice or three times as much as dividends from alternative energy companies. Figure out ways, in other words, to channel private money to the clean green cause. I realize that this recommendation could lead to some ambiguous outcomes. In the 1930s, the class of large private investors universally loathed Franklin Roosevelt. He doughtily acknowledged that fact on the radio, adding, 'And I welcome their hatred.' He still forcibly saved their system for them.

Although I have recommended loans from citizen-controlled banks, such loans can't do the whole job because they would finance mainly ideas that have already been tried and have proven their worth. Such ideas need to be put into practice, but those who do so will not be starting from scratch. This is why, besides loans, we also need grants. If private money and foundations in Europe and elsewhere are prepared to give grants, fine. If not, then governments must. Grants to people with novel ideas should be supported and such a fund should be part of every government fiscal stimulus plan. Here is a small item from the *New Scientist* as a case in point:

> The US Department of Energy has given $100,000 to Solar Roadways of Sagle, Idaho, to develop photovoltaic panels that can be embedded into roads and parking lots. Paving the entire US road network with solar panels would meet the country's energy needs.[12]

This idea may be unworkable or it may be brilliant – I have no idea. But that is not the point. The point is that we won't know unless it is further developed. The people who founded the Solar Roadways company don't have the cash themselves, and the banks think their idea is too far out to risk $100,000 on. But, *if it works*, $100,000 is peanuts compared to the possible payoff. Public money is the answer.

MONEY, LOTS OF IT, AND TAXES, WHAT ELSE?

In the spirit of going after the money where it is, we need new and better-targeted taxes, nationally and internationally. I recently received an e-mail from a professor in California, where the state government is virtually broke. He explained that 'Democrats in California are accepting the dismantling of public education and public health, while saying that they don't want a *complete* end to public support for health care for the poor and help for people moving off of welfare. Nobody is speaking up for taxing the rich.' California is also cutting environmental conservation budgets to the point that the state may no longer even protect such national parks as the world-renowned redwood (sequoia) forest.

Well, fortunately some people are speaking up for taxing the rich, even in the USA, where the Institute for Policy Studies, sister to the Transnational Institute, has developed a set of proposals for taxes they say could raise more than $450 billion from the American individuals and corporations best able to pay.[13] The IPS proposals deal only with the US tax structure, but many could be adapted and adopted for the situation in other countries.

Governments everywhere infected with neoliberalism have spent the past several decades relentlessly reducing taxes on their richest citizens and corporations, thus lopping off huge chunks of potential revenues they could otherwise have used for improving public services and the lives of *all* their citizens. Just as we could emulate the IPS report as a practical revenue-raising guide, so we could all begin by rescinding the tax cuts bestowed on the rich and restoring progressive taxes. Remember Republican President Eisenhower, who taxed the top slice of super-rich revenues at 90 per cent and got away with it.

Latvia, a country literally collapsing because of the crisis, has abandoned its 'flat tax', a system which taxes all revenues, consumption and profits at the same low rate whether the income is counted in hundreds, thousands or millions. This small country's action is a good sign because flat taxes are notoriously regressive, hitting the poor and middle-class much harder than the rich, but it's a shame Latvia had to find this out the hard way. Most other Eastern European countries also have flat taxes. Let's hope they imitate Latvia. One reason for Greece's sovereign debt crisis is that it has never taxed the Orthodox Church, the largest land and real-estate owner in the country. And many Greek companies conveniently relocated, at least on paper, to Cyprus, where the corporate tax rate is 10 per cent.

THE EUROPEAN UNION MANS THE TAX BARRICADES

Restoring fairer tax systems nationally, however vital, is difficult and unpopular with groups that have a great deal of influence, but there's no doubt we will face even more formidable obstacles to *international* taxation. Various provisions of European law, reaffirmed in the Lisbon Treaty, restrict international taxation. One is the dogma of the 'free movement of capital', which applies both to internal EU transactions and to those with third countries. The Commission and the European Court of Justice would undoubtedly see taxes on any kind of capital movements as violating this basic 'freedom'. Another barrier is the rule that makes unanimity a condition for changes in European fiscal and social legislation. Twenty-seven countries are never going to agree on anything substantial, and this organizes a 'race to the bottom', as member states compete to reduce taxes and give investors the most favourable concessions.

The Brits are at the head of a small coalition to make sure Brussels can't interfere in national fiscal affairs, much less levy European-wide taxes. Sometimes I wish the 'opt-out clause' the UK so often invokes were coupled with a 'kick-out clause', so that countries that want Europe to be more than just one big happy market could occasionally prevail, but that is going to be a long, perhaps endless battle. As the *Financial Times* reports,

> A majority of EU countries support tougher pan-European rules to avert future financial turmoil and are willing to give EU supervisors the power to impose binding decisions on governments in situations where two or more national supervisors cannot agree on how to treat a bank in difficulty. But a small group of EU states, led by the UK, opposed such an expansion of EU-wide supervisory powers, saying it would undermine the principle that taxation is a matter for national governments, not the EU.[14]

Our efforts will also be blocked by a European Central Bank that is totally independent of any political oversight and possibly the most conservative institution in Europe this side of the Roman Curia. To circumvent these daunting institutional obstacles, we would need a EuroGroup with some backbone that could act at least for the fifteen euro countries. We presently have the EuroGroup (the chair is Jean-Claude Juncker of Luxembourg) but not the backbone. Despite all this, when the sovereign debt crisis struck Greece and threatened to spread far and wide, the Lisbon Treaty was trampled underfoot and a clause, meant to cover natural disasters, was invoked to cover financial ones as well. Other loopholes could be found, and it's a shame to wait for new calamities before using them.

We should also encourage the formation of 'coalitions of the willing', made up of euro and non-euro states that want to cooperate on particular reforms, including tax reforms. The EU makes such 'enhanced cooperation' difficult but not impossible: those who sought to improve fiscal surveillance, harmonize their tax rates or even levy international taxes would have a chance to do so.

BREAKTHROUGH OR BREAKDOWN

The crisis provides an opportunity for a big emergency push towards international taxation, but we must try to do better and go faster in the twenty-first century than our ancestors were able to do in previous ones. Any history of taxation shows how tough it is to bring about change, but perseverance does pay off and the crisis provides a strong platform to popularize the idea. International taxes would not target the middle classes, much less the poor – only transnational corporations, traders and those who can easily afford them. They might, therefore, be marginally easier to achieve than national taxes were many decades ago, although they will be – they are already – bitterly opposed, just as taxes have always been bitterly opposed.

For example, the notion of income tax in the present sense doesn't seem to have occurred to anyone until William Pitt the Younger designed an amazingly modern progressive tax system for Britain in 1798. It was almost immediately beaten down and only revived to pay for the Napoleonic wars. In historical terms, taxes until quite recently were 'off again on again' emergency decisions relating to wars or other crises and carefully labelled 'temporary'. As soon as there no longer seemed an urgent need, legislators were keen to cash in on the political popularity that went with tax cuts or repeal.

For modern taxes, especially a progressive income tax, you need a modern money economy, accurate and verifiable accounts, and public finance expanding into new areas. So it is understandable that, until the late nineteenth and early twentieth centuries, most governments relied on property taxes, customs duties and those eternal revenue sources alcohol and tobacco. For as long as they could, they also levied a highly remunerative tax on sales of slaves.

The ever enlightened Norwegians had a progressive income tax by 1896, with the Swedes following in 1910. Campaigning that began in the 1870s got nowhere in France until 1909, and even then the conservative senate balked and prevented income tax from becoming law until it was passed as an emergency measure two weeks before the outbreak of the First World War. Prussia began state taxes in 1891, but there was no federal income tax in Germany until 1920. In Britain, income tax remained 'temporary' until 1913, and in the United States it took a constitutional amendment in 1916 to make the progressive income tax a permanent feature of the nation. Any progress on this rough road was naturally accompanied by the anguished cries of the rich proffering 'proof' that civilization as we know it would instantly succumb to such a wicked measure. The same loud objections will continue to accompany the struggle for international taxation and for any renewed or new taxes applied to those who can best pay or deserve to pay – all the more reason for demanding them now.

I certainly have no monopoly on ideas for new revenue sources: the more the better. It's said that Keynes and his younger Cambridge colleague and friend Roy Harrod liked to go out and drink together and invent new taxes. This must be an instance of some law stating that leisure rises to the same intellectual level as professional accomplishment. Well, we need Keynes and Harrod, and we need them now.

Another Cambridge economist, Arthur Cecil Pigou, whose misfortune it was to spend much of his life under the broad shadow of his younger colleague Keynes, invented taxes later named 'Pigovian' in his honour. These taxes are meant to correct what economists call 'negative externalities' – the side effects of economic activity. If a factory pollutes the air you breathe and the water you drink, you suffer, but the company doesn't compensate you for your suffering or pay for its negative impact in any way.

Global warming and runaway climate change are today the universal negative externality of collective as well as individual economic activity. Pigou's idea was to 'internalize the externalities' so that those responsible would pay for their impact, whether unintended or not. This is now often translated in ecological terms as the 'polluter pays principle'. One can state the Pigou principle even more simply: tax less what you want more of; tax more what you want less of. We need Pigou now as well. At the top of my own tax wish-list would be a Pigovian onslaught against greenhouse gases and climate change. The carbon tax is already a familiar idea that needs to be acted upon immediately. Unfortunately, the one proposed in France was unacceptable to progressives because it left companies out completely – the whole weight would have been borne by family incomes and consumers.

But a differently conceived tax is still necessary. CO^2 is a pollutant on a grand scale: at present levels it is life-threatening for humans and other living things, and greenhouse emissions should be curbed by taxing them and by simultaneously not taxing, but rather subsidizing, renewable energy sources. The Transnational Institute's environmental team at Carbon Trade Watch has developed strong arguments against trading CO^2 pollution rights which I won't reproduce here but simply recommend: such a market isn't going to solve the problem and neither are 'offsets' – what the TNI researchers calls 'the new indulgences for your carbon sins'.[15] The very notion of carbon trading supposes that CO^2 emissions must continue to exist – otherwise the price of emissions will collapse and some investors would be left holding the bag.

To get a carbon tax accepted faster, because we really are in an emergency, it would be worth taxing other corporate expenditures less, such as payrolls or other work-related taxes, in order to balance the new CO^2 tax burden, at least at the beginning. This would be a double application of the Pigovian principle: tax more what you want less of (greenhouse gases) and less what you want more of (employment). A carbon tax, even if accompanied by cuts in employment-related taxes, would not lead to cuts in other vital spending such as government budgets for health, education and public services, because an environmentally friendly economy is a huge source of employment, not to mention a healthier milieu. More people employed and contributing to the tax base would mean that other needs would still be adequately or better funded.

TOBIN OR NOT TOBIN?

Many people still call it the Tobin Tax; at Attac we call it simply a tax on financial transactions, because it would include all kinds of transactions, not just currency trades. The late Professor James Tobin proposed his tax on currency trading in the days when these trades amounted to around $80 billion a day. Tobin lived in simpler times. As the Bank for International Settlements, the central banks' central bank in Basel, reported in its *Triennial Survey* at the end of 2007, financial transactions had by then risen to a staggering $3,200 billion a day, 400 times what Tobin was up against, and they encompass a whole cookbook full of different operations.[16]

For starters, 'foreign exchange market' transactions come in three flavours – not chocolate, vanilla and strawberry but spot, outright forwards and swaps. These categories are all growing fast, but not nearly as fast as the 'over the counter (OTC) derivatives market turnover', which rises to positively dizzying heights. Please don't ask me to explain this in detail (the BIS does so very well) but, compared with the previous *Triennial Survey*, covering the years 2001 to 2004, these derivatives had climbed by 135 per cent, to $516 trillion ($516,000 billion), in 'notional terms', which tot up all the contracts bought/sold during a given period.

$516,000 billion dollars is of course more money than there is in the world, and the BIS cautions that 'notional amounts outstanding provide useful information on the structure of the OTC derivatives market but should not be interpreted as a measure of the riskiness of these positions'. The BIS prefers to measure risk by the measure of 'gross market value', which is the 'cost of replacing all open contracts at the prevailing market prices' at a given time. Using this measure in 2007, the heady notional $516 trillion could be reduced to a 'mere' $11 trillion ($11,000 billion).*

---

* Nominal or notional amounts outstanding are defined as the absolute gross nominal or notional value of all deals concluded and still open at the date of the survey. Another measure of the size of the derivatives markets is provided by outstanding contracts in terms of gross market values, which are comparable across different markets and products: they are defined as the sums of the absolute values of all open contracts with either positive or negative replacement values calculated at market prices prevailing on the reporting date. 'Reporting values' denote the price to be received or paid if the instrument were sold in the market at the time of reporting. Many thanks to Philippe Mesny of the Bank for International Settlements in Basel for kindly sorting out these arcane matters for me.

So we do not have an official interim estimate from the BIS on how much traffic still takes place daily on Forex and OTC derivatives markets and will have to wait for the one that should be issued at the end of 2010 to judge what impact the financial crisis has had on these transactions. We still know that, however great or small the sum may be compared with the daily $3,200 billion in 2007, taxing financial transactions even at a minuscule rate could bring in zillions for the environment and for eradicating hunger and misery. Using the 2007 tally of $3,200 billion a day, and, say, 240 trading days a year, we would hit $788,000 billion ($788,000,000,000,000) a year, and I'd be satisfied taxing it at 1 per 1,000 or 10,000 – wouldn't you? Taxing *notional* amounts – presently assumed to be about $600,000 billion a year – could be done at 1/10,000 and still amass enough to eliminate virtually every problem the world has ever known – hunger, environmental destruction, climate change, blatant inequalities . . . the mind reels. Whether you agree or not, I'll let you do the arithmetic and simply point out that all this speculation, so long as speculation lasts, could provide *a LOT* of money for good purposes.

A very low rate of one basis point* or less isn't going to hurt anyone, and it's too small to be worth trying to avoid illegally, but we still hear the objection that it could affect the real economy, not just the financial one. At least before the crash, only about 2 per cent of these financial transactions, particularly in foreign exchange, had anything to do with genuine economic activity – trades were simply intended to make a profit on fluctuations between currencies.

The real economy is something else. Imagine you run a

---

* The language of 'basis points' is easily translated by placing a comma before the last two digits to arrive at a percentage: e.g. '236 basis points' is 2,36 per cent.

company in the US and you want to buy a machine in Europe which you have ordered for delivery in six months. To know how much it's going to cost in a period when the euro has been steadily climbing, you buy a 'futures' contract for X euros today at a guaranteed price for delivery in six months. Or, for a small fee, you could purchase an 'option' to buy the euros in six months at today's rate. If the euros cost less then, you would choose not to exercise your option and just buy them at the going rate.

Compared with the purely speculative activity that makes its thin profits on small price spreads between currencies, these practical, real economy foreign exchange purchases are negligible. Most transactions on forex markets take place within a day, if not hours or minutes, and on the currency markets a week is eternity.* One could perfectly well exempt 'real economy' transactions from the tax, though I think this would be more trouble than it would be worth.

If the main objective of a transaction tax is to reduce speculation and stabilize markets, then the rate should be a bit higher – this was Tobin's goal. If it's to raise money for the environment and social progress, it should be lower, to the point where no one could possibly object.† This would be my priority, but the debate is open. We also talk about a 'Tobin–Spahn tax', since Professor Paul Bernd Spahn proposed to accompany the transaction tax with a 'circuit breaker' tax in cases where speculation gets out of hand. This is a high, punitive tax that kicks in automatically if the value of a particular currency moves up or down too far and too fast, beyond certain pre-established limits.

---

* 'Flash trading' takes place in a second or two and requires the most sophisticated, speediest computers.
† Of course the usual suspects would still object no matter how low the rate, because it's the principle of introducing international taxation that scares them.

Recall the wave of crises of the late 1990s that began in Asia, spread to Latin America and also infected countries like Russia and Turkey. In such cases, the central banks of even relatively wealthy countries like Thailand or Chile were completely powerless to defend their currencies with their own reserves. That's another reason we need international taxation, or at least very high exit taxes – 50 per cent or more – if capital is withdrawn within, say, less than a year after it was invested. The IMF has forced countries to drop exit taxes so as to leave capital entirely free to go where it likes as fast as it pleases, but the only countries in Asia that weathered the earlier crises were China and Malaysia, which applied them.

The Tobin–Spahn tax could protect national currencies against speculative attacks. These are far more frequent than most people realize: the International Labour Organization, which defines 'serious' as a drop in the value of a country's currency of 35 per cent or more within two months, has counted over ninety 'serious financial crises' between 1990 and 2002.[17]

How many times in the past ten years have I heard that collecting an international tax on financial transactions would be impossible because it would require legislation in every country in the world. This is another convenient but completely false argument against transactions taxes. The tax is applied to the currency itself, not to the legal jurisdiction or territory. A little-known institution called the Continuous Linked Settlement system settles these transactions every day and deals with seventeen currencies and 95 per cent of all transactions globally. The system is regulated by the Federal Reserve of New York. Since its PVP, or 'payment versus payment', system handles the buy/sell transactions simultaneously, it is foolproof and cheat-proof, and it could easily collect the tax at the point of settlement. Collection would be a matter of adding a few lines of software code.

The decision of a central bank to tax trades in its own currency can also be unilateral – the European Central Bank could decide tomorrow to levy a tax on all euro purchases. There is no need for universality. Brazil has a small tax on trades in its currency, the real. The transaction tax can and should easily be applied to purchases on other financial markets such as stocks and bonds as well; the United Kingdom already has a stamp tax of this kind. Transaction tax proposals have been around for a long time and happily are becoming more mainstream. After extended hearings, Belgium passed well-thought-out legislation for such a tax that could be used as a template by other parliaments. At a United Nations meeting in September 2004, over a hundred countries signed on for a transaction tax resolution sponsored by France, Spain, Brazil and Chile. Jacques Chirac was a champion of the idea and, to everyone's surprise, just before the German elections in September 2009, both the Social Democrat Frank Walter Steinmeier and Chancellor Angela Merkel came out in favour of it.

Even Gordon Brown wanted to join the growing chorus in favour of an international tax on financial transactions and recommended it to G-20 finance ministers in November 2009. He immediately got his wrist slapped by the US Treasury, the European Central Bank and Dominique Strauss-Kahn, head of the IMF, using specious arguments, and Brown backed down. Contrary to the lies still being put about, international taxes present no technical problems. The obstacles are purely political. Tax experts know exactly how to assess and apply international taxes, but bankers and those who support them fear the thin end of the wedge if any such measures at any rate are allowed.

The far more modest airplane ticket tax to finance the fight against HIV/AIDS, tuberculosis and malaria is now applied by about eighteen countries and collected by a small

UN agency. Although not a huge money-maker and not what we were campaigning for, it shows at least that international taxation can work.

TAX HAVENS ARE HEAVEN

Tax havens are also of concern to everyone seeking a greener world, greater social justice and a fairer sharing of the tax burden. According to the Tax Justice Network,[18] these off-shore secrecy jurisdictions probably shelter at least $12 or 13 trillion ($13,000 billion) in private or corporate deposits, thus depriving governments of at least $250 billion a year in revenues. I think the French, Spanish and Italian expressions for 'tax havens' – fiscal *paradis/paraiso/paradiso* – probably stem from a confusion between the English 'haven' and 'heaven', but, if so, in this case the confusion is accurate. These financial hideouts do provide a heaven of secrecy and opacity as well as a haven for large fortunes, and they give transnational corporations (TNCs) myriad opportunities to escape taxes through a variety of complex dodges.

Most international trade transits at least once via a tax haven and, according to the OECD, at least 60 per cent of trade is intra-company – that is, it takes place between the subsidiaries of the same parent transnational corporation. These TNCs make constant use of 'transfer pricing' to reduce their taxes, charging goods and services to themselves at totally unrealistic prices in totally unrealistic jurisdictions. It's quite possible to pay a healthy proportion of one's advertising expenses in Jersey or of one's research and development costs in Bermuda. Why else would the defunct US energy company Enron have had 692 subsidiaries in the Cayman Islands? Why else would Citicorp still have over 400 there?

The transfer pricing objective is simple: shift profits

from high- to low-tax jurisdictions. Prem Sikka, a chartered accountant, explains how: a company can design its products in country A, manufacture in country B, test in country C, hold patents in country D and assign marketing rights to a subsidiary in country E. Such a structure gives corporations huge discretion in allocating costs to each country and shifts profits through internal trade.

Transnational corporations are one of the greatest untapped sources of financing for a green and social New Deal. Over the years they have grown more and more adept at wriggling out of the taxes they ought to be paying in both the North and the South. Here, for example, is a headline in the *New York Times* that dates from 2004: 'U.S. multinationals shift their tax burden: Profit taken in offshore havens rose 68% over 3 years, report finds'.[19] The story, quoting the journal *Tax Notes*, explains that the 68 per cent increase of profits taken in offshore havens occurred between 1999 and 2002 at the expense of high-tax countries such as Britain and Germany where the TNCs had substantial sales – to the tune of $149 billion in profits not taxed where the real economic action was. Luxembourg, Bermuda and Singapore figured prominently as convenient places for US companies to park their profits. By 2002, United States TNCs were already booking 58 per cent of their profits in tax havens as the Republican-dominated Congress (but also the previous Clinton administration) provided incentives to use offshore jurisdictions and eroded the capacity of the Internal Revenue Service to enforce the tax laws. Purely national companies which could not avoid national taxes were thus automatically placed at a competitive disadvantage.

Transnational corporations see taxes as costs to be avoided, not as necessary contributions to the common good. In other words, when they get an educated and healthy workforce, well-managed water, gas and electricity supplies, efficient public transport to bring their employees to the workplace and law enforcement to protect their property, the companies, unlike the rest of us, have paid for none of this.

Rich-country governments are obviously losing revenue because they have the highest taxes and thus give TNCs the greatest incentives for avoiding them. But the British charity Christian Aid believes that developing countries are also losing more than $160 billion in tax revenues a year, mostly because of transfer pricing strategies. Tax havens thus contribute directly to poverty and hunger, and they hit both the North and the South.[20]

ACCOUNTING ISN'T BORING

TNCs also use lax reporting standards of accounting to their advantage. You can find out as much, or as little, as you want to know about how they manipulate the system by checking out Richard Murphy's detailed report on 'Country by Country Reporting'.[21] Murphy is a chartered accountant and his report is about accounting, but don't let that put you off, because Country by Country, or CbC, is the cleanest way to get the TNCs to come clean. With different accounting standards they could be legally obliged to report the names of their subsidiaries in every country where they operate, as well as their sales, purchases, labour costs, employee numbers and the taxes actually paid in each jurisdiction. The information would be public, and anyone, including their shareholders but particularly the tax authorities, could see at a glance that something fishy was going on if, for example, they reported that 30 per cent of their profits were earned in some small jurisdiction with insignificant sales and a zero tax rate.

It's more complicated than that, and the required information is more complex than the little I've cited, but, according to Murphy, and I believe him, putting these declarations in the public domain would make these giant corporations transparent and accountable, contribute to making trade fairer, reduce corruption, encourage genuine development and improve government revenues, particularly in the weaker states of the South. It would also ensure that their corporate social responsibility (CSR) talk was not just palaver and window dressing. Corporate types who like to go on about CSR should be reminded that social responsibility begins with paying one's taxes. I once reminded an audience of this from the platform at a CSR conference in Austria, whereupon my neighbour on the panel gave me a horrified look and explained, as he might to a small, not very bright child, that his job was to reduce his clients' taxes to the maximum, something I already knew. Murphy would add that transnational corporations should compete for the Man Booker Prize on the grounds that their accounts are works of fiction.

Tax sheltering and avoidance is a huge industry made up of people who know how to push the law to the limit while generally keeping their clients technically honest. The United States Senate in 2005 issued a blistering report in which it found three of the four largest transnational accounting firms – KPMG, PricewaterhouseCoopers and Ernst & Young (Deloitte somehow escaped) – guilty of a whole series of borderline or overtly illegal actions in avoiding US taxes for their clients, particularly through the creation and marketing of a series of tax shelters.[22]

Law firms and banks also attracted sharp Senate criticism for their facilitation and financing of tax dodges. Such ventures have naturally continued since this report was issued: the Bush years did nothing to control them and everything to encourage them. Meanwhile, the Big Four accounting firms routinely received multi-million dollar fees for approving, without raising an eyebrow, the accounts of banks and financial houses that later proved to be riddled with toxic assets. This has not stopped the United States government from retaining these very firms to help manage its TARP, or Troubled Assets Relief Program.

Well, the laws could be changed and the accountants could find other work helping the TNCs to prepare their Country by Country reports. Richard Murphy even shows them how. He is on the right track and the right side, but unfortunately, while the United States has its own set of too-flexible rules, the International Accounting Standards Board (IASB) now sets accounting rules in over a hundred countries, including the twenty-seven members of the European Union. This organization sounds quite official, public-spirited and impartial until you discover there's a slight problem with it.

The IASB is a private, privately funded group based in London, heavily dependent on the familiar Big Four transnational accounting firms, and it is not subject to government oversight or regulation of any kind. In January 2009, perhaps conscience-stricken, IASB set up a 'monitoring board' composed of public figures to oversee its 'trustees', who do the actual work of standard setting and are mostly top present or former accounting executives, plus present or former CEOs of transnational corporations such as Lafarge (cement) and Repsol (oil).

How much would you be willing to bet that this group will devise strict standards to govern the TNCs' accounting practices and that the TNCs themselves are eager to adopt Country by Country reporting? And how was it possible to give such an important task to a private body with no representation of public interests? The European Union, recognizing the need for common accounting standards to cover all the companies listed on the various European stock exchanges, gave the job of devising them to the International Accounting Standards Committee – an obscure group of private professionals of whom few had ever heard – which then quietly morphed into the now official board of the same name.

But surely these people are able to change hats and act for the common good? This is a doubtful proposition – transfer pricing is big business. Here is how one of the Big Four accounting firms, Ernst & Young, well represented on the IASB by its former chairman, markets its services:

> Successfully managing business and tax issues related to transfer pricing involves much more than documentation compliance. Transfer pricing affects almost every aspect of an MNE [multinational enterprise] and can significantly impact its worldwide tax burden. Our . . . professionals help MNEs address this burden . . . with leading solutions. Our multidisciplinary team helps MNEs develop transfer pricing strategies, tax-effective solutions, and controversy management approaches that best fit their objectives.[23]

Ernst & Young employs 900 professionals in its transfer pricing department alone. Perhaps it would be a good idea to provide them with some controversy and give the 'controversy management approaches' people something to do?

The G-20, true to form, has already expressed its full support for the International Accounting Standards Board and entrusted it with more power and prestige.

TRAFFIC, TRADE AND GREEN TECHNOLOGY

I wish we could also collect a tax on the miles travelled by our food between the producer and our kitchens. The voyages of vegetables and the peregrinations of potatoes should be put under control, and the best way is to try to eat as locally as possible, using the small farmer producer-to-consumer networks that are expanding in many countries. Most packaged foods, however, are still going to come from far away, and I don't see how we can be responsible consumers unless we have some way of measuring their environmental impact. In other words, we need an honest labelling system.

In a general way, both transport and trade have to be part of a green solution, and the rules of the World Trade Organization must be rethought if we hope to save the climate. Without being an addict of the 'technological fix', one should recognize that technology will be an important part of the green conversion package and cannot be rationed in a business-as-usual fashion if we are to survive.

Green tech must be not only financed in its various places of origin, sometimes using subsidies, but also traded and exported rapidly – as many people and countries as possible have got to be able to use it as fast as possible. Inventors and patent-holders are no longer lonely, obsessed men in makeshift garage labs – they are mostly corporations, and, if they insist on collecting royalties on every environmental technology for twenty years, as the Trade Related Intellectual Property (or 'TRIPs') agreement of the World Trade Organization specifically allows them to do, then the right equipment will never spread fast enough and coal-fired power plants will continue to supply energy to 80 per cent of the world. Either the rules of the TRIPs must change, or someone else must subsidize at least a part of the clean-tech transfer costs. And, since we in the West have 200 years of dirty development experience behind us, it seems to me we should help the rest of the world to catch up without forcing other countries to transit into the twenty-first century via the nineteenth. We also have the most power to change the trade rules.

The WTO is now timidly suggesting that, if some countries refuse to limit their CO^2 emissions, trading partners who accept to limit theirs might be allowed to apply compensatory taxes at their borders on the products of non-compliers. Ecological protectionism is a sensible idea and should increase rewards to virtue while penalizing vice.

EUROBONDS FOR EURONEEDS

Bonds issued by stable, wealthy governments are considered among the most reliable investments on earth. In times of uncertainty, people flock to them: witness the boom in US Treasury bonds despite the increasingly scary levels of debt the government has already incurred. Rich-country governments are expected to pay yearly interest without fail and give you back your capital at the end of a specified period; their bonds are therefore 'widows and orphans' investments *par excellence*. Some European investors (including my late French husband's grandfather) were hit by the Russian Revolution, which rendered their decorative Imperial Russian gold bond certificates worthless, but such events are rare.

If you want to invest in riskier bonds, you will get a higher interest rate if your chosen banana republic continues to pay – bonds are all appraised by our friends the ratings agencies, from AAA right down to the lowliest 'junk bond' level. For governments and companies, they provide a convenient way to borrow directly from the public and are marketed not by the companies or the governments themselves but by investment banks such as Goldman Sachs. If the European Union were to issue bonds they would be snapped up instantly, because little risk would be involved and because they would be a sound and sought-after alternative to those of the US Treasury. But Europe doesn't issue bonds (the Roman Curia, mentioned earlier as a competitor for 'most conservative institution', doesn't either).

Either the European Union's members have some sense of solidarity with fellow members or it's every small, poor, beleaguered country for itself. When Ireland and Greece fell afoul of the financial markets, with Portugal, Spain and Italy rapidly targeted as well, individual country sovereign debt in the eurozone was finally recognized as a source of instability. Other countries are likely to follow, and euro-countries cannot devalue their currencies individually so as to escape via higher exports and lower-value interest payments. The unpalatable choice is between exiting the euro and austerity, and, so far, they have chosen austerity, causing the less well-off in their societies to pay for the financial crisis yet again. I think going back to drachmas, pesetas, lire and what-have-you would be disastrous: the financial markets could pick them off one by one, forcing them to pay huge interest rates and accept massive unemployment – as Finland learned to its cost in the early 1990s before it joined the euro. Ask the Eastern Europeans who are not euro-group members. The EU imposes strict disciplines on such erring member states as Greece and tries to force them back into the iron arms of the Stability Pact, but it takes no responsibility at all for the vulnerable non-euro members, thus strengthening the arguments of those who say they were only admitted in the first place as reservoirs of cheap labour and low taxes.

No one is defending excessive government spending, particularly when huge amounts were spent on weapons purchases, as in Greece. But it's not fair either to look only on the expenditures side of the ledger. Revenues have also got to be improved through such already noted measures as taxing the Greek Orthodox Church and rich Greeks and forcing companies to come home from Cyprus. Above all, the European Central Bank should be lending to governments at 1 per cent – that is, at the same rate it charges banks. Europe also needs a budget worthy of the name – not the present measly 1 per cent of GDP. By way of comparison, the United States federal budget is 20 per cent of GDP.

Another way to counter these harmful effects that further deepen the inequalities between EU member states would be to issue European Union-level bonds. Many EU governments and even the IMF, with which I rarely find myself in agreement, think this could be a good idea. But Germany doesn't. As the largest, richest state in the Union, it doesn't want to have to pay, ever, if some other EU country gets into serious financial trouble. Yet, a country like Greece represents only 2 per cent of Europe's GDP, it's not a threat to anyone, and if European Union bonds existed then those troubled countries would be able to borrow more cheaply instead of paying high interest rates to their bondholders precisely because they're in trouble. It's a vicious circle. A country hard hit by the crisis is in debt and needs to borrow. To be able to borrow, it has to pay its creditors high rates. So it spends more paying them back than on fixing its economy. So it stays in trouble, and around we go again.

There must be some way to circumvent this dilemma, and Daniel Gros and Stefano Marcossi may have found it. In a short, sharp piece, they observe, quite rightly, that the European Union is sinking into recession as businesses cease to invest, consumers to consume and banks to lend. Meanwhile, although they panicked when the US subprime crisis spread to Europe and the European banking sector nearly collapsed, leaders have since relaxed and are no longer even paying lip service to forging a coordinated response. Instead they are going their separate ways with their different policies and divergent ways of implementing them. This, say Gros and Marcossi, is foolish because financial stability has definitely not yet been restored.[24]

Meanwhile, a great many European banks are already seriously exposed to the shaky European 'periphery' (not just Greece but, for example, Austrian banks). Sometimes these risks go even beyond risky Eastern Europe and right into financial-morass territory, such as Turkey, Ukraine and Iceland. These euro-zone banks hold something like $1,500 billion worth of dodgy claims and are closing the loan window to their erstwhile clients, thereby increasing the likelihood of the latter's default and of their own losses.

Gros and Micossi argue that the European Union is going to have to step in and save them or risk the dislocation of Europe itself. Where will it find the funds to provide balance of payments support in an emergency? This is what the IMF is doing now, under draconian conditions which, as usual, weaken the weak countries even more. 'Case-by-case' solutions along IMF lines won't work, so Europe should 'tap the gigantic global capital flows that more than ever are now in search of safety'. The euro and European financial markets would benefit from fresh incoming capital. Since the European Central Bank, so far at least, refuses to undertake such a change, 'the EU should set up a massive European Financial Stability Fund', which could then issue bonds with the explicit guarantee of member states. The cost of such a fund would be much less than if each country had to set up its own stimulus package, and Germany, which now objects to European bonds, would be the biggest winner because its banks would be the biggest customers and its export industries would gain the most from stabilization in Eastern European markets.

Gros and Micossi want to house the European Financial Stability Fund in the European Investment Bank because it is a solid institution, an agency that belongs to EU governments, and it already has the expertise for issuing bonds. They think investors would have such a huge appetite for this paper that the euro would displace the dollar as the world reserve currency. They also want – wrongly in my view – to close down the European Financial Stability Fund 'once financial markets operate normally again'.

But what if one conceived these bonds differently? Let's look seriously at the premise of these authors. If all those international investors really did beat down the doors to buy euro-bonds, and if the European Central Bank couldn't prevent it, why on earth close down the fund once the banks had drunk their fill? That would be insane. Such bonds should finance the Great Green Works programmes that no European country, not even the richest, could possibly undertake alone. Think of the possibilities: intra-European green transport and communications networks, renewable energy distribution systems, multinational green-industrial research poles, waste-transformation and recycling extraction facilities – the opportunities are endless.

If Europe doesn't soon decide to do something along these lines, the rotten assets can rot the whole system and the weaker EU countries will be left to the wolves and the vultures. Europe will miss its chance and in twenty years will be the place where rich Asians come to visit the museums and eat the delicacies – at least until the climate refugees overwhelm us – but wait! This is an optimistic chapter and I intend to keep it that way.

THE FUTURE

It would take too long here to enter into the debate that has found a niche in many societies and is called in French '*décroissance*', or 'de-growth'.[25] Elsewhere people speak of 'voluntary simplicity' or even my favourite, 'alternative hedonism', which certainly sounds sexy in an intellectual sort of way. Beyond the individual level, it means reducing economic activity, using fewer raw materials and less energy, producing fewer goods, and so on. Many people have written and continue writing on these questions, and

I wish them well. For reasons I've already touched on, this chapter is not about individual solutions, nor do I intend to repeat the arguments of the de-growth movement which are readily available. I am trying to write here about how to *scale up the response to the gravest problem that has ever confronted humanity*, but this in no way invalidates the worth or necessity of individual efforts or of reducing economic 'throughput'.

I agree with the obvious postulate that material growth cannot continue forever, although the growth of education, culture, music, games, information, friendship, love can. Remember Kenneth Boulding's observation that, 'to believe that the economy can grow indefinitely on a finite planet, you have to be a madman or an economist.' It's now common knowledge that we're already using more resources than the planet can provide and drawing down our environmental capital. I expect you already know the arguments about needing three to five planets if everyone were to live as Europeans and US citizens do. Yes, we are destroying natural capital, but that is also because a large part of our economic activity is a cost rather than a benefit to us. 'Growth' is encouraged by having more automobile accidents, cancer cases and, when they can be arranged, wars. Clearly we need a GPI, or genuine progress indicator, rather than a GDP, or gross domestic product, which tells us little or nothing about the real state of our economies. All this and more has been endlessly repeated, alas to relatively little effect.

The best theoretical analysis by far in my view is Herman Daly's *Steady-State Economics*. If you don't know Daly's work, please put down this book now and look him up (but please return to this book afterwards; I'm not quite finished). What's more, he writes clearly and often amusingly despite the seriousness of his subject. Another splendid book was published in 1997 by the ecological scientist and thinker Ernst-Ulrich von Weizsäcker. Called *Factor Four* (*Faktor Vier*), it promised, and delivered, the ideas and techniques needed to reduce raw material throughput by half while doubling wealth and well-being. Weizsäcker told me he had wanted to call his book 'Factor Ten' because he was convinced you could both divide resources and multiply wealth by five – but his publisher refused, saying no one would believe it. I did – particularly because all of the practical techniques he put forward already existed twelve years ago. His latest book has now appeared in English: called *Factor Five*, it reinforces his previous arguments.

Concrete ideas and encouragements spur action, but hectoring and trying to shame people into ecologically correct behavioural change produce the opposite effect. George Monbiot, in one of his invariably brilliant pieces for *The Guardian*, thinks resistance to change has a lot to do with the way our brains are wired. He quotes scientific authorities to the effect that following the routine, like driving along a familiar road, is a job for the brain's basal ganglia, the cerebral automatic pilots that use much less energy than the prefrontal cortex, the part of the brain to which we turn for more difficult, unusual tasks. The problem is that we perceive greater use of brain energy just as we perceive pain. So the answer to why we resist change is literally a no-brainer: because it's painful. Exhortation won't help – at least not at the mass level.

Monbiot goes on to say that 'everything we need to do [for the environment] has been made harder by debt'. The national debt of the UK is set to hit 150 per cent of GDP by the end of 2010, and two awful consequences ensue: there's no money left to fund a green new deal and the only way to pay back the debt is to resume economic growth. Monbiot sees the only solution in cutting back on useless government expenditures, above all arms production and defence spending, particularly as wars make the country not more but less safe. His conclusion is unassailable: 'Last time we faced a crisis on the scale of the global climate crash, the rational solution was to build tanks. Now the rational, least painful solution is to stop building tanks, and use the money to address a real threat.'[26]

We managed to build the tanks and it cured the Depression of the 1930s. Now, much as I agree with Monbiot that reducing defence spending would be a great leap forward, I hope to have shown that it's not the only way to pay for the environmental conversion we need, not only in individual countries but worldwide, including the new industrial powerhouses such as India and China. Voluntary simplicity will work even less in places where a relatively large proportion of the population still lives in dire poverty and where the emerging middle classes can't wait to taste the delights of the Western-style good life. It won't even fly for majorities in the West with far higher per capita incomes, because the basal ganglia will be doing their usual humdrum, probably destructive jobs, but sparing us pain.

Forty years ago, the biologist Garrett Hardin made a hugely influential speech to the American Association for the Advancement of Science entitled 'The Tragedy of the Commons'.[27] His objective was basically to advocate limiting population growth through coercion, just as we limit bank robbery through law because money is not a free good of which everyone can take as much as they want. Nor can people have as many children as they want, because the 'commons' is now the whole planet.

Hardin believed that appealing to conscience was useless and built his argument on the metaphor of the common pasture, where each 'rational herdsman' will try to take advantage of all the others by adding one extra animal after another – to be imitated, naturally, by all the other herdsmen, until the common pasture collapses. In his view, the only effective strategy to counter such phenomena is mutual constraint. Too bad Hardin's purpose was to prevent 'over-breeding' through coercion rather than taking his 'commons' argument in the opposite direction.

People cooperate when they know they are part of a group, feel strong ties to the other members of that group and have a say in managing the common resource. One can call it 'mutual constraint' – I prefer 'mutual support' or 'coopera-tion': what is clear is that groups can and do manage their common resources efficiently and productively, so long as they can collectively decide who can and cannot be a member of the group. This is crucial and has been proven over and over, from medieval pastures to present-day Maine lobster fisheries to Indian forests. This doesn't mean the commons dwellers are more noble or worthier than the rest of us – they simply realize they're going to remain a member of their group for the foreseeable future. Maybe you can afford to cheat or be unfair to someone you will probably never see again, but you can't do that if you are going to be dealing with the same people day after day. In that case, reciprocity is the only strategy for guaranteeing your own survival, much less prosperity. But, in order to work, the group has to retain the right to say who is a member and who isn't, and this is what capitalism and World Bank global manager-types can't tolerate. They intervene more and more in the allocation of resources along 'all for ourselves and nothing for other people' lines.

There are other solutions, from the individual to the institutional level, and the social psychologist Mark van Vugt proposes another perspective on commons management in today's world. He too confirms what we know about the impacts of inequality. He says that it is even possible to appeal to our better natures and pull back from the 'all for ourselves', 'grab what I can now' mentality. For that to happen, we must perceive that our societies are fair and trust other people: these are the indispensable preconditions for cooperation. Van Vugt offers the '4i' framework of information, identity, institutions and incentives as a plan of action to combat global environmental disaster. People must have accurate *information* on how bad a situation is (for example, if they know how bad the drought is, they save more water) and what they can do about, say, resource conservation or energy saving (information on recycling or buying an A-rated electrical appliance instead of a B- or C-rated one). In psychological experiments, people manage a fixed supply (of money, of food, etc.) much better than if it fluctuates. Uncertainty leads people to underestimate the damage their actions can cause so they need accurate information.

Identity means feeling one is a part of a group, like the Maine lobstermen – but it can also be more anonymous, like a neighbourhood. A US energy company started sending out invoices with a smiley or frowny face to tell its customers if they were consuming more or less than the neighbourhood average. Consumption was reduced dramatically.* People like to compare themselves favourably with others. Polluting companies or institutions can be effectively named, shamed and compared into changing their behaviour.

Institutions, like people, may or may not be perceived as trustworthy: when the British railways were privatized, many did not trust that the network would be run efficiently and fairly and switched back to driving. *Incentives* work too when they punish overuse and reward responsible

---

* Mark van Vugt (Free University of Amsterdam and Oxford and Kent universities in the UK), 'Triumph of the commons', *New Scientist*, 22 August 2009. He doesn't say, but I wonder if this energy company was public. A private one would have had no interest in reducing energy consumption with the smiley–frowny comparisons.

behaviour, but economic incentives appear not to make much difference if people are already committed to a greener lifestyle. Government subsidies, can, however, encourage that commitment.

Going green requires more equality and more trust, as well as institutions that contribute to both. This is the way the individual and the local can be linked to, and have a bearing on, the global. For me, hope lies in identifying all the ways we can find to scale up the local so that it becomes regional, national and global, so that it mobilizes and motivates everyone in a conscious effort to make our societies fairer and more cohesive, just as happened during the Second World War. The environmental threat to us may seem more diffuse and more distant than that of war, but this illusion will soon be dissipated by events if it hasn't been already.

To undertake a genuine clean, green and *fast* conversion, we need money, and I've suggested some ways to find it. But, more than money, more than machinery or technology or political incentives, I still believe that, in the end, if anything saves us it will be the *mythos* – not a lie, a legend or a fairy tale, but the grand narrative a disenchanted world cries out for. It will be the song everyone can sing together, telling us we can behave like intelligent, sentient, loving human beings, the song that unites us in belief, the hope that gives strength and links us to a future promising not perfection – not utopia, but a world at once rational and beautiful, with enough space and a good life for all. Yes, sings the *mythos*, in hundreds of languages, in every key, in scores of countries, Yes, we can.

CONCLUSION

In 1919, an Italian immigrant who had arrived penniless in Boston a dozen years earlier perpetrated a financial fraud that ever since has borne his name. Other con-men had operated similar scams since at least the seventeenth century, but Charles Ponzi brought off the biggest swindle of his time before being caught and jailed. The Ponzi or pyramid scheme operates with one simple rule: you make good on your promises to those who come in first using the fresh funds supplied by those who come in later. Finally, no 'greater fools' can be enticed to give you their money and the pyramid crumbles. Bernie Madoff's caper lasted for decades but was simply a far more ambitious and rather more sophisticated Ponzi scheme. The twenty-first century has added a new twist: it has made scams, dressed up with triple A ratings and fancy mathematics, legal. Now the entire system is based on illusion, and it has also sought and found greater fools in ever more exotic places. Our unaccountable Ponzi people, our corporate and media elites, our weak-willed, banker-infiltrated governments and high-level international bureaucrats who together make up the Davos class have come together to plunge the world to the bottom of the bathtub. You can almost hear the poor planet gasping and spluttering as it tries to emerge, like a prisoner being water-boarded. This near-drowning is far from the first of the neoliberal era; there were many dress rehearsals, but they never quite did the trick of killing the prisoner and inflicting total, worldwide devastation.

And yet the financial fiascos are accelerating in frequency and severity with more and more devastating social consequences. A quick list of the worst in recent years could start in 1982 with the Mexican default that triggered the third world debt crisis still plaguing many of the poorest countries. The unravelling of US Savings & Loans (equivalent to the building societies in the UK) began in 1985–6, lasted well into the 1990s, caused 745 S&L failures and cost the government about $130 billion. On 19 October 1987, the Dow Jones stock index nosedived by 23 per cent, wiping out about a trillion dollars' worth of paper wealth before spreading to other markets. Japan has been in the economic doldrums the longest, beginning in 1990 and lasting to this day.

Major currency crises struck about ninety developing countries from the early 1990s, culminating in the 1997–8 Asian financial debacle and the virtual shutdown of Thailand, Korea, Indonesia and several other countries. It then leapfrogged as far as Russia, Turkey, Argentina and beyond. In each case, speculators attacked, governments spent all their foreign exchange reserves trying to save their currency, businesses failed massively, and unemployment, poverty and destitution rose inexorably.

Back in the USA, the energy giant Enron had been systematically cooking its books, setting up hundreds of real or fake subsidiaries in the Cayman Islands, borrowing heavily and trading in every conceivable resource while looting the public purse and its employees' pension funds as a benevolent White House looked on. Enron had to admit in late 2001 that it had overstated its profits by the bagatelle of $567 million and understated its debts by a cool $25 billion. The 'dot.com' bubble was meanwhile steadily inflating: at the turn of the millennium the overvalued stocks of high-tech Silicon Valley companies began to tank, eventually bringing down the stock market by half.[1] Our very own misnamed subprime crisis that took off in 2007 inaugurated the latest and most severe in the series, with the sovereign debt crisis in Europe hard on its heels.

We know, as surely as we know that lightning will continue to strike, that highly leveraged debt, deregulation, shadow banking, excessive risk-taking and unalloyed greed, so long as they are left free to wreak havoc, will provoke other break-downs. We know that concentration in the financial industry and the implicit or explicit guarantee of government bailouts will encourage ever greater risk-taking and hasten the next disaster. The world is now more often in crisis than out of it, thus proving once more that the term 'crisis' scarcely applies. This landscape of sharp peaks and deep valleys is the place where we live today and, if nothing changes, tomorrow.

Nor have these breakdowns remained cloistered in the financial districts. They have concentrated wealth in fewer hands and imposed the most savage social and economic inequalities since before the Second World War. Although people can be exploited in a hundred different ways by our present system, today it's almost a privilege to be exploited by an employer – it means that at least you have a job. Access to necessities of life, such as adequate food and clean – or even dirty – water, has also moved beyond the reach of a sizeable fraction of humanity and threatens their survival. In such a situation, conflicts are inevitable; many are already occurring to secure a place under the ever more blazing sun.

We inflict such grave damage on the earth that our planet can no longer passively accept the abuse. It is reacting, gradually making the very possibility of human existence more fragile, more problematic. The force of positive feedbacks is also intensifying. Each of the ills we have examined in these pages worsens the others in ways often impossible to predict or measure until too late; they all strengthen the walls of the prison.

My purpose here has been to delineate those walls and to trace ways of escaping this prison where we are kept under lock and key, not just by governments or financial institutions but also by newly minted authorities such as the G-20. Strangely, they all appear to believe they know what the future holds and that they are equipped to deal with it, using the same tools as in the past, allowing the same devastating forces to remain in place, refusing to impose binding rules and structural change. They refuse to recognize we are on a knife-edge, that the crises they pretend are separate are in fact coalescing. Nor do they understand that 'next time', whatever and whenever that may be, will be worse. It could even be what the philosopher-urbanist Paul Virilio has called the 'integral accident'.

Civilizations are mortal. This too we have known at least since Paul Valéry pointed it out after the First World War.* Yet present rulers forget this too. Their eyes are not on the spectacular failures of the past like Babylon, Athens, Rome or Teotihuacan; they do not remember that every era's great powers can slide from magnificence to decay in a few decades if not a few years. Rather than learning from the ancient or the more recent past, our institutions and the people in charge of them cling to the illusion that they

---

* 'Nous autres civilisations savons maintenant que nous sommes mortelles.' Also Shelley's sonnet 'Ozymandias' of 1817, quoted in full on p. 198.

can shape the future without taking seriously the realities and the dangers of the present. And yet, if we don't take them seriously, the increasing complexity of our societies will drag us inevitably down. We pride ourselves on the efficiency of our systems, but the search for efficiency and the relentless drive for maximum profits leaves no slack, no play, no space in the system for mistakes, for accidents or the improbable.

Every cultivated field must produce a maximum without fallow or rest; every worker must be infinitely flexible; every factory must produce at lowest cost or perish; every bank must out-risk its rivals. Hundreds of millions are excluded because they are 'not productive enough' or 'cost too much'. Hundreds of millions more produce and consume so little that they serve little or no purpose in a capitalist marketplace. They are dispensable or worse; their perceived uselessness is nothing but another drag on the system. As far as the rich are concerned, so long as they accept to do so quietly, they can rot. If they protest, they will be dealt with. The rich can do without them. Our societies are stretched financially, economically, socially, ecologically to the breaking point and we have no shock absorbers.

If your body or brain suffers degeneration or injury, often another seemingly redundant function can take over and compensate for the loss, but when systems – of food supply, water, communications, sanitation, energy, disease prevention, transport, housing, and so on – are stretched too tight, and become too complex, a minor shock can shake the entire structure. The longer the supply chain for some vital component, the more potential points of failure it possesses. The more we allow individual life and social support systems to deteriorate, the greater the probability of their breakdown, spilling over and infecting the whole.

You have surely heard of the 'butterfly effect' – in which the beating of a tiny creature's wings is supposed to be sufficient, through successive amplifications, to cause a hurricane halfway around the world. Others may refer to the older, more proverbial image of the kingdom lost for want of a nail.* I prefer to think about 'self-organized criticality', a more general scientific expression of the way systems react to stress as a central concept that helps us better to understand both our prison and our means of escape.

The concept of self-organized criticality allows us to look at a system – any system – and recognize that it can reach a critical point and change profoundly its properties when a single, seemingly insignificant element is added at some unpredictable point in its evolution. The simplest example of a critically organized system, and the one used most often, is the sandpile with a steep gradient. As each extra grain of sand falls on the pile, its instability increases. One grain may, now and then, trigger a minor movement, but nothing much happens until finally a single extra grain triggers a major avalanche and the system 'resets' itself ; the slope of the sandpile will be much less steep and it will reset to a much more stable state. No grain of sand or snowflake or drop of water has special properties – all are, by themselves, insignificant. But as the instability of the system, whatever it is, increases, so do the chances that one small element can provoke a critical event – an avalanche, a blizzard or a flood.

A sandpile is a simple structure; it's mostly orderly and stable, but if it continues to grow it will always reach, at some point, the brink of chaos. A system in a state of self-organized criticality is one that lies somewhere on that boundary between

---

* For want of a nail a shoe was lost, for want of a shoe a horse was lost, for want of a horse a rider was lost, for want of a rider a battle was lost, for want of a battle a kingdom was lost – and all for want of a horseshoe nail.

order and chaos. Earthquakes, avalanches and, perhaps more surprisingly, forest fires also behave that way. At some unpredictable point the critical moment arrives, the system is plunged into disorder, instability and turbulence, then settles down again in some new, less complex, more nearly stable state. Critical systems have another important property:

> Even though individual sand avalanches are impossible to predict, their overall distribution is regular [and] avalanches of all possible sizes occur. They also follow a 'power law' distribution which means bigger avalanches happen less often than smaller avalanches, according to a strict mathematical ratio. [For example,] earthquakes of magnitude 5.0 on the Richter scale happen 10 times as often as quakes of magnitude 6.0 and 100 times as often as quakes of magnitude 7.0.[2]

Self-organized criticality hit the scientific scene only in 1987, but now scientists are finding these systems operating far beyond the physics of sandpiles and avalanches – in fact they are being discovered just about everywhere. The analytical tools self-organized criticality gives us seem to apply to the dynamics of biological evolution and of periodic mass extinctions of life – or to the human brain, whose networks of cells seem to alternate between periods of orderly calm and 'avalanches' of electrical activity at unpredictable moments. Some believe that self-organized criticality also applies to historic events. Civilizations too may exist on the brink of chaos.

I claim no scientific expertise; my own approach is through analogy alone, but I do not find it in the least absurd to believe that modern financial systems and governmental laxity positively *invite* periodic and repeated plunges into chaos. We do not even give them time to 'reset' in some more stable configuration acquired thanks to bailouts before they head off once more on the path to chaos.

I also see the disintegration of order at work in increasing inequalities and concentrations of wealth. Recall all the demonstrable outcomes of huge inequalities – lower life expectancies, poor health, mental illness, more crime, more prisoners, and so on – all these are signals of mounting chaos. Each added sand grain of injustice leads – at some unpredictable point – to social upheaval and breakdown.

It seems obvious as well that climate change is an incremental phenomenon in which the system of the biosphere appears to be stable but undergoes relatively small but steady additions of greenhouse gases. Positive feedbacks increase their impact on humans, as in the increasing severity of storms, droughts and floods, but also on the biospheric system itself – the more it heats up, the more greenhouse gases are ejected into the atmosphere. For example, the melting permafrost in Siberia is releasing millions of tonnes of methane, a far more powerful gas than CO_2. Without immediate, radical and conscious human intervention, the system can only collapse and reset itself – perhaps at a point incompatible with civilized life or with human life itself.

Once you start thinking in terms of self-organized systems and the critical events that punctuate their existence, you begin seeing them everywhere. Take a practical example such as European governments bickering, say, about fishing rights. Pretty soon, amid the futile words, as one fish species after another reaches the critical point, the stocks suddenly collapse. Then there is nothing left to argue about.

Could the collapse of entire civilizations follow a similar pattern? Are our own systems so intrinsically unstable that, unbeknown to those whose existence depends on them, they are approaching a critical moment? I believe they are, largely because we think they are so 'efficient'. So long as we define efficiency as faster, higher, bigger, tighter, richer, more concentrated and more connected, we are asking for trouble. In a word, the gradient of our sandpiles is too steep; our systems are growing too complex. They are therefore unpredictable and vulnerable to small accidents and events that may prove devastating. What we need is far more slack, to stop stretching the rubber band to the snapping point, to stop adding another card and then another to the house of cards, not understanding that feedbacks are at work and that they are steadily weakening the very structures we believe are strongest.

Mainstream economists still think you can keep adding another unit of growth or another tonne of CO_2 forever and the graph will always show a nice straight ascending line. No rational person should believe them. Especially if governments believe them, we will all be driven to chaos and be 'reset' at a much lower, more stable – and far less liveable – level. We cannot prevent chance occurrences, further negative inputs to our systems and 'tipping points', as the popular press has labelled self-organized criticality. We can, however, do two things. The first is to *introduce far more resilience into our systems* and stop stretching the rubber band so taut. In complex systems, resilience and genuine efficiency are the same thing. This means preventing accidents in so far as they can be foreseen and therefore exerting far more control over the more fragile systems such as banking. We can't allow unruly, irresponsible children to dump entire trucks full of sand on the sandpile just because they find it fun and momentarily profitable.

Social resilience means consciously striving for more equal, more inclusive societies with more public services, more social protection and more democratic participation of employees and consumers. The system that drives poverty, exclusion and inequality can be brought under greater control, so that winners do not take all but are constrained to share. Adam Smith's observation 'All for ourselves and nothing for other people seems in every age of the world to have been the vile maxim of the masters of mankind' must be consigned to the dustbin of history by cajoling or forcing the erstwhile masters to cooperate.

Resilience means back-up systems for food, water and energy supplies and incentives to encourage conservation, decentralization and maximum diversity. People must be helped to grow their food within systems adapted to the natural parameters of their own place and their own climate – not rigid, productivist and imported frameworks. And I cannot stress too strongly the need for a radical, massive and immediate conversion to renewable energy. Rules must be clear and democratically arrived at, they must be binding on everyone and they must carry severe penalties if broken. But extra-legal coercion and violence are bad because they reintroduce more 'noise' and unpredictability into complex systems. Democracy, on the contrary, builds flexibility and 'slack'.

To explain the second thing we can do, I need to end on another personal note. People often ask me 'What keeps you going?' It's true that I've spent decades writing, speaking and campaigning on issues I care passionately about. The banal answer to their question is simply that all the activists I know, including myself, are simply trying to achieve a more just world and to live honourably in the circumstances of their own time and place, which are the product of chance. But the longer I've done my work, the more I have realized that all kinds of work in all kinds of places is increasingly coalescing and forming a genuine movement which many now call the 'alter-globalization' movement, or the Movement for Global Justice. The name doesn't matter: what counts is that a great number of apparently isolated undertakings can, in time, form a critical mass.

No one can say when or even if they will provoke the self-organized critical moment in history, which probably will not be recognized at the exact date and hour it takes place anyway. But we are – of this I am sure – engaged in a new moment in the long history of human emancipation. No one can foresee, either, what action, what text, what organization, what person might be the grain of sand that changes the configuration of the whole. All of us are conscious, however, that we could not have done our own work without the presence of innumerable comrades, known and unknown.

This does not mean we feel we are somehow 'winning', and it's even rare to be able to prove progress. Happy is the social activist who can claim a victory – I have found victories elusive, partial and fleeting, especially when a temporarily outflanked but powerful adversary figures out how to get what he wants in a different way.

So, I am asked, why don't people like me grow discouraged? Sometimes we do – we wouldn't be human if we didn't. But I've known dozens, hundreds, who have continued, no matter what. Why? Are we simply fools? The explanation of my friend the late Teddy Goldsmith for persistence was simple: 'What else is there to do?' What indeed? But, beyond that, I believe one is justified in taking complexity theory and self-organized criticality seriously, even – perhaps especially – in social and political and economic systems. I know that I cannot predict or know today, or probably ever, what may be the impact of my actions. They may have none at all. One can make every effort not to leave the world as one found it and still have no guarantee of success. This is why I do not answer the recurrent question 'Are you optimistic or pessimistic?'

I am neither. I don't know the future. But I have hope and I believe, because of the certain existence of criticality, that my hope is not grounded merely in faith. Faith may comfort but may also be based on illusion, the irrational and the impossible. I prefer the world of reason, sense and possibility and to recognize that I might write something or reach someone with an idea; I might act or inspire others to take action of their own. I might be the crucial, though insignificant grain of sand that causes the system to reset in a pattern at once safer, greener, fairer, more humane and more civilized.

So might you.

Notes

Introduction

1   Adam Smith, *The Wealth of Nations*, Book III, Chapter IV; p. 512 in the Pelican Classic edition, ed. Andrew Skinner (Harmondsworth and New York: Penguin, 1974).

2   Susan George, *Hijacking America: How the Religious and Secular Right Changed What Americans Think* (Cambridge: Polity, 2008).

3   Jenny Anderson, 'Wall Street pursues profit in bundles of life insurance', *New York Times*, 'Back to Business' series, 6 September 2009, and Marshall Auerback and L. Randall Wray, *Banks Running Wild: The Subversion of Insurance by 'Life Settlements' and Credit Default Swaps*, Policy Note no. 2009/9, Levy Economies Institute, Bar College, New York, October 2009.

4   Andy Coghlan, 'You don't get many of those to the shekel', *New Scientist*, 26 May 2001 (a summary of an article in *Nature*, 411, 24 May 2001, p. 437).

5   Personal communication.

Chapter 1 The Wall of Finance

1 An author who does this admirably, with an almost day-to-day account of the build-up to meltdown, is the *Financial Times* journalist Gillian Tett in *Fool's Gold* (London: Little, Brown, 2009), which is highly informative and, if you enjoy market disasters, fun to read.

2 Hundreds of Hamilton's drawings can be found in the *New Yorker's* 'Cartoon Bank' on its site: www.cartoonbank.com. I have taken the cited captions from this bank, which provides great pleasures and needs no bailouts.

3 See Susan George, *Hijacking America: How the Religious and Secular Right Changed What Americans Think* (Cambridge: Polity, 2008).

4 For a graphic example, see *What's the Matter with Kansas: How Conservatives Won the Heart of America* (New York: Metropolitan Books, 2004), in which Thomas Frank shows how ordinary, ill-paid workers in dead-end jobs could be brought to identify culturally with the very people keeping them in their place.

5 International Labour Organization, *Economic Security for a Better World* (Geneva: ILO, 2004).

6 For a blow-by-blow description of the rise and eventual fall of the Glass–Steagall Act, see www.pbs.org/wgbh/pages/frontline/shows/wallstreet/weill/demise.html.

7 Gillian Tett and Paul J. Davies, 'Out of the shadows: how banking's hidden system broke down', *Financial Times*, 17 December 2007.

8 United Nations Conference on Trade and Development, *World Trade and Development Report 2009* (Geneva: United Nations, 2009), pp. 94–5. Gillian Tett, in *Fool's Gold*, explains how JPMorgan invented and launched and later suffered from these instruments.

9 Wolfgan Münchau, 'Time to outlaw naked credit default swaps', *Financial Times*, 28 February 2010.

10 Details can be found in the thorough investigation of the Center for Public Integrity: http://www.publicintegrity. org.

11 Dean Baker, 'Investigating the collapse: looking for the killer we already know', www.truthout.org, 1 June 2009.

12 Tett, *Fool's Gold*, p. 163.

13 Alan Greenspan, 'The Fed didn't cause the housing bubble', *Wall Street Journal*, 11 March 2009. The refutation by John Taylor is summarized in Susan Lee, 'It really is all Greenspan's fault', *Forbes*, 3 April 2009.

14 The 231-page report *Sold Out: How Wall Street and Washington Betrayed America* is the product of two US civil society organizations, Essential Information and the Consumer Education Foundation, which performed a notable public service in publishing it.

15 'Cash for trash', *New York Times*, 22 September 2008.

16 Center for Responsive Politics, Open Secrets Blog, 'TARP recipients paid out $114 million for politicking last year', www.opensecrets.org/news/2009/02/tarp-recipients-paid-out-114-m.html, 4 February 2009. Some of the juiciest returns went to Bank of America ($45 billion from TARP), Citigroup ($50 billion), AIG (a further $40 billion), and so on.

17 To download the reports (about 250 pages each) or consult the Treasury press releases, go to www.sigtarp.gov.

18 Barofsky in an interview with ABC News, 'Inspector general for TARP: Treasury Department is not being transparent', 22 July 2009.

19 Jason Palmer, 'Financial markets driven wild by hormones', *New Scientist*, 19 April 2008; Linda Geddes, 'Are good financial traders born, not made?', *New Scientist*, 14 January 2009. The investigators were John Coates and Joe Herbert at Cambridge, with additional information from Bruce McEwen of Rockefeller University

in New York. Both articles based on reports published in the *Proceedings of the National Academy of Sciences*: DOI: 10.0173/pnas.0704025105 and DOI: 10.1073/pnas.0810907106.

Chapter 2 The Wall of Poverty and Inequality

1 Eric Holt-Giménez and Raj Patel with Annie Shattuck, *Food Rebellions: Crisis and the Hunger for Justice* (Oakland, CA: Food First Books; Boston: Grassroots International, 2009). Other information from Holt- Giménez et al., pp. 134–58; from the Bill and Melinda Gates Foundation website; and from my own work on the earlier Green Revolution – chapter 5 of *How the Other Half Dies: the Real Reasons for World Hunger* (Harmondsworth: Penguin, 1976), available on my website, www.tni.org/users/susan-george.

2 Holt-Giménez et al., *Food Rebellions*, pp. 134–5.

3 Tukundane Cuthbert, quoted by Aileen Kwa, 'Privatisation of seeds moving apace', InterPress Service, 21 February 2008.

4 'Monsanto failure', *New Scientist*, 7 February 2004; Mariam Mayet, *Comments on the National Biotechnology Safety Bill of Uganda* (Johannesburg: African Centre for Biosafety, Briefing Paper no. 8, June 2009). For numerous well-referenced critiques of AGRA and its components, see www.biosafetyafrica.org, and search under 'Gates Foundation'.

5 David Rieff, 'A Green Revolution for Africa?', *New York Times Magazine*, 10 October 2008.

6 Shiva is quoted by Rieff, ibid.

7 Jules Pretty et al., 'Reducing food poverty by increasing agricultural sustainability in developing countries', *Agriculture, Ecosystems & Environment*, 95/1 (2003): 217–34; cited in Holt-Giménez et al., *Food Rebellions*, p. 147.

8 Lim Li Ching, 'Is ecological agriculture productive?', briefing paper for the Oakland Institute with a number of scientific references; see www.oaklandinstitute. org/?q=printpage&nid=499.

9 This farmer is cited in Institute for Food and Development Policy, Food First Facts on AGRA, n.d.

10 The Canadian ecological watchdog ETC Group, cited in David Rieff, 'A Green Revolution for Africa?'

11 Abhijit Banerjee (of MIT), Angus Deaton (Princeton University), Nora Lustig (UNDP), Ken Rogoff (Harvard) and Edward Hsu (International Finance Corporation), *An Evaluation of World Bank Research, 1998–2005* (Washington, DC: World Bank, 24 September 2006), p. 53.

12 *How the Other Half Dies* is available on my website: www. tni.org/users/susan-george.

13 The CIA – the United States Central Intelligence Agency – *World Factbook* is a useful source for such statistics.

14 Richard Wilkinson, *Mind the Gap: Hierarchies, Health and Human Evolution* (London: Weidenfeld & Nicolson, 2000); and with Kate Pickett, *The Spirit Level: Why More Equal Societies Almost Always Do Better* (London: Allen Lane, 2009).

15 Betsey Stevenson and Justin Wolfers, *Economic Growth and Subjective Well-Being: Reassessing the Easterlin Paradox*, Brookings Papers on Economic Activity, 16 April 2008.

16 Wilkinson and Pickett, *The Spirit Level*, p. 19.

17 Kevin Watkins and Patrick Montjourides, *Global Monitoring Report* (Paris: UNESCO, 2009). Towards the end of 2009, commodity prices were fortunately on the upswing again, partly because of increased demand from China and a few other cash-rich Asian societies.

18 International Labour Organization, *Global Employment Trends*, January 2010, p. 10.

19 International Labour Organization, *The World of Work 2008* (Geneva: ILO, 2008); www.ilo.org/public/english/bureau/inst/download/world08.pdf.

20 James Boyce and Léonce Ndikumana, *New Estimates of Capital Flight from Sub-Saharan African Countries: Linkages with External Borrowing and Policy Options*, Working Paper Series no. 166, Political Economy Research Institute [PERI], University of Massachusetts, Amherst, April 2008.

21 Norwegian Commission on Capital Flight from Developing Countries, *Tax Havens and Development* (Oslo: Norad, 2009); www.regjeringen.no/upload/UD/Vedlegg/Utvikling/tax_report.pdf.

22 BBC World Services poll executed by Globescan and the Program on International Policy Attitudes [PIPA], University of Maryland, between 31 October 2007 and 25 January 2008.

23 Vincente Navarro, 'What we mean by the social determinants of health', *International Journal of Health Services*, 39/3 (2009): 423–41 [a speech given by Navarro at a health professionals congress on 9 September 2008].

Chapter 3 The Most Basic Basics

1 FAO, *The State of Food Insecurity in the World 2009* (Rome: FAO 2009).

2 These events were the proximate cause of my first book, *How the Other Half Dies: the Real Reasons for World Hunger* (Harmondsworth: Penguin, 1976; and several later editions in many languages), now available in English on my website www.tni.org/users/susan-george.

3 Independent Evaluation Group, *World Bank Assistance to Agriculture in Sub-Saharan Africa 1991–2006* (Washington, DC: World Bank, 2008).

4 Stephen Marks, 'China and the great global landgrab', *Pambazuka News*, 11 December 2008; www.pambazuka.

org/en/category/africa_china/52635. *Pambazuka News* is a project of Fahamu, an Oxford-based think tank on Africa with offices in Nairobi, Cape Town and Dakar. The name means 'consciousness' or 'knowledge' in Kiswahili.

5 Ramesh Chand (National Centre for Agricultural Economics and Policy Research, New Delhi), 'The global food crisis: causes, severity and outlook', *Economic and Political Weekly* [New Delhi], 28 June 2008.

6 P. J. Crutzen et al., 'N2O release from agro-biofuel production negates global warming reduction by replacing fossil fuels', *Atmospheric Chemistry and Physics Discussions*, 7 (2007): 11191–205; and Zoe Corbyn, 'Biofuels could boost global warming, finds study', *Chemistry World* [Royal Society of Chemistry], September 2007.

7 Stefan Tangermann, director of Trade and Agriculture, OECD, 'What's causing global food price inflation?', 22 July 2008, www.voxeu.org/index.php?q=node/1437. Vox is a 'research-based policy analysis and commentary from leading economists'.

8 The excellent and thorough report of the Carbon Trade Watch project of the Transnational Institute contains an enormous amount of documentation for any serious European student of this issue: *Paving the Way for Agrofuels: EU Policy, Sustainability Criteria and Climate Calculations* (Amsterdam: TNI, September 2007; updated 2nd edn, February 2008). The authors much prefer the term 'agrofuels' to 'biofuels' because the latter 'implies inherent environmental advantages' that are notably absent in reality.

9 FAO *Policy Brief: Food Security*, June 2006. The definition of food security evolved from the time it was first mentioned at the World Food Conference in 1974.

10 FAO data tables on freshwater resources (incorporating UN and World Bank statistics) for all countries, at http://

earthtrends.wri.org / pdf_library / data_tables / wat2_ 2005. pdf.

11 WHO, 'Water, sanitation and health', www.who.int/ water_sanitation_health; WHO, 'Domestic water quantity, service level and health', www.who.int/water.

12 David Chandler, 'Influence of global warming seen in changing rains', *New Scientist*, 23 July 2007, citing an article which initially appeared in *Nature*.

13 Maude Barlow, *Blue Covenant: The Global Water Crisis and the Coming Battle for the Right to Water* (Toronto: McClelland & Stewart, 2007); see also Maude Barlow and Tony Clarke, *Blue Gold: The Fight to Stop Corporate Theft of the World's Water* (Toronto: Stoddart, 2002).

14 Various authors, *Reclaiming Public Water: Achievements, Struggles and Visions from around the World* (Amsterdam: Transnational Institute, 2005). See also www.tni.org; Focus on the Global South, www.focusweb.org; M.A. Manahan et al., *Water Democracy: Reclaiming Public Water in Asia* (Amsterdam: TNI, 2007). I must declare an interest: I am chair of the board of the Transnational Institute and very proud of the TNI team that produced this remarkable publication.

Chapter 4 The Wall of Conflict

1 John Gray, *Straw Dogs* (London: Granta, 2002), pp. 165–6.

2 Matthew Garrahan and Kenneth Li, 'Caged violence rises from the canvas to land fistful of dollars', *Financial Times*, 16 July 2009.

3 This and the following information on the origins and decline of warfare is drawn from John Horgan, 'The end of war', *New Scientist*, 4 July 2009, quoting numerous anthropologists and other scientists. Horgan is himself

director of the Center for Science Writings at Stevens Institute of Technology, Hoboken, New Jersey.

4 I quoted this in a chapter, entitled 'The fundamentalist freedom fighter', about Larry Summers, then the World Bank's chief economist, in *Faith and Credit: the World Bank's Secular Empire* (with Fabrizio Sabelli; London: Penguin; Boulder, CO: Westview Press, 1994), p. 109. The source is Kirsten Garrett ('Background Briefing', Australian National Radio, broadcast on Australian Broadcasting Company, 10 November 1991), in an interview with Summers at the bank's annual meeting in Bangkok, which I transcribed from the tape kindly supplied by Ms Garrett.

5 'Summers on sustainable growth', *The Economist*, 30 May 1992.

6 Peter Schwartz and Doug Randall, *An Abrupt Climate Change Scenario and its Implications for US National Security*, United States Department of Defense, October 2003.

7 Pacific Institute for Studies in Development, Environment and Security, www.worldwater.org; Peter Gleick's chronology of water conflict can be found at www.worldwater.org/conflictchronology.pdf (regularly updated).

8 Answers to the 'FP Quiz' about water in the July–August 2009 issue of *Foreign Policy*. I was rather annoyed not to get all eight questions right because I thought I knew the literature, but I still think it is a great magazine, and I'm not alone – in 2009, and for the third time in seven years, it received the US National Magazine Award for General Excellence.

9 Marc Levy et al. and CIESIN; see www.ciesin.org/levy.html.

10 For a comparatively early but comprehensive example, see Kent Hughes Butts (Professor of Political Military Strategy at the US Army War College), 'The strategic importance of water', *Parameters* [the army's scholarly quarterly journal], spring 1997.

11 The figure of 47 per cent is that given in the *Foreign Policy* quiz cited above, but Peter Gleick's chronology cites 'sources' that put the proportion of the world population dependent on the Tibetan plateau/Himalayan glaciers at 25 per cent. Whichever figure is correct, it's still a huge number of people.

12 Stephan Faris, 'The last straw', in the 'Failed States Index' feature in *Foreign Policy*, July–August 2009.

13 Dispatch from the Euro-Mediterranean Information System on know-how in the Water Sector (EMWIS), 17 June 2009.

14 Curtis Abraham, 'Don't exaggerate climate change link to conflict', *New Scientist*, 20 October 2007.

15 Javier Solana, *Climate Change and International Security*, paper from the high representative and the European Commission to the European Council, S113/08, 14 March 2008.

16 Janet Redman et al., *Dirty is the New Clean: A Critique of the World Bank's Strategic Framework for Development and Climate Change* (Washington, DC: Institute for Policy Studies, 2008).

17 Lies Craeynest and Daisy Streatfeild, *The World Bank and its Carbon Footprint: Why the World Bank is Still Far from Being an Environment Bank* (WWF-UK, 23 June 2008); http://assets.wwf.org.uk/downloads/world_bank_report.pdf.

18 Andrew Revkin, 'World Bank should improve environmental record, review says', *International Herald Tribune*, 22 July 2008. For the full 181-page report, see www.worldbank.org/oed.

Chapter 5 Our Future

1 Matt Taibbi, 'The great American bubble machine', *Rolling Stone*, 2 July 2009.

2 '... highlighting the trading bonanza sweeping Wall Street as central banks continue to pump billions into the financial system.' Franceso Guerrera and Michael Mackenzie, 'Goldman reaps benefits as trading boom returns', *Financial Times*, 5 November 2009. See also Justin Baer, 'Goldman beats its record for $100m-plus days', *Financial Times*, 2 March 2010.

3 Susan George, 'Of capitalism, crisis, conversion & collapse: The Keynesian alternative'. For those interested, the full text is on my site, www.tni.org/users/susangeorge. The event was sponsored by the International Forum on Globalization and the Institute for Policy Studies.

4 Green New Deal Group, *A Green New Deal: Joined-Up Policies to Solve the Triple Crunch of the Credit Crisis, Climate Change and High Oil Prices* (London: New Economics Foundation, 2008). The NEF has continued to reflect and publish on this question.

5 For the WWF study on Europe, see http://assets.panda. org/downloads/low_carbon_jobs_final.pdf; for the Pew Center Report on the 'clean energy economy' and more, see www.pewcenteronthestates.org/uploadedFiles/ Clean_Economy_Report_Web.pdf.

6 In and around Porto Alegre, Brazil, the city where the World Social Forum originated, over 1,300 SMEs are integrated in a credit–debit network that operates with no interest payments. They no longer need the banks at all. Smaller, similar networks are in operation elsewhere: see www.socialtrade.org.

7 Philip Inman, 'Goldman to make record bonus payout', *The Observer*, 21 June 2009.

8 John Authers, 'Economic solution that dare not speak its name', *Financial Times*, 1 March 2009.

9 'Response by the presidency on behalf of the G8 to the

Jubilee 2000 Petition', 19 May 1998; see http://hartford-hwp.com/archives/27c/015.html.

10 Thanks to the CADTM (Comité pour l'annulation de la dette du Tiers Monde) and to Eric Toussaint and Damien Millet, who provided the HIPC information and the debt figures that allowed me to make these calculations. From the CADTM Debt Report, 2009.

11 Justin Mullins, 'The greening of Silicon Valley', *New Scientist*, 28 May 2008.

12 'Good week for solar power', *New Scientist*, 5 September 2009, p. 25.

13 For the Institute for Policy Studies Report, see www.ips-dc.org/reports/reversing_the_great_tax_shift_seven_steps_to_finance_our_economic_recovery, April 2009.

14 Tony Barber, 'UK wins EU bank concession', *Financial Times*, 10 June 2009.

15 Carbon Trade Watch, *The Carbon Neutral Myth: Offset Indulgences for your Climate Sins*, Transnational Institute, February 2007.

16 Bank for International Settlements, *Triennial Central Bank Survey of Foreign Exchange and Derivatives Market Activity in 2007: Final Results*, 19 December 2007. Both the thorough explanatory press release and the full survey with all the statistics are available on the BIS site at www.bis.org. Quotations are from the press release.

17 International Labour Organization, *Economic Security for a Better World* (Geneva: ILO 2004).

18 The Tax Justice Network provides a wealth of information on tax evasion and avoidance, tax havens and much other financial lore, in several languages: www.taxjustice.net/cms/front_content.php?idcatart=2.

19 Story by David Cay Johnston, *International Herald Tribune*, 13 September 2004.

20 Christian Aid, *The Morning after the Night Before: The*

Impact of the Financial Crisis on the Developing World, November 2008.

21 www.financialtaskforce.org/wp-content/uploads/2009/06/ Final_CbyC_Report_Published.pdf.

22 United States Senate, Committee on Homeland Security and Governmental Affairs, Permanent Subcommittee on Investigations, *The Role of Professional Firms in the US Tax Shelter Industry*, 8 February 2005.

23 Cited from the Ernst & Young website by Prem Sikka, 'Shifting profits across borders', *The Guardian*, 12 February 2009. Anton Valukas's 2,200-page report on the Lehman Brothers bankruptcy, made public in March 2010, also questions the professional conduct of Ernst & Young in helping Lehman to disguise debt on its balance sheet.

24 Daniel Gros and Stefano Micossi, 'A bond-issuing EU stability fund could rescue Europe', *Europe's World*, no. 12, summer 2009; www.europesworld.org/ NewEnglish/Home/Article/tabid/191/ArticleType/ ArticleView/ArticleID/21306/language/en-US/ AbondissuingEUstabilityfundcouldrescueEurope.aspx.

25 See its major theoretician, Serge Latouche, *Le Pari de la décroissance* (Paris: Fayard, 2006)

26 George Monbiot, 'Let's divert the money spent on arms to addressing the real strategic threat', *The Guardian*, 23 June 2009.

27 Later published under the same title in *Science*, 13 December 1968.

Conclusion

1 Niall Ferguson, in *The Ascent of Money: A Financial History of the World* (London: Allen Lane, 2008), provides a lot of fascinating detail on all these crises and much more.

2 David Robson, 'Disorderly genius: how chaos drives the brain', *New Scientist*, 29 June 2009.

INDEX

acolyte:
spate : 53